Revenue Recognition

Understanding and Implementing the New Standard

Joanne M. Flood

WILEY

Cover design and image: Wiley

Library of Congress Cataloging-in-Publication Data

Names: Flood, Joanne M., author.
Title: Wiley revenue recognition plus website : understanding and
    implementing the new standard / Joanne Flood.
Description: Hoboken, New Jersey : John Wiley & Sons, Inc., [2017] | Includes index. |
Identifiers: LCCN 2016053413 (print) | LCCN 2017018484 (ebook) | ISBN
    9781119351696 (pdf) | ISBN 9781119351689 (epub) | ISBN 9781118776858 (pbk.)
Subjects: LCSH: Financial statements–Law and legislation–United States. |
    Financial statements–Standards–United States. | Financial
    disclosure–Law and legislation–United States. |
    Revenue–Accounting–Standards–United States. |
    Accounting–Standards–United States.
Classification: LCC KF1446 (ebook) | LCC KF1446 .F59 2017 (print) |
    DDC 346.73/063–dc23
LC record available at https://lccn.loc.gov/2016053413

ISBN 978-1-118-77685-8 (paperback)
ISBN 978-1-119-35169-6 (ebk)
ISBN 978-1-119-35168-9 (ebk)
ISBN 978-1-119-35164-1 (ebk)

CONTENTS

EXECUTIVE SUMMARY

WHAT IS REVENUE?

> **U.S. GAAP**
>   Revenue: Influx or other enhancement of assets of an entity or settlements of liabilities (or a combination of both) from delivering or producing goods, rendering services, or other activities that constitute the entity's ongoing major or central operations. (ASC 606-10-20)
>
> **IFRS**
>   Revenue: Income arising in the course of an entity's ordinary activities. (IFRS 15, Appendix A)
>   Income: Increases in economic benefits during the accounting period in the form of inflows or enhancements of assets or decreases in liabilities that result in an increase in equity other than those relating to contributions from equity participants. (IASB Framework)

Revenue versus Gains

U.S. GAAP. The U.S. Financial Accounting Standards Board (FASB) distinguishes revenue from gains. Gains are defined in Statement of Financial Accounting Concept 6 (CON6), *Elements of Financial Statements*, as

> *Increases in equity (net assets) from peripheral or incidental transactions of an entity and from all other transactions and other events and circumstances affecting the entity except those that result from revenues or investments by owners.*

Revenue is commonly distinguished from gains in U.S. GAAP for the three reasons listed below.

Exhibit ES.1   Distinguishing between revenue and gains in U.S. GAAP

Revenue	Gains
Results from an entity's central operations.	Result from incidental or peripheral activities of the entity.
Is usually earned.	Result from nonreciprocal transactions (such as winning a lawsuit or receiving a gift) or other economic events for which there is no earnings process.
Is reported gross.	Are reported net.

IFRS

The IASB's definition of income includes revenue and gains. Gains are defined as increases in economic benefits and other items of revenue. They may or may not occur in the ordinary course of business.

THE NEW REVENUE STANDARD[1]

The revenue recognition standard represents a major milestone in our efforts to improve and converge one of the most important areas of financial reporting. It will eliminate a major source of inconsistency in GAAP, which currently consists of numerous disparate, industry-specific pieces of revenue recognition guidance.

—*Russell Golden, Chairman of the FASB*

The successful conclusion of this project is a major achievement for both boards. Together, we have improved the revenue requirements of both IFRS and U.S. GAAP, while managing to achieve a fully converged standard. Our attention now turns to ensuring a successful transition to these new requirements.

—*Hans Hoogervorst, Chairman of the IASB*
FASB/IASB Press Release May 28, 2014

In May 2014, the FASB and the IASB jointly issued *Revenue from Contracts with Customers* as, respectively,

- Accounting Standards Update (ASU) 2014-09 and
- IFRS 15.

DEVELOPMENT OF REVENUE GUIDANCE

Revenue numbers are a critical metric for investors. Revenue recognition has often been a source of restatements and comments from regulators, such as the U.S. Securities and Exchange Commission (SEC). Over the years, regulators have increased their enforcement activities in this area.

U.S. GAAP

Revenue recognition guidance in the U.S. was initially found in

- CON 5, which specifies that an entity should recognize revenue when realized or realizable and earned, and
- CON 6, which defines revenue as inflows or other enhancements of assets and/or settlements of liabilities from delivering goods or services as a result of the entity's ongoing major or central operations.

In 1999, the SEC provided additional guidance to public companies in Staff Accounting Bulletin (SAB) No. 101 (amended in 2003 by SAB No. 104 and codified in Topic 13).

U.S. GAAP related to revenue developed piecemeal, with specific, often industry-related requirements, but also has broad concepts. In some cases, the guidance resulted in different accounting for economically similar transactions. In addition to the guidance in ASC Topic 605, *Revenue Recognition*, U.S. guidance can be found in numerous pieces of industry-specific guidance, such as that for the software industry, construction contracts, real-estate

---

[1] The Financial Accounting Standards Board (FASB) and the International Accounting Standards Board (IASB) (the Boards) issued two separate standards. For ease of reference, this publication refers to them as "the revenue standard" or "the Standard."

sales, and multiple-element arrangements. Industry guidance often addressed narrow issues and was not built on a common framework. This led to economically similar transactions being accounted for differently. Even though in the U.S. there were 200 separate pieces of guidance, there were still transactions for which there was no guidance, in particular for service transactions.

IFRS

IFRS does not have as many rules, but the standards can be confusing and difficult to apply, and were sometimes based on different principles. The guidance was limited for some significant topics, like contracts with multiple-element arrangements. This lack of guidance made it difficult to account for some complex transactions. When IFRS guidance was absent, preparers at times turned to industry-specific U.S. literature.

THE REVENUE RECOGNITION PROJECT

Driven by the need to achieve simplification and consistency, the FASB and the IASB (the Boards) began a joint project in 2002.

The Boards issued an exposure draft (ED) in June 2010 that elicited over 1,000 comment letters. The Boards issued a revised ED in November 2011 and conducted numerous meetings and outreach activities before issuing the final Standard. The basically converged, new Standard is principles based, eliminating the existing transaction- and industry-specific guidance. This move away from prescriptive guidance and bright lines increases the need for professional judgment, which in turn increases the need for expanded disclosures. To compensate for the lack of rules, the revenue standard provides extensive application guidance.

The New Standards

In the U.S., ASU 2014-09

- superseded 200 separate items of FASB Accounting Standards Codification® (ASC) guidance, most of it industry specific
- created Topic 606, *Revenue from Contracts with Customers* and Subtopic 340-40, *Other Assets and Deferred Costs—Contracts with Customers*.
- created Topic 610, *Other Income*

ASU 2014-09 is over 700 pages long and was released in the following sections:

- Amendments to the FASB Accounting Standards Codification

  - Section A—Summary and Amendments That Create Revenue from Contracts with Customers (Topic 606) and Other Assets and Deferred Costs—Contracts with Customers (Subtopic 340-40)
  - Section B—Conforming Amendments to Other Topics and Subtopics in the Codification and Status Tables

- Background Information and Basis for Conclusions

  - Appendix: Comparison of Topic 606 and IFRS 15

- Amendments to XBRL Taxonomy.

IFRS 15 replaces the previous standards IAS 11, *Construction Contracts* and IAS 18, *Revenue* and several interpretations:

- IFRIC 13, *Customer Loyalty Programmes*
- IFRIC 15, *Agreements for the Construction of Real Estate*
- IFRIC 18, *Transfers of Assets from Customers*
- SIC-31, *Revenue—Barter Transactions Involving Advertising Services.*

IFRS 15 is over 300 pages long and was released in these sections:

- IFRS 15 with Appendices
- Defined Terms
- Application Guidance
- Effective Date and Transition
- Amendments to Other Sections
- Basis for Conclusion with Appendices
- Comparison of IFRS 15 and Topic 606
- Amendments to the Basis for Conclusions in Other Sections
- Illustrative Examples
- Appendix
- Amendments to the Guidance in Other Standards.

Project Goals

The FASB and the IASB believe that the final documents meet two major goals—simplification of revenue recognition guidance and consistency globally and across entities, jurisdictions, markets, and industries. According to *FASB in Focus*,[2] the Boards believe that the Standard meets their goals to

- remove inconsistencies and weaknesses in existing revenue requirements
- provide a more robust framework for addressing revenue issues
- improve comparability of revenue recognition practices across entities, industries, jurisdictions, and capital markets
- provide more useful information to users of financial statements through improved disclosure requirements, and
- simplify the preparation of financial statements by reducing the number of requirements to which an organization must refer.

The revenue standard provides a robust framework that is expected to simplify the preparation of financial statements by reducing the sources of guidance and replacing them with a single source that users can understand. The Standard adds new guidance for contract modifications and offers consistent application for service contracts. The Standard also provides guidance for related topics, such as warrantees, licenses, and when to capitalize the cost of obtaining a contract and some costs of fulfilling a contract.

Customer Loyalty Programs. In addition, the changes may affect customer loyalty programs. Companies will have to make new estimates. It is expected that entities will be reviewing their loyalty programs to evaluate their effects, if any, on revenue, and some companies may choose to amend their contracts with customers.

---

[2] *FASB in Focus*, May 28, 2014, FASB, Stamford, CT.

Exhibit ES.2   Key differences between ASU 2014-09 and IFRS 15

EFFECTIVE DATES

While the FASB and IASB standards are generally aligned, the implementation dates are different. (See the section in this chapter on effective dates.) Also, the IASB allows early implementation and has no relief for nonpublic entities. IFRS for small and medium-sized public entities is available for those entities. The FASB allows early implementation but only for annual reporting periods beginning after December 15, 2016. (ASC 606-10-65-1; IFRS 15.C)

COLLECTIBILITY THRESHOLDS

In order for an entity to apply the revenue standard to a contract, collectibility must be probable. The collectibility threshold for recognizing revenue, introduced late in the process, is an area of FASB/IASB difference. R. Harold Schroeder, the lone dissenter on the FASB, pointed out that "probable" does not mean the same under U.S. GAAP and IFRS because the definitions of probable are different under each. According to Schroeder's dissenting opinion, the IASB's threshold is lower because it defines probable as "more likely than not," which is greater than 50%, whereas the FASB Topic 450 defines probable as "likely to occur," which some have historically interpreted as a 75–80% threshold. The Boards acknowledged this difference, but decided to be consistent with their own definitions. The IASB's Mackintosh and the FASB's Golden both believe that the difference will have a small impact on results. [ASC 606-10-25-1(e); IFRS 15.9(e)]

The FASB, but not the IASB, amended its guidance to clarify that when assessing collectibility, an entity should evaluate the consideration for the goods or services it expects to receive rather than the consideration promised for all the goods or services.

In addition, the FASB subsequently decided to clarify that when assessing collectibility, an entity should consider its ability to mitigate its exposure to credit risk. The IASB concluded that its guidance and discussion in the Basis for Conclusions is sufficient. (Also, see the appendix to this summary for information on proposals to amend the Standard as originally issued.)

INTERIM REQUIREMENTS

Disclosures are another source of FASB/IASB differences. The Boards generally kept their existing interim requirements. However, the IASB amended its guidance to require interim disclosure of disaggregated information. The FASB amended Topic 270 similarly for public entities, but also added requirements to disclose on an interim basis revenue recognized in the current period that was included in the contract balances at the beginning of the period, revenue recognized in the current period for performance obligations satisfied in previous periods, and remaining performance obligations. The FASB generally prescribes interim disclosures, whereas the IASB leans toward only annual disclosures. (ASC 270-10-50-1A; IAS 34.16A)

PROMISED GOODS OR SERVICES IMMATERIAL IN THE CONTEXT OF THE CONTRACT

The FASB, but not the IASB, clarified that an entity is not required to assess whether promises that are immaterial in the context of the contract are performance obligations.

PRESENTATION OF SALES TAXES

The FASB, but not the IASB, provides an accounting policy election that allows an entity to exclude sales and similar taxes from the measurement of transaction price.

SHIPPING AND HANDLING ACTIVITIES

The FASB, but not the IASB, includes a practical expedient that allows entities to account for as fulfillment activities shipping and handling activities that occur after the customer has obtained control of a good.

NONCASH CONSIDERATION

The FASB, but not the IASB, requires noncash consideration to be measured at fair value at contract inception. The FASB also specifies that the constraint on variable consideration applies only to the variability in the fair value of the noncash consideration that arises from reasons other than the form of the consideration.

LICENSING

Both the FASB and the IASB made changes subsequent to the issuance of ASU 2014-09 and IFRS 15 on guidance regarding licenses. Those changes are incorporated into Chapter 6 and relate to

- determining the nature of the entity's promise in granting a license of intellectual property
- contractual restriction in a license and the identification of performance obligations
- renewals of licenses of intellectual property
- when to consider the nature of an entity's promise in granting a license.

COMPLETED CONTRACTS

The FASB amended its definition of a completed contract, but the IASB did not. (See Chapter 9.) The IASB contains a practical expedient to allow an entity applying the full retrospective method of adoption not to restate contracts that are completed contracts at the beginning of the earliest period presented.

PRACTICAL EXPEDIENT FOR CONTRACT MODIFICATION—DATE OF APPLICATION

For entities applying the modified retrospective method, the FASB requires entities to apply the practical expedient at the date of initial application. The IASB allows entities to apply the expedient either at the beginning of the earliest period presented or at the date of initial application.

DISCLOSURE RELIEF FOR NONPUBLIC ENTITIES

The FASB provides specific relief related to disclosure, transition, and effective dates for nonpublic entities, while the IASB does not. IFRS 15 applies to all entities, except for small and medium-sized entities. (ASC 606-10-50-7, 50-11, 50-16, 50-21, 340-40-50-4; IFRS 15.5)

IMPAIRMENT LOSS REVERSAL

U.S. guidance does not permit impairment loss reversal for an asset that is capitalized under the guidance on costs to obtain or fulfill a contract. IASB guidance requires an entity to reverse an impairment loss, consistent with the guidance of IFRS 36, *Impairment of Assets.* (ASC 340-40-35-6; IFRS 15.104)

In addition to these major differences, the FASB and the IASB have some differences in the articulation of the principles of the Standard. Those differences and the differences above are included in the relevant chapters in this volume.

Source: Clarifications to IFRS 15, Appendix A; ASU 2014-12, Appendix.

SCOPE

The scope of the Standard is wide. It affects all public companies, nonpublic companies, and nonprofit organizations. The Standard applies to contracts with customers and defines a customer as:

> *a party that has contracted with a company to obtain a good or service that is an output of the company's ordinary activities in exchange for consideration.*

(ASC 606-10-20)

Practice Pointer: Care should be taken to determine whether a contract is with a customer or if it is a collaborative effort. To make the recognition and measurement consistent with revenue transactions, the Standard applies to transfers of nonfinancial assets, such as property and equipment, that give rise to revenue. Revenue can be generated by contracts that are not with customers. Examples are alternative revenue programs of utilities and not-for-profit contributions. The Standard is applicable to those transactions.

Scope Exceptions

The following are outside the scope of the Standard:

- Lease contracts in the scope of ASC 840, *Leases* and IAS 17, *Leases.*
- Insurance contracts issued by insurance entities within the scope of ASC Topic 944, *Financial Services—Insurance* or IFRS 4, *Insurance Contracts.* Note: Insurance contracts issued by entities that do not apply insurance industry-specific guidance under U.S. GAAP are in the scope of the revenue standard. Under IFRS, insurance contracts are scoped out no matter who issues them. Warranty contracts considered insurance contracts under IFRS I are also scoped out.
- Financial instruments and other contractual rights or obligations in the scope of

  - ASC 310, *Receivables*
  - ASC 320, *Investments—Debt and Equity Securities*
  - ASC 323, *Investments—Equity Method and Joint Ventures*
  - ASC 325, *Investments—Other*

- ASC 405, *Liabilities*
- ASC 470, *Debt*
- ASC 815, *Derivatives and Hedging*
- ASC 825, *Financial Instruments*
- ASC 860, *Transfers and Servicing*
- IFRS 9, *Financial Instruments*
- IFRS 10, *Consolidated Financial Statements*
- IFRS 11, *Joint Arrangements*
- IAS 27, *Separate Financial Statements*
- IAS 28, *Investments in Associates and Joint Ventures.*

- Guarantees other than product or service warranties, in the scope of ASC 460, *Guarantees.*
- Nonmonetary exchanges between entities in the same line of business to facilitate sales to customers or potential customers.

(ASC 606-10-15-2)

Revenue from transactions or events that do not arise from contracts with customers is not in the scope of the Standard, such as

- dividends
- non-exchange transactions, like donations or contributions
- IFRS only:

  - changes in the fair value of biological assets, investment properties, and the inventory of broker-traders

- U.S. GAAP only:

  - changes in regulatory assets and liabilities arising from alternative revenue programs for rate-regulated activities in the scope of ASC 930, *Regulated Operations.*

The guidance included in new subtopic ASC 340-40 applies only if the costs incurred are related to a contract under ASC 606. (ASC 606-10-5)

The guidance in new topic ASC 610 specifies the standards for income that is not in the scope of ASC 606, including gains and losses from the derecognition of nonfinancial assets and from gains and losses on involuntary conversions.

Example ES.1: Nonmonetary Exchanges to Facilitate Sales to Customers or Potential Customers

ABC Road Salt sells road salt to municipalities. ABC determines the optimum amount of salt on hand to meet a typical winter's demand in New York State. ABC enters into a contract with Penn Road Salt to provide road salt to the other if needed. ABC and Penn are in different regions and rarely experience the same winter storms. The parties provide each other no other consideration.

This transaction is outside the scope of the Standard because it involves nonmonetary exchanges between parties in the same line of business to facilitate sales to customers or potential customers.

Contracts Partially in Scope

If a contract is partially within the scope of the Standard and partially within the scope of other guidance, the entity should apply the other guidance first. That is, if the other standard specifies how to separate or initially measure parts of the contract, then the entity should apply those requirements first. The remaining portion is accounted for under the requirements of the new Standard. If the other standard does not have applicable separate and/or initial measurement guidance, the entity should apply the revenue standard to separate and/or initially measure the contract. (ASC 606-10-15-4)

Example ES.2: Contract Partially Out of Scope

Power Rentals leases power equipment to builders and provides maintenance for the leased equipment. To record the transaction, Power Rentals must first separate the contract price related to leasing the equipment and account for that under the leasing guidance. The remaining maintenance portion would be accounted for under the revenue standard.

Sale of Transfer of Nonfinancial Assets

Transactions that are not part of the entity's ordinary activities, such as the sale of property, plant, and equipment, nonetheless fall under certain aspects of the Standard. An entity involved in such activities applies the guidance related to transfer of control (Chapter 5) and measurement of the transaction price (Chapter 3) to evaluate the timing and amount of the gain or loss. U.S. GAAP reporters should also apply the guidance in the Standard to determine whether the parties are committed to perform under the contract and, therefore, whether a contract exists (Chapter 1).

EFFECTIVE DATES

In deciding on effective dates, the Boards wanted to strike the right balance between improving reporting standards as soon as possible and giving entities enough time to implement the broad and potentially significant changes. Ultimately, the Boards decided on a longer than usual implementation period because of the number of entities and line items affected. Despite that added time, soon after the release of the Standard, the Boards heard from many entities that they needed more time to implement the new guidance.

Changes to Effective Dates

U.S. GAAP. In response to constituent concerns, the FASB issued ASU 2015-14, *Revenue from Contracts with Customers (Topic 606): Deferral of Effective Dates.* The ASU allows for all entities a one-year deferral from the original effective dates and for early adoption using the original adoption dates.

The ASU is effective as follows:

- For public entities, the guidance in the Standard is effective for annual reporting periods beginning after December 15, 2017, including interim reporting periods within that period; that is, beginning in the first interim period within the year of adoption. Early application is permitted but not earlier than the original effective date of December 15, 2016.
- For nonpublic entities, the new guidance is required for annual reporting periods beginning after December 15, 2018, and interim periods within annual periods beginning after December 15, 2019. A nonpublic entity may elect early application, but no earlier than the original effective date for public entities.

IFRS. IFRS 15 was originally effective for annual periods beginning on or after January 1, 2017. Partly because in the near future some companies will transition from national to international standards, the IASB allows for early adoption for current IFRS preparers, provided that fact is disclosed and for first time preparers. In September 2015, the IASB issued an amendment to IFRS 15 deferring the effective date for one year until 2018. Entities still have the option of applying early.

Other Changes to the Standard

In addition to the ASU deferring the effective date, the FASB responded to feedback by issuing several other EDs to amend ASU 2014-09:

- Accounting Standards Update 2016-08, *Revenue from Contracts with Customers (Topic 606): Principal versus Agent Considerations (Reporting Revenue Gross versus Net)*
- Accounting Standards Update 2016-10, *Revenue from Contracts with Customers (Topic 606): Identifying Performance Obligations and Licensing*
- Accounting Standards Update 2016-12, *Revenue from Contracts with Customers (Topic 606): Narrow-Scope Improvements and Practical Expedients*
- Proposed Accounting Standards Update, *Technical Corrections and Improvements to Update 2014-09, Revenue from Contracts with Customers.* As this volume goes to press, the FASB expects to issue a final document in the fourth quarter of 2016.
- Proposed Accounting Standards Update, *Technical Corrections and Improvements to Update 2014-09, Revenue from Contracts with Customers-Additional Corrections*

As a purchaser of this book, you have exclusive access to a companion website, with the latest technical developments and other useful information. The website will contain updated information about exposure drafts and other technical guidance from the standards' setters. See the back of the book for information on how to access the site.

The IASB decided to issue its changes in one comprehensive document: *Clarifications to IFRS 15.* For more on the FASB's and IASB's changes, see the appendix to this summary.

IMPLEMENTATION OPTIONS

Entities have the option to implement the guidance through

- full retrospective application, or
- modified retrospective application.

Full Retrospective Approach

Under this method, all prior periods presented must be restated in equity in accordance with ASC 250, *Accounting Changes and Error Corrections.* That is, entities must report the cumulative effect for the earliest year reported.

Modified Retrospective Approach

Using the modified retrospective approach, the entity recognizes the cumulative effect of initially adopting the standard as an adjustment to the opening balance of retained earnings in the annual period when the standard is adopted. If the entity issues comparative statements, then it reports revenue for prior years under the guidance in effect before adoption.

OBJECTIVE OF THE STANDARD

The objective of the Standard is

. . . to establish the principles that an entity shall apply to report useful information to users of financial statements about the nature, amount, timing, and uncertainty of revenue and cash flows arising from a contract with a customer.

(ASC 606-10-10-1)

The Standard provides principles to help entities meet this objective when measuring and reporting on revenue.

CORE PRINCIPLE AND THE FIVE STEPS OF THE REVENUE RECOGNITION MODEL

The Standard takes an asset and liability approach and articulates a core principle on which the new guidance is based.

Exhibit ES.3   The five steps

Core Principle:

. . . recognize revenue to depict the transfer of promised goods or services to customers in an amount that reflects the consideration to which the entity expects to be entitled in exchange for those goods or services. (FASB ASC 606-10-05-3 *et al.*, IFRS 15.IN7)

This core principle reflects the asset and liability approach that underlies the Standard. This approach recognizes revenue based on changes in assets and liabilities. The Boards believe that this is consistent with the conceptual framework approach to recognition and brings more consistency to the measurement compared with the "earned and realized" criteria in previous standards. To achieve the core principle, entities should follow the five steps above, explained through the following simple example.

Example ES.3: Application of the Core Principle Through the Five Steps

Assume that on May 1, 20X1, ACME enters into a contract to sell 50 desktop computers to XYZ Company for CU 50,000 with delivery promised on July 15, 20X1. On July 31, 20X1, ACME completes a performance obligation by delivering all the computers and makes the following entries:

	Debit		Credit
Accounts Receivable	CU 50,000	Revenue	50,000
Cost of Goods Sold	CU 30,000	Inventory	30,000

On August 15, 20X1, the customer makes the payment and ACME makes the following entry:

	Debit		Credit
Cash	CU 50,000	Accounts Receivable	50,000

Under the Standard, entities account for assets and liabilities arising from customer contracts. Entities must carefully analyze their contracts for

- terms,
- measurements, and
- promises.

In reviewing a transaction, each of the five steps in Exhibit ES.4 may not be needed, and they may not always be applied sequentially. Be aware that the Standard is not organized by these five steps, but the Boards believe that the steps offer a methodology for entities to use when deciding on the appropriate accounting for a transaction. As mentioned, the model is based on an assets and liabilities or control approach as opposed to the risks and rewards approach under previous standards. However, risks and rewards are a factor when determining control for point-in-time revenue recognition.

Each of the steps encompasses new concepts, and entities will have to carefully analyze their contracts with customers as they transition to the new guidance.

DISCLOSURES REQUIRED BY THE STANDARD

Because there is a greater need to estimate, there is a greater need to disclose.
—*Russell Golden, FASB Chairman, May 2014*

Revenue is arguably the most significant financial reporting metric, and the Standard requires all entities to make new disclosure requirements designed to provide better information to financial statement users about contracts with customers. The Standard requires entities to disclose both quantitative and qualitative information that enables users of financial statements to understand the nature, amount, timing, and uncertainty of revenue and cash flows arising from contracts with customers. The additional disclosures are partially driven by the increased judgment related to estimates required in the new guidance. The requirements are comprehensive

Exhibit ES.4   Overview and application of the five steps in the revenue recognition model

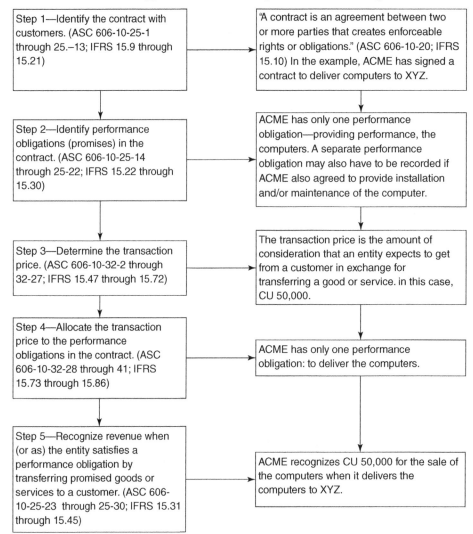

Step 1—Identify the contract with customers. (ASC 606-10-25-1 through 25.–13; IFRS 15.9 through 15.21)	"A contract is an agreement between two or more parties that creates enforceable rights or obligations." (ASC 606-10-20; IFRS 15.10) In the example, ACME has signed a contract to deliver computers to XYZ.
Step 2—Identify performance obligations (promises) in the contract. (ASC 606-10-25-14 through 25-22; IFRS 15.22 through 15.30)	ACME has only one performance obligation—providing performance, the computers. A separate performance obligation may also have to be recorded if ACME also agreed to provide installation and/or maintenance of the computer.
Step 3—Determine the transaction price. (ASC 606-10-32-2 through 32-27; IFRS 15.47 through 15.72)	The transaction price is the amount of consideration that an entity expects to get from a customer in exchange for transferring a good or service. in this case, CU 50,000.
Step 4—Allocate the transaction price to the performance obligations in the contract. (ASC 606-10-32-28 through 41; IFRS 15.73 through 15.86)	ACME has only one performance obligation: to deliver the computers.
Step 5—Recognize revenue when (or as) the entity satisfies a performance obligation by transferring promised goods or services to a customer. (ASC 606-10-25-23 through 25-30; IFRS 15.31 through 15.45)	ACME recognizes CU 50,000 for the sale of the computers when it delivers the computers to XYZ.

and include quantitative and qualitative information. The FASB's ASU includes some exceptions for disclosure by nonpublic entities.

Forming and Documenting Professional Judgment

At a conference in September 2015,[3] Wesley R. Bricker, the SEC's Deputy Chief Accountant, spoke of the Standard's increased need to exercise judgment and how preparers can be sure they are making reasonable judgments that will withstand scrutiny. Mr. Bricker suggested as a

---

[3]   Remarks at the Bloomberg BNA Conference on Revenue Recognition by Wesley R. Bricker, Deputy Chief Accountant of the SEC, New York, September 17, 2015.

resource the Center for Audit Quality's *Professional Judgment Resource*.[4] That document lists five elements of an effective process:

1. Identify and define the issue.
2. Gather the facts and information and identify the relevant literature.
3. Perform the analysis and identify alternatives.
4. Make the decision.
5. Review and complete the documentation and rationale for the conclusion.

DISCLOSURES REQUIRED FOR A NEW STANDARD

IAS 8 requires an entity to disclose that it has not applied a new standard that has been issued but is not yet effective. The entity must also disclose:

- The new standard's title.
- The nature of the change in accounting policy.
- The date the entity intends to apply the standard.
- Any discussion of the anticipated impact of the new requirements on the financial statements or if unknown or if not reasonably estimable, a statement to that effect.

SEC registrants are required by SAB 74 to disclose the material impact of a recently issued accounting standard when it is expected to be implemented in the future. A public entity may predict the effect. If not able to do so, it may disclose that it has not yet assessed the impact. As the implementation deadline approaches, entities can anticipate that the SEC will expect more specificity.

Wesley R. Bricker, in remarks at the 2015 AICPA National Conference on Current SEC and PCAOB Developments, indicated that the SEC will be reviewing the disclosures about the expected effect. The SEC expects to see more robust and detailed disclosures and entities to provide more useful information to investors as the implementation dates near. Mr. Bricker further suggested registrants may consider advising investors when that assessment is expected to be complete.[5]

OTHER CHANGES INCLUDED IN THE STANDARD

In addition to the items mentioned above, the standard includes changes on

- contract costs,
- right of returns,
- warranties,
- principal versus agent considerations,
- licenses,
- repurchase agreements,
- customer acceptance terms, and
- other areas.

---

[4] Center for Audit Quality's "Professional Judgment Resource" available at http://www.thecaq.org/docs/reports-and-publications/professional-judgment-resource.pdf?sfvrsn=4

[5] http://www.sec.gov/news/speech/bricker-remarks-2015-aicpa-conference-sec-pcaob-developments.html

SEC RESPONSE

The revenue standard does not supersede the SEC guidance. In the US, the SEC is currently considering the new guidance. It is expected to adopt the changes, and significant changes are expected to SAB 13, *Revenue Recognition*. The SEC has indicated that it will be keeping a close eye on implementation. The Chief Accountant has indicated that registrants are expected to follow Transition Resource Group (TRG) conclusions, or discuss differing conclusions with the SEC staff.

Soon after the release of the Standard, the SEC offered relief on revenue recognition implementation. Entities electing full retrospective adoption will not be held to a five-year presentation of restated revenue figures. Shelley Luisi of the SEC's Office of the Chief Accountant has stated that the SEC "will not object if the retrospective application only applies to selected financial data in the years that are included in the audited financial statements. So any additional years included in selected financial data will not need to be retrospectively restated." Ms. Luisi emphasized that disclosure will be critical to investors understanding the inconsistency. The SEC has also indicated that it will not object if entities

- do not recast the ratio of earnings to fixed charges disclosures, while disclosing the lack of comparability;
- continue to use the pre-transition significance test for equity method investors for S-X Rules 3-09 and 4-08(g).

Item 11(b) of Form S-3, Registration Statement Under the Securities Act of 1933, requires entities to recast annual financial statements upon adoption of a new accounting principle. The SEC has said that it is clear that retrospective revision of the financial statements is required for registrants applying the full retrospective method, provided the change is material. Therefore, a calendar-year registrant filing a Form S-3 registration statement in 2018 after adoption of the Standard retrospectively in a Form 10-Q would have to recast its prior-period 2015, 2016, and 2017 financial statements.

At the date of this publication, the SEC has announced rescission, effective upon an entity adopting the Standard, of four SEC Staff EITF Observer comments related to these four narrow issues.

EITF	Issue
90-22	Accounting for gas-balancing arrangements
91-09	Revenue and expense recognition for freight services in process
00-10	Accounting for shipping and handling fees and costs
01-09	Accounting for consideration given by a vendor to a customer (including a reseller of the vendor's products)

INDUSTRY-SPECIFIC GUIDANCE SUPERSEDED

IASB Vice Chairman Ian Mackintosh and FASB Chairman Russell Golden both identified software, telecommunications, and real restate as industries that will be most affected.

—*May 2014 Revenue Recognition*
Standard Announcement

Entities that currently apply industry-specific guidance will see the greatest impact and may face complex implementation challenges. Industries most affected include

- telecommunication companies selling telephones and phone services,
- computer software,
- construction,
- aerospace,
- defense,
- real estate, licensors (pharmaceuticals, film and entertainment, franchisors), and
- asset management.

Vendor-specific objective evidence (VSOE) is no longer required for companies selling software. Entities can use it but if it is not available, estimates may be used. This is an area that will require a high degree of judgment.

For some, but not all, of the industries listed above, revenue recognition may be accelerated. For instance, revenue recognition in the telecommunications industry may be accelerated, but for the asset management industry, revenue generally may be recognized later under the new requirements.

AICPA INDUSTRY COMMITTEES

In response to the issuance of the Standard, the AICPA has established 16 industry task forces. The task forces are charged with identifying implementation issues and aiding in the development of an AICPA accounting guide on revenue recognition. The industries included in the project are

- Aerospace and Defense
- Airlines
- Asset Management
- Broker-Dealers
- Construction Contractors
- Depository Institutions
- Gaming
- Health Care
- Hospitality
- Insurance
- Not-for-Profit
- Oil and Gas
- Power and Utility
- Software
- Telecommunications
- Timeshare.

Comments submitted to the task forces can be viewed on aicpa.org.

CHANGES TO INDUSTRY-SPECIFIC GUIDANCE

Exhibit ES.5 lists the changes made by the ASU to industry-specific guidance.

Exhibit ES.5 Status of industry-specific guidance in ASU 2014-09 for affected industries

ASC Section	Status	Comments
905-605 Agriculture—Revenue Recognition	Retains a portion of the 905-605 guidance	
908-605 Airlines	Superseded	
910-605 Contractors—Construction	Superseded	
912-605 Contractors—Federal Government	Superseded	For guidance on the presentation of a loss on a termination of a contract for default, see paragraph ASC 912-20-25-4
920-605 Entertainment—Broadcasters	Superseded	
922-605 Entertainment—Cable Television	Superseded	
924-605 Entertainment—Casinos	Superseded	
926-605 Entertainment—Films	Superseded	
928-605 Entertainment—Music	Superseded	
932-605 Extractive Activities—Oil and Gas	Superseded	
940-605 Financial Services—Brokers and Dealers	Superseded	
942-605 Financial Services—Depository and Lending	Superseded	
944-605 Financial Services—Insurance	Superseded	For guidance on recognizing revenue from contracts that are not within the scope of this topic by insurance entities, see ASC Subtopic 944-605
946-605 Financial Services—Investment Companies	Superseded	
948-605 Financial Services—Mortgage Banking	Superseded	
952-605 Franchisors	Superseded	
954-605 Health Care Entities	Retains a portion of the 954-605 guidance	For guidance on determining whether a liability should be recognized for a continuing care retirement community for its obligation to provide future services and the use of facilities to current residents, see Sections 954-440-25 and 954-440-35

ASC Section	Status	Comments
958-605 Not-for-Profit Entities	Retains a portion of the 958-605 guidance	For guidance on determining when to recognize a loss under prepaid health care services contracts, see paragraph 954-450-30-4 For guidance on recognizing revenue from contracts that are not within the scope of this topic by not-for-profit entities, see Subtopic 958-605
970-605 Real Estate—General	Superseded	
972-605 Real Estate—Common Interest Realty Associations	Superseded	
974-605 Real Estate—Real Estate Investment Trusts	Superseded	
976-605 Real Estate—Retail Land	Superseded	
78-605 Real Estate—Time-Sharing Activities	Superseded	
980-605 Regulated Operations	Retains a portion of the 980-605 guidance	For guidance on recognizing a loss on long-term power sales contracts, see paragraph 980-350-35-3
985-605 Software	Superseded	

TRANSITION RESOURCE GROUP

The FASB and the IASB established a joint TRG to solicit, analyze, and discuss stakeholder issues and inform the Boards about potential implementation issues that could arise during the transition period. The Boards then consider whether amendments or additional guidance is needed. The TRG does not issue authoritative guidance. The TRG consisted of 19 members, representing U.S. and international preparers, auditors, users from various industries, and public and private companies and organizations. At its first meeting, the TRG defined its role as insuring that comparability actually occurs upon implementation.

Over 80 issues were brought to the TRG. For 98% of those issues, the TRG decided that they did not need action by the Boards or the issues were discussed with and resolved with the FASB and IASB staff. At a joint meeting of the Boards on February 18, 2015, two issues were discussed, and the Boards agreed to issue clarifying guidance on

- licenses of intellectual property, and
- identifying performance obligations.

However, the Boards came to different conclusions on the substance of some of the changes and the methods to communicate those changes. The FASB issued an ED in May 2015 on the two issues above—licenses and identifying performance obligations. On the latter, the ED aims to reduce cost and complexity. For the former, the ED seeks to increase the clarity and operability of the guidance.

The Boards held a second joint meeting on March 18, 2015 to discuss

- practical expedients upon transition—contract modifications and completed contracts
- sales tax presentation—gross versus net
- noncash consideration
- collectibility—accounting for cash received
- principal versus agent—gross versus net reporting.

At the June 22, 2015 joint meeting of the FASB and the IASB, principal versus agent issues were discussed. In August 2015, the FASB issued an ED on principal versus agent considerations with comments due October 1, 2015. In addition, the FASB has directed its staff to draft an ASU on narrow scope improvements and practical expedients.

On July 30, 2015, the IASB issued a proposal with clarifications to IFRS 15. The proposal includes two practical expedients to help entities transition to the Standard and aims to clarify

- how to identify the performance obligations in a contract,
- how to determine whether a party involved in a transaction is the principal or the agent, and
- how to determine whether a license provides the customer with a right to access or a right to use the entity's intellectual property.

The issues and actions being taken by the FASB and the IASB are summarized in the appendix to this summary.

On December 16, 2015, the Boards held a joint meeting and affirmed their proposals related to

- principal versus agent, and
- application of the control principle.

The Boards decided to eliminate exposure to credit risk as a control indicator [ASC 606-10-55-39(e); IFRS 15.B37(e)]. The FASB approved drafting of a final ASU.

At its January 2016 meeting, the IASB directed its staff to draft the final amendments to its clarification of IFRS 15, with expectation of publication of a final document in March 2016 and an effective date of January 1, 2018. The IASB also stated that it does not plan to schedule any more meetings of the IFRS constituents of the IASB. The TRG will not be disbanded. It will be available for consultation if needed. The IASB will continue to collaborate with the FASB and monitor future FASB discussions with the U.S. GAAP constituents of the TRG. The IASB pointed out that IFRS reporters are not required to consider FASB's pronouncements or public discussions when applying the Standard. The IASB did point out, however, that IAS 8 allows entities to consider the most recent pronouncements of other standards setters as long as that guidance does not conflict with IFRS standards and the *Conceptual Framework*.[6]

See the appendix to this summary for subsequent developments. For the most recent developments, readers should consult the FASB and IASB project pages.

---

6 http://www.ifrs.org/Current-Projects/IASB-Projects/Clarifications-IFRS-15-Issues-from-TRG-discussions/Project-news/Pages/Project-news-January-2016.aspx

APPENDIX: STATUS OF ISSUES BROUGHT TO THE BOARDS

The table that follows summarizes the issues and the path forward chosen by the FASB. Additional information and background papers can be found on the FASB website.

Issue	FASB Decisions	IASB Decisions
Licenses of Intellectual Property (IP)		
Determining the nature of an entity's promise in granting a license	Update the standard to affirm that functional IP is a separate performance obligation unless the functionality is expected to change substantively as a result of activities that do not transfer a promised good or service to the entity and the customer is required to use the updated IP resulting from that change.	Update the standard to clarify the effect of the entity's activities on the functionality of a license.
Determining when the entity should determine the nature of the entity's promise in granting a license	Update the standard to clarify that an entity may need to determine the nature of a license that is not a separate performance obligation in order to apply the guidance on whether a performance obligation is satisfied over time or at a point in time and the appropriate measure of progress.	No update to the standard. Referenced paragraphs 59–64 of Agenda Paper 7B.
Determining when the sales-based and usage-based royalties constraint applies	Update the standard to clarify that rather than splitting a royalty (and applying both the royalty and general constraints to it), an entity would apply the royalty constraint if the license is the predominant feature to which the royalty relates. Revise the related illustrations.	
Contractual restrictions in license arrangements	Update the standard to clarify that the contractual restrictions, such as those described in ASC 606-10-55-64, are attributes of the license and do not affect the identification of the promised goods or services.	No updates to the standard. Referenced analysis in paragraphs 68–73 of Agenda Paper 7B.
Identifying Performance Obligations		
Identifying promised goods or services	Update the standard to permit entities to evaluate the materiality of promises at the contract level and that, if the promises are immaterial in the context of the contract, the entity would not need to evaluate such promises further.	No updates to the standard.

	Requires that if as a result of not identifying immaterial goods or services, revenue is recognized before all of the goods or services in the contract are transferred to the customer, the entity should accrue the costs to transfer those goods or services.	
The concept of distinct within the context of the contract	Add illustrative examples and update the standard to define "separately identifiable," reframe the separation criteria to focus on a bundle of goods or services.	Add illustrative examples but not otherwise amend the standard's guidance. IASB noted that the analysis in paragraphs 34–43 of Agenda Paper 7C could help educate preparers.
Shipping and handling services	Add guidance clarifying that shipping and handling activities that occur before control transfers to the customer are fulfillment activities and allow entities to elect a policy to treat shipping and handling activities as fulfillment costs if they do not represent the predominant activity in the contract and they occur after control transfers. If revenue is recognized before the shipping and handling activities occur, the entity should accrue the related costs of the shipping and handling activities.	No updates at this time because staff unsure of the extent of issue for IFRS constituents.
Narrow Scope Improvements and Practical Expedients Upon Transition		
Contract modifications that occur prior to the date of initially applying the standard	Allow a practical expedient that would permit an entity to account for a modified contract by determining the transaction price at the contract modification adjustment date (CMAD) and perform a single standalone selling price allocation (with the benefit of hindsight) to all satisfied and unsatisfied performance obligations in the contract from inception. Entities using the full retrospective method should use the beginning of the earliest period presented as the CMAD, whereas entities using the modified retrospective method	Entities using either the full retrospective or modified retrospective method should use the beginning of the earliest presentation as the CMAD.

	should use the date of initial application as the CMAD.	
Definition of a completed contract	FASB clarified its definition of a completed contract and added the phrase "substantially all."	The IASB did not change its definition.
Contracts completed at transition	Add a practical expedient to allow entities using the modified retrospective approach to apply it to all contracts.	Add a practical expedient to allow entities electing the full retrospective approach to apply the Standard retrospectively only to contracts that are not complete as of the beginning of the earliest period presented.
Transition disclosures	The Boards added guidance to require entities to disclose use of either of the practical expedients mentioned above and, to the extent reasonably possible, a qualitative assessment of the estimated effect of applying the expedient.	
Technical correction	FASB made a technical correction to transition guidance to clarify that an entity using the full retrospective approach does not need to disclose the effect of the accounting change on affected financial statement line items in the period of adoption.	
Presentation of sales taxes— gross versus net	Add a practical expedient for presentation of sales taxes, allowing an election for net reporting for all in-scope sales taxes with disclosure of the policy. FASB reporters must disclose if they opt for the policy election.	Decided not to add a practical expedient.
Measurement date for determining the fair value of noncash consideration	Clarify the guidance to require that noncash consideration be measured at contract inception.	No additional guidance at this time.
Application of the constraint on variable consideration to changes in the fair value of the noncash consideration	Add guidance to apply the constraint on variable consideration only to a transaction in which the fair value of noncash consideration might vary for reasons other than the form of the consideration.	No additional guidance at this time. The IASB will monitor the FASB's actions and revisit if necessary.
Collectibility Considerations		
The application of the collectibility criterion in Step 1 of the Standard	Amend the guidance in Step 1 to clarify when a contract is "terminated" per ASC 606-10-25-7. The contract need not be	IASB postponed a decision and will perform more research.

	legally terminated and the entity does not have to stop pursuing collection in order for the contract to be considered terminated for purposes of recognizing cash under the new standard. Add a criterion to the alternate recognition model so that if collectibility is not probable, an entity should recognize revenue in the amount of consideration received when control has transferred, an entity has stopped transferring and has no obligation to transfer additional goods or services, and consideration is nonrefundable. Add guidance to clarify that the objective of the collectibility threshold [ASC 606-10-25-1(e)] is to assess an entity's exposure to credit risk for a product transferred to the customer. Under some circumstances, entities may not assess their ability to collect all of the consideration in order to meet the threshold.	
Principal versus Agent (Reporting Revenue Gross versus Net)		
Determining whether an entity's promise is to provide or to arrange	The Boards reaffirmed the standard's principle that an entity is the principal when it controls the promised good or service. The entity is an agent when it does not control the specified good or service before it is transferred.	
Unit of account for the principal versus agent evaluation	Entity determines principal versus agent role for each specified good or service promised to the customer. Clarify that a specified good or service is a distinct good or service. And, depending on the circumstances, a good or service may be a right to an underlying good or service provided by another party.	
Application of the control principle	Update the guidance to clarify the application of the control principle for services.	
Control indicators	Update the guidance to clarify the role of the indicators in ASC 606-10-55-39 and IFRS 15, B37, specifically: that the indicators help the evaluation of control, rather than override the evaluation; how each indicator relates to the control principle; and that one or more indicators may be more or less relevant depending on the contract. Eliminate credit risk as an indicator. Also, update to reframe when the indicators indicate when an entity is a principal rather than an agent.	

Illustrative examples	Amend principal versus agent examples and add examples.	
Estimating gross revenue as a principal	The Boards discussed including the issue of estimating gross revenue as a principal in cases where the entity is a principal but does not know the price paid by the end customer to an agent. Boards decided not to include the issue, but requested that the staff add the Board's reasoning on this issue in the Basis of Conclusion in the ASU on principal versus agent considerations, including that Topic 606's transaction price guidance addresses the issue and the Board does not support gross revenue in those cases.	
Technical Corrections and Improvements (Proposed Changes)		
Preproduction costs	Supersede the guidance on preproduction costs related to long-term supply arrangements in ASC 340-10 so that entities apply the guidance in ASC 340-40.	
Impairment testing	Amend the impairment testing guidance in ASC 340-40 so that entities would consider contract renewals and extensions and measure the consideration it expects to receive as the sum of consideration received but not recognized and the amount it expects to receive. The order of impairment would be assets outside the scope of ASC 340, assets within the scope, and then asset groups within the scope of ASC 350.	
Scope	Specify that contracts within the scope of ASC 944 are excluded for ASC 606. Clarify scope for incentive-based capital allocations.	
Contract modifications	Amend Example 7.	
New subtopic	Subtopic 924-815 that includes a scope exception from derivatives guidance for fixed odds wagering contracts.	
Cost capitalization guidance	Align the guidance in ASC 946 for public and private funds.	
Remaining performance obligations	FASB decided to add a practical expedient for entities applying the requirement to disclose remaining performance obligations. Those entities can	

| | use the expedient and not disclose remaining performance obligations related to the following types of variable consideration:

• Sales-based or usage-based royalties promised in exchange for a license of IP and
• Variable consideration that is allocated entirely to a wholly unsatisfied performance obligation or to a distinct good or service that forms part of a single performance obligation and meets the criteria in ASC 606-10-32-40. | |

1 STEP 1—IDENTIFY THE CONTRACT WITH THE CUSTOMER[1]

OVERVIEW

For the most part, guidance for Step 1 in applying the revenue recognition model is straightforward. However, the new guidance for contract modifications might be an aspect of this guidance that is somewhat trickier. Contract modifications are explored in detail in Chapter 6.

---

[1] The Boards issued two separate standards. For ease of reference, this volume refers to them as a single standard, "the revenue standard" or "the Standard."

Contract: *Agreement between two or more parties that creates enforceable rights and obligations.*
  (ASC 606-10-20; IFRS 15 Appendix A)

Note: The IASB has, in effect, two definitions of contract. The revenue standard emphasizes legal enforceability, whereas IAS 32, *Financial Instruments: Presentation*, stops short of *requiring* legal enforceability. (IAS 32.13) The IASB decided not to amend IAS 32 because of concerns over creating unintended consequences in accounting for financial instruments.

Exhibit 1.1   Overview of Step 1 of the revenue recognition model—identify the contracts

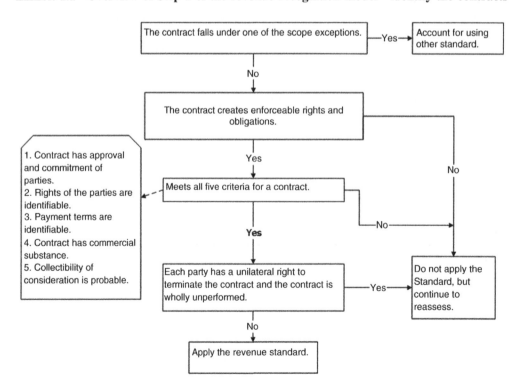

To apply the revenue standard, entities should first determine whether a contract is specifically excluded from the guidance in the Standard. Scope exceptions are detailed in the Executive Summary chapter. The Executive Summary chapter includes a list of transactions excluded from the Standard and a related example regarding nonmonetary exchanges. After determining that a contract is not specifically excluded, entities must identify the contracts that meet the criteria in Step 1 of the revenue recognition model. If the entity determines that a contract does not meet the criteria for Step 1, the contract does not exist for the purposes of the Standard and the entity does not apply Steps 2 through 5. A contract as articulated in the Standard must exist before an entity can recognize revenue from a customer.

ASSESSING WHETHER CONTRACTS ARE WITHIN THE SCOPE OF THE STANDARD

To be within the scope of the revenue standard, and in accordance with the definition of contracts in the Standard, the agreement must not fall under one of the scope exceptions listed in the Executive Summary chapter and must

- create enforceable rights and obligations, and
- meet the five criteria listed in the Standard.

Enforceable Rights and Obligations

The enforceability of the contract

- is a matter of law
- varies across legal jurisdictions, industries, and entities
- may vary within an entity
- may depend on the class of customer or nature of goods or services.

Determining whether an arrangement has created enforceable rights is a matter of law, and evaluating the legal enforceability of the contract can be particularly challenging. This is particularly true if multiple jurisdictions are involved. Entities also need to consider whether, in order to comply with jurisdictional or trade regulation, a written contract is required. Significant judgment may be involved for some cases, and qualified legal counsel may need to be consulted.

The Boards clarified that even though the contract must be legally enforceable to be within the scope of the guidance, the performance obligations within the contract may not be legally enforceable, but may be based on the valid expectations of the customer.

The Five Contract Criteria

The Standard lists five criteria that are assessed at contract inception and that must be met for agreements to be considered contracts subject to the guidance of the Standard.

The five criteria, shown in Exhibit 1.2, are essentially a financial accounting definition of a contract. The entity needs to exercise judgment when applying the criteria. The entity must also be aware that the parties may enter into amendments or side agreements that change the substance of the contract. So, it is important to understand the entire contract, including the amendments and side agreements.

A contract that has enforceable rights and obligations between two or more parties is within the scope of the revenue standard when *all* five of the above criteria are met. The criteria are discussed in more detail below.

Exhibit 1.2   The five contract criteria (ASC 606-10-25-1; IFRS 15.9)

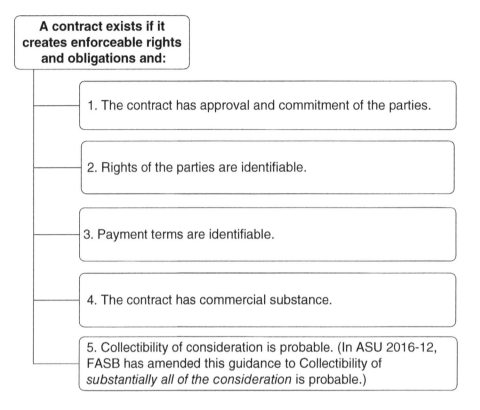

The Contract has Approval and Commitment of the Parties. The approval of the parties can be

a. written,
b. oral, or
c. implied by the entity's customary business practice.

This criterion is included because if not approved, a contract may not be legally enforceable. The Standard focuses on the enforceability of the contract rather than its form (oral, written, or implied). An entity may take into consideration its past business practices when assessing this criterion. For example, an entity that has a practice of performing based on oral agreements may determine that those oral agreements meet the requirement. If an oral agreement meets the requirement, an entity may need to account for the contract as soon as performance begins rather than wait for a signed agreement.

Example 1.1: Oral Contract

Scan Safe provides virus scanning services over the Internet. A customer calls to sign up for the service and provides the sales representative with credit card authorization. The customer agrees to the terms, and the service begins immediately. The oral agreement that Scan Safe and the customer have entered into is legally enforceable in its jurisdiction. The agreement meets the criteria for a contract with a customer, and the agreement falls under the guidance in the Standard.

Example 1.2: Product Delivered, but No Written Contract Exists

Office Supplier usually delivers products based on a written contract. However, a regular customer had a flood that destroyed furniture and computers. Because of the customer's urgent need, Office Supplier provides replacement products without a written contract. To determine whether an enforceable contract exists even though Office Supplier has deviated from its usual business practice and has no written agreement, Office Supplier must determine if it has legally enforceable rights and the oral agreement meets all five of the criteria to be a contract.

Automatic Renewal   Some contracts may automatically renew. Entities should apply the Standard to the period for which the parties have enforceable rights and obligations.

Example 1.3: Contract Extension

LMS provides web hosting services to Publishing Company. The written contract calls for Publishing Company to pay CU 1,500 per month for the services. The contract expires on June 30, 20X1 and contains no provision for automatic extensions. There are no performance issues and no expected changes in performance requirements. While the entities negotiate new payment terms, LMS continues to provide the hosting services for July and August and Publishing Company continues to pay CU 1,500 per month. The entities sign a new contract on August 27, 20X1 that requires Publishing Company to pay CU 2,000 per month.

In this case, a contract appears to exist because LMS performed and Publishing Company paid for the service under the terms of the previous contract. LMS should analyze the contract for legal enforceability and recognize revenue accordingly.

Commitment to Perform   The Boards concluded that it is not necessary for the parties to be committed to fulfilling all of their rights and obligations, but there must be sufficient evidence that the parties are substantially committed.

Termination Clauses and Wholly Unperformed Contracts   When determining the parties' commitment to perform under a contract, termination clauses are a key element to consider. Termination clauses are an indicator of both parties' commitment to perform under the contract. The contract *does not exist*, for the purposes of the revenue standard, if

- each party has a unilateral right to terminate, and
- the contract is wholly unperformed without compensating the other party.

However, the contract does exist for the purposes of the revenue standard if only one party has the right to terminate the contract without penalty. If both parties have a unilateral right to terminate the agreement, then the TRG members agreed that the agreement should be treated as a month-to-month contract. The TRG members also agreed that where a substantive termination clause exists, the contract term is the stated contract term or, if earlier, the date when the termination payment is no longer due.

A contract is considered *wholly unperformed* if the entity has

- not satisfied any part of its performance obligation
- not transferred any of the promised goods or services to the customer, and
- the customer has not paid, or is obligated to pay, any other consideration under the contract.

(ASC 606-10-25-4; IFRS 15.12)

Example 1.4: Meeting the Termination Criteria

Office Supplier enters into an agreement with Business Center to supply furniture and computers for an office complex under development in an economically disadvantaged country. Business Center agrees to pay an advance deposit. Office Supplier determines that the agreement does not meet the collectibility criteria. Office Supplier determines that it has fulfilled its performance obligations and Business Center has paid the consideration it was obligated to pay under the contract. The contract does not meet the wholly unperformed criteria for a terminated contract, therefore, the contract has not been terminated.

Rights of the Parties are Identifiable. This criterion is relatively straightforward and is necessary in order to assess when the entity has transferred control of the goods or services. If the rights of each party cannot be identified, revenue cannot be recognized.

Payment Terms are Identifiable. This criterion is necessary to determine the transaction price. It does not mean that the transaction price has to be fixed or explicitly stated. There must be an enforceable right to payment and sufficient information to estimate the transaction price. For more on determining the transaction price, see Chapter 3.

The Contract has Commercial Substance. Designed to prevent entities from artificially inflating revenue by transferring goods back and forth, this criterion requires the entity to demonstrate a substantive business purpose for the transaction. Commercial substance means that the contract is expected to change the risk, timing, or amount of the entity's future cash flows. No changes in cash flow likely indicate there is no commercial substance. This criterion also applies to noncash transactions. A noncash transaction may have commercial substance because it might result in reduced cash outflows in the future.

Collectibility of Consideration is Probable. For an entity to apply the Standard, it must be probable that the entity will receive the consideration it is entitled to for the goods and services that will be transferred to the customer. The transaction price may be less than the consideration stated in the contract if the consideration is variable. The assessment of collectibility is not based on all the consideration promised in the contract for all of the promised goods or services.

Technical Update

TRG discussions with the Boards raised a concern that there are potentially different interpretations of how to apply the collectibility criterion when it is not probable that the total consideration in the contract is collectible. Some interpreted the criterion to mean that all of the consideration must be collectible. Others interpreted it to mean that the contracts would meet the criterion if the entity could protect itself from credit risk.

The Boards pointed out that the assessment of collectibility considers

- the entity's exposure to the customer's credit risk, and
- business practices that would enable the entity to mitigate that risk.

These business practices include stopping services or delivery of goods or requiring advance payments. The Basis of Conclusion, paragraph 46, states that the entity would not consider the likelihood of payment for those goods or services that will not be transferred.

The IASB concluded that the current guidance and the explanatory information in the Basis for Conclusion are sufficient, and pointed out that an entity generally will not enter into a contract with a customer if the entity does not consider it to be probable that the entity will collect the consideration for which it will be entitled in exchange for the goods or services transferred to the customer. (Clarifications to IFRS 15.BC88–93)

The FASB, in contrast, decided to amend its implementation guidance and examples. The FASB changes confirm that the collectibility assessment may be based on a portion of the consideration promised in the contract to which it will be entitled in exchange for the goods or services transferred to the customer. This clarification was added by ASU 2016-12, where the FASB changed this criterion to: "Collectibility of substantially all of the consideration is probable." [ASC 606-10-25-1(e)] The IASB has not added a similar clarification.

As a purchaser of this book, you have exclusive access to a companion website, with the latest technical developments and other useful information. The website will contain updated information about exposure drafts and other technical guidance from the standards' setters. See the back of the book for information on how to access the site.

The assessment of collectibility must reflect the customer's *ability and intent* to pay. This criterion acts as a collectibility threshold. A more detailed discussion of the collectibility threshold can be found below.

Source: ASC 606-10-25-1(e); IFRS 15.9(e).

COLLECTIBILITY THRESHOLD

Comparison with Legacy Guidance

The revenue standard includes some significant changes from legacy guidance. Under legacy U.S. guidance (ASC 605-10-25-1), revenue must be earned and realized or realizable before it can be recognized. The revenue standard is not based on the realization principle. Revenue is recognized based on what the entity expects to receive—what is collectible. For SEC filers, SAB Topic 13 clarifies that collectibility is one of four criteria for revenue recognition and must be reasonably assured. For IFRS filers, IAS 18.14 includes a similar criterion: for revenue to be recognized, it must be probable that the economic benefits associated with the transaction flow to the vendor.

To be considered a contract with a customer under the Standard, it must be probable that the entity will collect the consideration to which it is entitled. In addition, under legacy guidance, collectibility is evaluated when revenue is recognized, whereas in the new revenue standard, collectibility is assessed when determining whether a contract exists. The Boards consider the customer's credit risk an important part of determining whether a contract is valid. It is not an indicator of whether revenue is recognized, but an indicator of whether the customer is able to meet its obligation.

The criterion replaces specific guidance in U.S. GAAP for health care entities and real estate transactions.

Differences between IFRS and U.S. GAAP

Collectibility is an area of difference between ASU 2014-09 (codified as ASC 606) and IFRS 15. Both documents use the term "probable." However, there is a difference in the underlying definition of probable. U.S. GAAP defines probable as "likely to occur." This is generally interpreted as a 75 to 80% probability. The collectibility threshold is similar to that in ASC 985-605, *Software: Revenue Recognition*. The threshold is slightly higher than that in SEC

SAB Topic 13, which is "reasonably assured." IFRS define probable as "more likely than not," interpreted as greater than 50%. This opens the door to some differences in practice between what is considered a contract with customers under the two standards. The boards believe that the number of instances of differences will be minimal because an entity would not likely enter into a high-credit-risk contract without protection to ensure it can collect. On the contrary, there could be a subsequent deterioration of the customer's ability to pay.

Assessing Collectibility

To be accounted for under the Standard, a contract must have commercial substance. To have commercial substance, the consideration must be collectible. So, the underlying objective of the collectibility assessment is to determine if there is a substantive transaction.

Collectibility is a "gating" question designed to prevent entities from applying the Standard to problematic contracts and recognizing revenue and an impairment loss at the same time.

Judgment. Applying the collectibility criterion requires judgment. It is partly a forward-looking assessment and requires the entity to look at all the factors and circumstances, including the entity's customary business practices and knowledge of the customer.

Timing of Assessment. Collectibility must be evaluated, like the other criteria, at contract inception, but also must be re-evaluated when significant facts and circumstances change. Most entities will not enter into a contract where there is a significant credit risk. However, even in cases where at contract inception there is no significant credit risk, there could be a subsequent deterioration in the customer's ability to pay.

Collectibility = Intent and Ability to Pay. Collectibility refers only to the company's credit risk—the customer's intent and ability to pay—and in making the collectibility assessment not to any other uncertainty or risk. Credit risk is the risk that the entity will not be able to collect the contract consideration to which it is entitled from the customer.

Consider Only Transaction Price. When making the collectibility assessment, entities should be aware that collectibility relates to the *transaction* price, a term introduced in the revenue standard, not the *contract* price. The transaction price is the amount the entity expects to be entitled to. The transaction price is not adjusted for credit risk. The entity may have to consider the transaction price in Step 3 before making a conclusion regarding Step 1's collectibility threshold.

Technical Update

In ASU 2016-12, the FASB clarified that U.S. GAAP reporters should take into account factors that might mitigate credit risk, such as

- payment terms, like upfront payments, or
- the ability to stop transferring goods or services.

A factor that should not be considered is the ability of the entity to repossess an asset. (ASC 606-10-55-3c)

Variable Consideration in the Transaction Price   The revenue standard requires an entity to consider whether the price is variable because if so, the entity may wind up offering a price concession. The collectibility assessment is made after taking into account any price concessions that may be made to the customer. The transaction price may be less than the stated contract price if the entity intends to offer a price concession.

Basis of Assessment May Be Less than Total Consideration. The assessment is not necessarily based on the entire amount of consideration for the entire duration of the contract. For example, the entry may have the ability and expectation to stop transferring goods or services if the customer stops paying consideration when due. In another example, if an entity expects to receive only partial payment for performance, the contract may still meet the contract criteria. The expected shortfall is similar to a price concession. The entity must determine if the partial payment is

- an implied price concession
- an impairment loss
- a contract lacking commercial substance.

When an entity expects a shortfall, the entity must exercise significant judgment to determine the proper accounting.

Example 1.5: Assessing Collectibility—Implied Price Concession

ACME enters into a contract to sell 1000 desks to a customer for CU 200,000. The customer is based in a geographic area suffering significant economic difficulty. This is a new customer and a new region for ACME. ACME expects that it will not be able to collect the full contract amount. However, because it wants to establish a customer base in the region, ACME enters into the contract expecting to accept a lower amount of consideration. With the implied price concession, ACME expects to be entitled to CU 160,000. Considering the customer's intent and ability to pay, and the region's economic difficulty, ACME concludes that it is probable that it will collect the CU 160,000.

Example 1.6: Assessing Collectibility—Meeting the Collectibility Threshold

Truman Construction, a real estate developer, enters into a contract to sell to Pearl River, Inc. a commercial building in the downtown area. The consideration is CU 1,000,000 broken down as follows:

- CU 50,000 nonrefundable fee paid at the contract inception, and
- CU 950,000 financed long term by Truman Construction.

The financing is provided on a nonrecourse basis. This means that if Pearl River defaults on the debt, Truman can repossess the property and keep the deposit, but cannot seek further compensation.

Pearl River intends to open an Asian fusion restaurant in the facility. Pearl River has business experience from its previous import–export endeavor, but this is its first venture into the highly competitive restaurant industry. Truman evaluates the facts and circumstances of the agreement. It determines that the factors below put the entity's intent and ability to pay substantially all of the consideration in doubt and, therefore, the agreement does not meet the collectibility threshold:

- The debt will be repaid by proceeds from the risky restaurant venture.
- Pearl River has no other assets or income to repay the debt.
- Pearl River's liability under the terms of the loan is limited because the loan is nonrecourse.

Truman does not recognize the receivable from the real estate asset. Because the contract does not meet the collectibility threshold, the contract does not meet the criteria for a contract and is out of scope of the Standard. So, initially Truman

- monitors the situation to determine if, and when, the contract does meet the contract criteria, and

- looks to the guidance in ASC 606-10-25-7 through 25-8 or IFRS 15.15–16 to determine the accounting for the nonrefundable deposit.

CONTRACT RECOGNITION

Exhibit 1.3 summarizes the qualifications of contracts that fall under the guidance in the Standard and those that do not.

Exhibit 1.3 Contracts in or out of scope

Apply the revenue standard if the contract creates enforceable rights and obligations and:	Do *not* apply the revenue standard to a contract if:
1. The contract has approval and commitment of the parties. 2. The rights of the parties are identifiable. 3. Payment terms are identifiable. 4. The contract has commercial substance. 5. Collectibility of consideration is probable. (ASC 606-10-32-17; IFRS 15.62)	Each party has a unilateral right to terminate the contract **and** The contract is wholly unperformed.

A contract that meets the qualifications for recognition under the Standard

- gives the entity the right to receive consideration, and
- creates obligations for the entity to deliver goods and services.

This combination of rights and obligations gives rise to net assets or net liabilities. These assets and liabilities are not recognized until one or both parties perform. Entities must monitor contracts for when performance has begun. Once performance has begun, a contract that is enforceable and meets the five contract criteria exists for the purposes of the revenue standard. Even if a contract has not been signed, the entities may determine that a contract exists and may need to account for a contract as soon as performance begins rather than delay revenue recognition for an executed contract. In some cases, timing of revenue recognition may differ from that under legacy standards.

ARRANGEMENTS WHERE CONTRACT CRITERIA ARE NOT MET

What happens if the entity receives consideration from the customer, but the contract fails Step 1? In that case, the entity should apply what is sometimes referred to as the alternate recognition model and recognize the consideration received only when *one* of the following occurs:

a. The entity has no remaining obligations to transfer goods or services to the customers, and all or substantially all of the consideration promised by the customer has been received by the entity and is nonrefundable.

b. The contract has been terminated, and the consideration received from the customer is nonrefundable.

c. For U.S. GAAP only—The entity has transferred control of the goods or services to which the consideration that has been received relates, the entity has stopped transferring goods and services to the customer and has no obligation to transfer additional goods or services, and the consideration received from the customer is nonrefundable.

(ASC 606-10-25-7; IFRS 15.15)

Technical Update

Subsequent to issuance of the Standard in May 2014, the TRG brought an issue to the Boards regarding the criteria in ASC 606-10-25-7 and IFRS 15.15. Some TRG members and other stakeholders held the view that for certain arrangements, the criteria were unclear. Therefore, in ASU 2016-12, the FASB added criterion "c" to clarify when revenue would be recognized if an entity did not meet the criteria in Step 1 above of the revenue recognition model.

The IASB did not propose similar amendments. In its 2016 Clarification to the Revenue Standard, the IASB has included in its Basis of Conclusion additional discussion of collectibility. The additional discussion states that when assessing collectibility, entities should consider their ability to mitigate exposure to credit risk throughout the contract by, for example, stopping providing goods or services or requiring advance payments. The difference in the two approaches to this issue should not result in significant differences in financial reporting in most cases. Example 1 of the Standard is changed by the FASB and those changes result in different conclusions as to the timing of transfer of control for the fact pattern presented.

If an arrangement does not meet the contract criteria in the revenue standard, then consideration received should be accounted for as a liability until

- "a" or "b" or, for U.S. GAAP reporters only, "c" above occur, or
- the arrangement meets the contract criteria.

The liability is measured at the amount of consideration received from the customer. The liability represents the entity's obligations to

- transfer goods or services in the future, or
- refund the consideration received.
(ASC 606-10-25-8; IFRS 15.16)

This can be contrasted with current standards where revenue may be recognized in the amount of cash received. Chapter 5 has a detailed discussion of recognizing revenue, contract assets, and contract liabilities.

Exhibit 1.4   No contract exists, consideration received

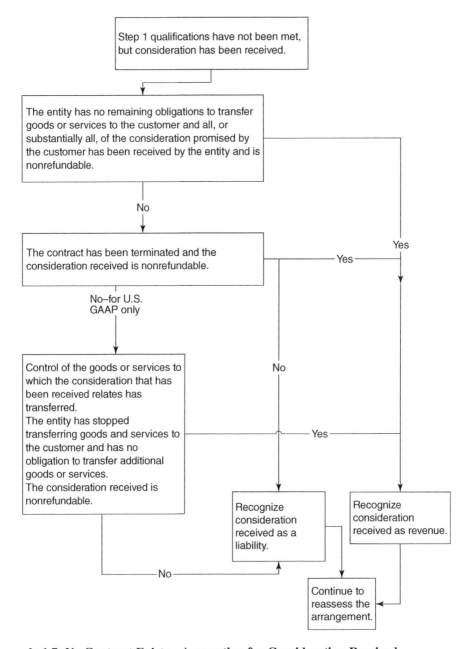

Example 1.7: No Contract Exists—Accounting for Consideration Received

Use the facts in Example 1.6. Because the contract between Truman Development and Pearl River does not meet the Step 1 qualifications, and the entity has not received substantially all of the consideration and has not terminated the contract, Truman accounts for the nonrefundable CU 50,000 as a liability and does not derecognize the real estate asset. Truman also does not recognize a receivable. Truman continues to assess the contract until the five contract criteria have been met or the contract meets the termination criteria.

Reassessment

When an arrangement has been assessed and is considered a contract under the revenue standard, the entity is not required to reassess the contract unless there is an indication of a significant change. A significant change might be, for example, a significant deterioration in the customer's ability to pay. (ASC 606-10-25-5; IFRS 15.13) In that case, the entity needs to assess whether it is probable that the customer will pay the consideration for the remaining goods or services. In contrast, if the arrangement is not initially considered a contract and if there is an indication that there has been a significant change in facts and circumstances, the entity should reassess to determine whether the criteria are met subsequently. (ASC 606-10-25-6; IFRS 15.14) The entity applies the provisions of the Standard from the date the criterion are met.

Only the rights and obligations that have *not* transferred are reassessed. Therefore, a reassessment will not result in any reversal of revenue, receivables, or assets already recognized. Those assets are assessed for impairment under the relevant financial instruments standard. The entity does not recognize any additional revenue from the agreement.

The TRG members have acknowledged that the assessment of whether significant changes have occurred requiring a reassessment of collectibility or even a determination that a contract no longer exists under the Standard will be situation-specific and require judgment.

THE PORTFOLIO APPROACH AND COMBINING CONTRACTS

The revenue standard includes

- a practical expedient for combining groups of contracts, and
- a new requirement to combine contracts.

A Practical Expedient

An entity normally applies the revenue standard to individual contracts. However, in certain circumstances, an entity may use a practical expedient and apply the revenue standard to a group of contracts. This expedient allows for the portfolio approach—applying the revenue standard to a group of contracts or performance obligations under the following conditions:

- the contracts must have similar characteristics *and*
- the entity must reasonably expect that the effects of applying the guidance to a portfolio would not differ materially from applying it to individual contracts or performance obligations.

(ASC 606-10-10-4; IFRS 15.4)

It is expected that in most cases entities will apply the revenue model to an individual contract. However, entities need to evaluate the cost versus benefit of using the portfolio approach. For some, the effort to assess what constitutes a portfolio and develop the processes needed to account for the portfolio may outweigh any benefit of this practical expedient.

Combination of Contracts Required

IFRS 11, *Construction Contracts*, provides that two or more contracts *must* be accounted for as a single contract if certain conditions are met, and IAS 18 has a similar provision. Under legacy

U.S. GAAP (ASC 605-25-25-3), the entity is *allowed* to combine contracts if certain conditions are met. The Standard *requires* a combination of contracts under certain circumstances. Entities have to assess existing contracts to determine whether combination is required and should also be mindful of the combination requirement when writing new contracts. The decision to combine contracts is made at the inception of the contracts.

Exhibit 1.5   Combination of contracts required

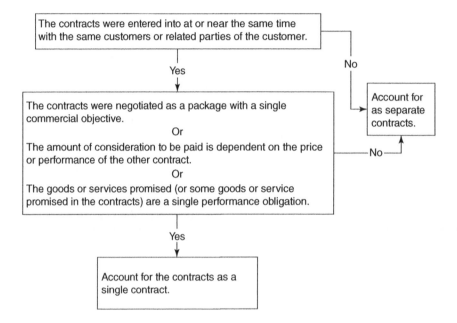

The entity needs to assess whether the substance of the contract is that the pricing or economics of the contracts are interdependent. The Standard offers guidance to help make that judgment. The contracts should be accounted for as a single contract when the contracts are entered into at or near the same time with the same customers or parties related to the customer and if *any* of the following conditions are met:

a. The entity negotiates the contracts as a package with a single commercial objective.
b. The amount of consideration to be paid in the contract depends on the price or performance of the other contract.
c. The goods or services promised in the contracts (or some goods or services promised in the contracts) constitute a single performance obligation.

(ASC 606-10-25-9; IFRS 15.17)

The entity should apply the guidance on identifying performance obligations when assessing "c." (See Chapter 2.)

The fact that multiple contracts are negotiated at the same time is not sufficient evidence to demonstrate that the contracts represent a single arrangement. (ASC 2014-09 BC73; IFRS 15.BC73)

Tip: The entity needs to exercise significant judgment in determining what constitutes "at or near the same time." If the time period between execution of the contracts is short, contracts may meet the "at or near the same time" condition. Also, subsequent promises not considered at contract inception are generally accounted for as contract modifications.

If the criteria are met, contracts between the same customer or related parties of the customer should be combined. Related parties are those defined in the guidance ASC 850, *Related Parties Disclosures* and IAS 24, *Related Party Disclosures.*

In U.S. GAAP, related parties include

- affiliates of the entity
- entities for which investments in their equity securities would be required, absent the election of the fair value option under the Fair Value Option Subsection of Section 825-10-15, to be accounted for by the equity method by the investing entity
- trusts for the benefit of employees, such as pension and profit-sharing trusts that are managed by or under the trusteeship of management
- principal owners of the entity and members of their immediate families
- management of the entity and members of their immediate families
- other parties with which the entity may deal if one party controls or can significantly influence the management or operating policies of the other to an extent that one of the transacting parties might be prevented from fully pursuing its own separate interests
- other parties that can significantly influence the management or operating policies of the transacting parties or that have an ownership interest in one of the transacting parties and can significantly influence the other to an extent that one or more of the transacting parties might be prevented from fully pursuing its own separate interests.

(ASC 850-10-20)

IAS 24, *Related Party Disclosures* includes the following definition of related parties:

A related party is a person or entity that is related to the entity that is preparing its financial statements (in this Standard referred to as the 'reporting entity').

a. A person or a *close member of that person's family* is related to a reporting entity if that person:

    i. has control or joint control of the reporting entity;
    ii. has significant influence over the reporting entity; or
    iii. is a member of the *key management personnel* of the reporting entity or of a parent of the reporting entity.

b. An entity is *related* to a reporting entity if any of the following conditions applies:

    i. The entity and the reporting entity are members of the same group (which means that each parent, subsidiary and fellow subsidiary is related to the others).
    ii. One entity is an associate or joint venture of the other entity (or an associate or joint venture of a member of a group of which the other entity is a member).
    iii. Both entities are joint ventures of the same third party.
    iv. One entity is a joint venture of a third entity and the other entity is an associate of the third entity.
    v. The entity is a post-employment benefit plan for the benefit of employees of either the reporting entity or an entity related to the reporting entity. If the reporting entity is itself such a plan, the sponsoring employers are also related to the reporting entity.
    vi. The entity is controlled or jointly controlled by a person identified in (a).

    vii. A person identified in (a)(i) has significant influence over the entity or is a member of the *key management personnel* of the entity (or of a parent of the entity).

    viii. The entity, or any member of a group of which it is a part, provides key management personnel services to the reporting entity or to the parent of the reporting entity.

(IAS 24.9)

Assessing Collectibility of a Portfolio of Contracts

An issue was raised with the TRG regarding how to deal with situations in a portfolio of homogenous contracts where some customers will pay amounts owed, but the entity has historical experience indicating that some customers will not pay the full consideration. In that case, the entity should record revenue, but separately evaluate the contract asset or receivable for impairment. The entity will have to exercise judgment regarding whether to record a bad debt expense or reduce revenue for an anticipated price concession.

IDENTIFYING THE CUSTOMER

> Customer: A party that has contracted with an entity to obtain goods or services that are an output of the entity's ordinary activities in exchange for consideration.
>   (ASC 606-10-20; IFRS Appendix A)

Collaborative Arrangements

A collaborative arrangement is not in the scope of the Standard unless the collaboration meets the definition of a customer. In most cases, the identification of the customer is straightforward. However, the Boards decided not to offer additional application guidance and, therefore, a collaborative arrangement requires more careful analysis of the facts and circumstances. For example, an arrangement with a counterparty where both parties share the risks and benefits will most likely not result in a counterparty meeting the definition of a customer, and, therefore, the arrangement will not fall under the Standard. (ASC 606-10-15-3; IFRS 15.6) On the contrary, an arrangement where the entity is selling a good or service, even if the arrangement is labeled a collaboration, will likely fall under the scope of the Standard.

It is also possible that portions of the contract will be a collaboration, while other portions will be a contract with a customer. The latter portion will be in the scope of the revenue standard.

After a thorough analysis of the agreement, the entity should decide whether to apply the revenue standard and/or other guidance, such as ASC 808, *Collaborative Arrangements*, or IFRS 11, *Joint Arrangements*.

Example 1.8: Collaborative Arrangement

A company in the biotech industry enters into an agreement with a company in the pharmaceutical industry to share equally in the revenue from work on the development of a specific new drug. If the companies agree to simply work together, this collaborative arrangement is not in the scope of the revenue standard because there is no customer. If, on the contrary, the biotech company is selling its compound to the pharmaceutical company, then the arrangement is likely in the scope of the Standard.

Arrangements with Multiple Parties

There are cases where multiple parties are involved in the transaction. For example, pharmaceutical companies provide products to customers and parts of the fees are paid by an insurer and the remaining fees are paid by the customer. Or, manufacturers issue coupons directly to the consumer and reimburse the retailer for the coupons.

> **Tip:** Careful analysis is needed to evaluate the substance of the transaction to determine
>
> - who are the customers,
> - whether the entity is a principal or an agent, and
> - if the contracts can be combined.

The entity must also determine if it is the principal or agent in the transaction. This matters because the principal recognizes the revenue for the gross amount, and the agent recognizes the transaction at net—the amount that the entity expects to retain after paying the other party for goods or services provided. Principal versus agent guidance is discussed in detail in Chapter 6.

2 STEP 2—IDENTIFY THE PERFORMANCE OBLIGATIONS

Technical Alert

Subsequent to issuance of the Standard, the TRG surfaced several issues related to identifying performance obligations:

- determining whether a good or service is separately identifiable from other promises in the contract;
- shipping and handling activities;
- immaterial goods or services.

Although on some issues the Boards took different approaches, the FASB and the IASB both issued changes to the Standard related to identifying performance obligations. Those changes are discussed in the relevant sections of this chapter.

As a purchaser of this book, you have exclusive access to a companion website, with the latest technical developments and other useful information. The website will contain updated information about exposure drafts and other technical guidance from the standards' setters. See the back of the book for information on how to access the site.

Performance obligation: A promise in a contract with a customer to transfer to the customer either:

    a. A good or service (or a bundle of goods and services) that is distinct.
    b. A series of goods or services that are substantially the same and that have the same pattern of transfer to the customer.
(ASC 606-10-20; IFRS 15.22)

OVERVIEW

The purpose of identifying the performance obligations in a contract is to establish the unit of account to which the transaction price should be allocated. The accounting unit affects when and how revenue should be recognized. Because the revenue recognition model is an allocated transaction price model, identifying a meaningful unit of account is critical. (ASU 2014-09 BC85; IFRS 15.BC85) Once the performance obligations are identified, the entity can then assess whether they are immaterial.

The Standard uses the term "performance obligation" to distinguish obligations to provide goods or services to a customer from other obligations. Although it is a new term, "performance obligation" is similar to the notions of deliverables, components, or elements of a contract in legacy guidance. In the definition above, the Standard essentially provides two categories of performance obligations:

- a distinct good or service *and*
- a series of goods or services with the same pattern of transfer.

This chapter will examine both in depth.

To apply Step 2 of the revenue standard, at the inception of the contract, the entity should assess the contract and

a. identify all promised goods or services or bundle of goods or services, then
b. identify the contract's performance obligations.

The purpose of the first part of the assessment is to identify the promises in the contract, taking note of terms and customary business practices. The entity must identify all promises, even if they seem inconsequential or perfunctory. In ASU 2016-10, the FASB clarified that an entity is not required to assess whether promised goods or services are performance obligations if they are immaterial in the context of the contract. (ASC 606-10-25-16A) Materiality should be assessed in the context of the arrangement as a whole, and the quantitative and qualitative nature of the promised goods or services should be considered. (ASU 2016-10 BC13) The IASB did not make a similar clarification because it believes the IFRS 15 requirements are clear.

In the second part of the assessment, the entity determines which of those promises are performance obligations that should be accounted for separately. Some contracts contain single performance obligations and are relatively straightforward. Multiple elements in a contract may present more challenges.

The process for implementing Step 2 is outlined in Exhibit 2.1.

PROMISES IN CONTRACTS WITH CUSTOMERS

When identifying the promises in a contract, the entity must identify not only the explicit promises, but also the implicit promises and those activities associated with the contracts that do not meet the criteria for performance obligations.

Promises to provide goods or services are performance obligations even if they are satisfied by another party.

Implicit Promises

In addition to promised goods or services explicitly detailed in the contract, a contract may include implicit promises for goods or services. Promises are normally specified, but may include those implied by, for example,

- the customary business practices of a particular industry,
- an entity's published policies, and
- specific statements.

These implicit promises may create a valid (IFRS) or reasonable (U.S. GAAP)[1] expectation on the part of the customer that the entity will transfer a good or service. (ASC 606-10-25-16; IFRS 15.24) It is important, therefore, to understand the entity's customary business practices, marketing materials, and representations made during contract negotiations. The entity must determine if the customer has a valid or reasonable expectation that the entity will provide a good or service. (ASC 606-10-25-16; IFRS 15.25)

---

[1] In ASU 2016-10, the FASB replaced "valid expectation of the customer" with "reasonable expectation of the customer" to clarify that promises do not need to be enforceable. The IASB did not make that change, opining that "valid" is consistent with the requirements for constructive obligations in IAS 37, *Provisions, Contingent Liabilities, and Contingent Assets*.

Exhibit 2.1   Step 2—Identifying the performance obligation

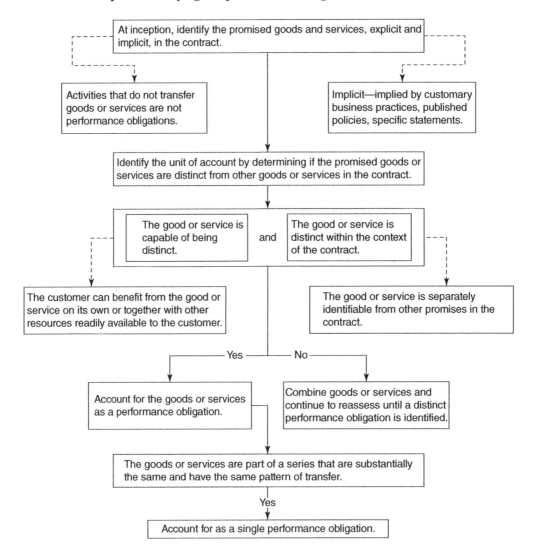

Constructive Performance Obligations.   As noted in Chapter 1, the customer's expectation may arise from a constructive performance obligation outside a written contract. So, in evaluating whether a reasonable expectation exists, the entity must consider industry norms, past business practice, etc. Examples of constructive performance obligations are, for instance, customer loyalty points, free handsets provided by telecommunication companies, or free maintenance with the purchase of a car. These kinds of implied promise may not be enforceable by law, and the entity itself may consider them marketing incentives or incidental to the goods or services for which the customer is paying. However, the customer may see them as part of the negotiated exchange. The Boards decided that they are goods or services for which the customer pays and that the entity should include them in performance obligations for the purpose of recognizing revenue under the

Standard. (ASU 2014-09 BC87–88; IFRS 15.BC87–88) That said, some incentives do not represent performance obligations if they are provided independently.

Goods to Be Provided in the Future

The Boards also concluded that goods or services to be provided in the future give rise to performance obligations. In some industries it is common practice to provide services to the customer's customer. For example, an automotive manufacturer may promise to provide service to a vehicle sold by a dealer. This type of promise is a performance obligation if it can be identified in the contract with the customer, either explicitly or implicitly. (ASU 2014-09 BC92; IFRS 15. BC87)

Example 2.1: Implied Performance Obligation

WPS, a manufacturer of project management software, enters into a contract with Big Box Office Supply Company to sell 250 units of its project management software. Big Box intends to resell the software to its end customers—small business owners. WPS has historically offered free online support directly to the end user. WPS and Big Box expect that this support will continue. The online support meets the definition of a performance obligation when WPS transfers control of the products to Big Box. Because WPS and Big Box are not related parties, the contracts will not be combined.[2] Therefore, WPS accounts for the online support as a separate performance obligation.

Activities Not Included as Performance Obligation

Performance obligations *transfer* goods or services to the customer. In line with the core principle of the Standard, only promises that transfer goods or services to the customer can be performance obligations. (ASU 2014-09 BC93; IFRS 15.BC93) An entity may need to undertake setup activities to fulfill performance obligations. If those activities transfer goods or services to the customer, they are part of the performance obligations. However, activities that do not transfer goods or services, like administrative tasks, are not promised goods or services in the contract with the customer. (ASC 606-10-25-17; IFRS 15.25) Some organizations may have a significant number of performance obligations, especially, for example, if "free" items are included, and now they have to be recognized under the standard.

Example 2.2: Activities Not Included as Performance Obligations

Main Street Sports sells annual memberships. The process includes sale of the membership, enrolling the customers, and activating the customer's gym membership card. Selling the membership, enrolling a customer, and activating the service are considered administrative tasks and are not performance obligations.

What is a Promised Good or Service?

The Standard offers some clarity by providing examples of promised goods or services. Bear in mind that this is not an exhaustive list. Promised goods or services may include

- sale of goods produced by an entity
- resale of goods purchased by an entity

---

[2] See Chapter 1 for more information on combining contracts between related parties.

- resale of rights to goods or services purchased by an entity
- a contractually agreed-upon task for a customer
- standing ready to provide goods or services
- arranging for another party to transfer goods or services to a customer
- rights to goods or services to be provided in the future that a customer can resell or provide to its customer
- licenses
- constructing, manufacturing, or developing an asset on behalf of a customer
- options to purchase additional goods or services.

(ASC 606-10-25-18; IFRS 15.26)

Shipping and Handling Services

Stakeholders had diverse views about accounting for shipping and handling under the Standard. These concerns were brought to the TRG. Many entities do not consider goods and the related shipping to be multiple deliverables. To account for them as such would create operability issues in terms of systems, processes, and internal controls. Requiring entities to account for shipping as a separate performance obligation might diminish the usefulness of the information. Cost/benefit concerns led the FASB to offer relief. Consequently, the FASB in ASU 2016-10 clarified the requirements.

The FASB clarified that shipping and handling services performed prior to the customer obtaining control of the goods are not promises to the customer. They are activities to fulfill the promise. However, the FASB gave entities the choice to account for shipping and handling services performed after the customer takes control as a fulfillment cost. Entities electing this practical expedient must disclose it in accordance with the Standard's disclosure requirements. Be aware this is an election and not a requirement. (ASC 610-10-25-18A and 25-18B)

The IASB took a different path and chose not to issue an amendment. The IASB believes that creating an accounting policy election would create an exception to the revenue recognition model and, possibly, cause comparability problems for entities with significant shipping and handling costs. IFRS reporters must consider whether shipping and handling create a separate performance obligation. This difference in approach may result in diversity in practice that may have a material effect on the financial statements.

DETERMINING WHETHER A GOOD OR SERVICE IS DISTINCT

After the entity identifies a contract's promises, where there are multiple promises in a contract, the entity must determine which are separate performance obligations. That is, the entity must identify the separate units of account. Performance obligations are the accounting unit for applying the revenue standard.

The Standard has guidance to help entities identify types of item that may be goods or services in the contract. (See above for list of "What is a Promised Good or Service.") In some situations, it requires judgment to determine whether promised goods should be accounted for as a group or separately. This is a key decision because

- determining the unit of account dictates how and when revenue is recognized, and
- the key determinant when identifying a separate performance obligation is whether a good or service or bundle is distinct.

Remember that the first category in the performance obligation definition dictates that the entity determines if promises of goods or services are distinct and, therefore, the promises are performance obligations and are accounted for separately. To determine whether an entity has to account for multiple performance obligations, the entity must assess whether the good or service is distinct, that is, separately identifiable from other promises in the contract.

In some cases, even though a good or service is capable of being distinct, accounting for it as a separate performance obligation might not reflect the entity's performance in that contract.

A good or service is distinct if it meets *both* these criteria:

1. Capable of being distinct. The customer can benefit from the good or service on its own or together with other resources that are readily available to the customer and
2. Distinct within the context of the contract. The entity's promise to transfer the good or service to the customer is separately identifiable from other promises in the contract.

(ASC 606-10-05-4B; IFRS 15.IN7.b)

> **Tip:** The assessment of whether or not a good or service is distinct must be done for a *specific contract* with a customer. It cannot be based on assessments performed on other contracts with the customer.

Therefore, the entity uses a two-part process for determining whether a promised good or service or bundle of goods or services is distinct:

1. Assess at the level of the good or service, that is, is the good or service inherently capable of being distinct
       and
2. Assess in the context of the contract, that is, is the promise to transfer the good or service separately identifiable from other promises in the contract?

(ASC 606-10-25-19; IFRS 15.27)

Legacy IFRS includes only limited guidance on separately identifiable components. Criterion number 1 is similar to the standalone value criterion in extant U.S. GAAP, but criterion number 2 is a new concept. If *both* these criteria are met, the individual units of account must be separated. The Standard includes indicators to help the entity determine whether the distinct criterion is met. Exhibit 2.2 below gives an overview of the information to consider when determining if a good or service is distinct and more detailed information follows the exhibit.

Criterion 1: Good or Service is Capable of Being Distinct

A good or service is capable of being distinct if the customer can benefit from it on its own or together with other resources readily available to the customer. (ASC 606-10-25-19a; IFRS 15.27a)

Customer Can Benefit from a Performance Obligation. A good or service is capable of being distinct if the customer can benefit from it. What does it mean to "benefit from a good or service"? To benefit, the customer must be able to

- use
- consume,
- sell for an amount greater than scrap value, or
- otherwise generate economic benefit.

Exhibit 2.2 Determining whether a good or service is distinct[3]

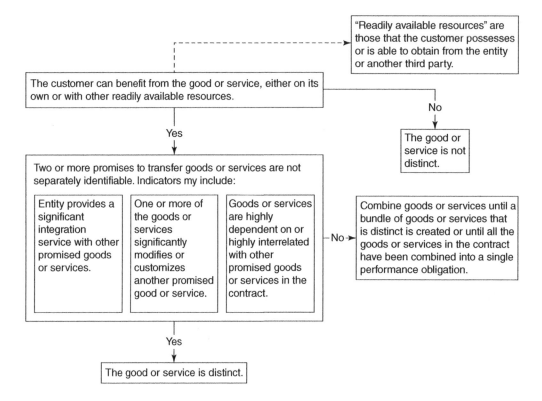

The ability to sell the good or service at scrap value would not necessarily support a conclusion that the good or service is capable of being distinct.

The assessment of whether the customer can benefit from the good or service on its own is based on the characteristics of the goods or services themselves, rather than how the customer might use them. The benefit may come from one good or service on its own or in conjunction with other readily available resources. A readily available resource is

- a good or service that is sold separately by the entity or by another entity, or
- a resource that the customer has already obtained either from the entity or through other transactions or events.

One indication that the customer can benefit from the goods or services is that the entity regularly sells them separately. (ASC 606-10-25-20; IFRS 15.28)

Example 2.3: Capable of Being Distinct

Builder enters into a contract to remodel a kitchen. Builder will supply the design, demolition services, cabinets, flooring, and other materials, in addition to the plumbing and electrical work. Builder regularly sells these goods and services individually.

---

[3] The language in the flowchart reflects FASB ASU 2016-10.

Builder must identify the performance obligations in the contract. Because Builder sells the items individually and the homeowner could benefit from them on their own or together with other readily available services, the promised goods and services are capable of being distinct.

However, the goods and services are not distinct within the context of the contract because they are not separately identifiable. Builder provides significant integration services when remodeling the homeowner's kitchen.

Example 2.4: Not Capable of Being Distinct

Machine Manufacturing sells a complex piece of equipment to a manufacturer. The contract includes a provision that Machine Manufacturing will install the equipment. Because Machine Manufacturing is the only entity capable of installing the equipment, the equipment is not capable of being distinct. The customer cannot benefit from the equipment on its own or in conjunction with readily available resources.

In order to assess whether to combine goods or services and account for them as one performance obligation, the entity must understand what the customer expects to receive. For instance, a contract may promise to deliver multiple goods, but the customer may be buying the finished good that those items create.

Criterion 2: Distinct within the Context of the Contract

After an entity has determined that a good or service is capable of being distinct, the second step in the assessment of whether the performance obligations are distinct is to determine if they are distinct within the context of the contract.

The concept of distinct within the context of the contract is based on the idea of "separable risks," which the Boards explain as follows:

> . . . *the individual goods or services in a bundle would not be distinct if the risk that an entity assumes to fulfill its obligation to transfer one of those promised goods or services to the customer is a risk that is inseparable from the risk relating to the transfer of the other promised goods or services in the bundle.*

(ASU 2014-09 BC103; IFRS 15.BC103)

Because the notion of separable risks is not a practical criterion, the Standard requires the entity to determine if the good or service is separately identifiable or distinct within the context of the contract.

Separately Identifiable Indicators. The objective when assessing whether an entity's promise to transfer goods or services to the customer is separately identifiable is to determine whether the nature of the promise, within the context of the contract, is to transfer each of those goods or services individually or, instead, to transfer a combined item or items to which the promised goods or services are inputs. (ASC 606-10-25-21; IFRS 15.29)

The Standard provides indicators rather than criteria to help determine when two or more promises to provide goods or services are distinct within the context of the contract. Providing guideposts rather than hard and fast rules allows the entity to exercise its judgment to reflect the underlying economic substance of the transaction. Some indicators that goods or services are not separately identifiable are:

- The entity *provides a significant integration service*. That is, the entity is providing the goods or services as an input for the combined output specified by the customer. In the Basis of Conclusion, the Boards noted that a good or service is not separately identifiable from other promises in a contract when an entity uses the good or service as an input into a single process or project that is the output of the contract. This indicator is especially relevant to the construction industry and might be relevant to some software installations, as well as other applications.

- One or more of the goods or services *significantly modifies or customizes* or is significantly modified or customized by one or more of the other goods or services promised in the contract. The software industry illustrates this indicator.
- The goods or services are *highly interdependent on, or highly interrelated with*, other goods or services promised in the contract. In other words, each of the goods or services is significantly affected by one or more of the other goods or services in the contract. (ASC 606-10-25-21; IFRS 15.29)

The entity will have to exercise significant judgment when considering these factors. There is no hierarchy to these factors. One does not carry more weight than the others. The entity will have to make the assessment and determine how to weigh the factors in specific situations. (ASC 606 BC102; IFRS 15.BC102)

Example 2.5: Significant Integration Service

If an entity contracts to construct a building, all the goods or services involved in the construction are probably capable of being distinct, but would likely not be considered distinct within the context of the contract. That is, the customer could benefit from each on its own. For instance, many of the materials used in the construction might be delivered before actual construction begins. However, the entity would likely take the position that the materials are an input to building the structure and there is a significant level of integration required to transform the materials into the building. Therefore, the materials and the construction services are a single performance obligation. It would be impractical to account for each item of construction separately, and to do so, would not faithfully represent the promise in the contract or result in a useful reflection of the entity's performance.

Other common examples of this can be found in the construction industry. Many long-term construction and service contracts will be identified as single performance obligations because they tend to include significant integration services. For instance, a house painter will likely consider the paint as an input to produce the painted house. The service is a significant integration service and, therefore, the paint and the painting services are a single performance obligation.

Example 2.6: Significant Customization

An entity contracts to sell a software system. The customer is not a typical consumer-driven business. It is a membership organization that produces publications and sells them to its members at a discount and at full price to the general public. During the purchasing process, the customer wants to interact differently with its members than it does with nonmembers. It also wants to maintain detailed information on its members' purchases. Because of its unique needs, the customer requires the entity to perform extensive customization of the software. The sale includes

- the software license
- help desk support for three years
- any available software updates, including the resources to integrate the customized elements.

Element	Step 1—Capable of Being Distinct?	Step 2—Distinct in the Context of the Contract?
Software license and customization	Can be used without help desk support and upgrades. Is capable of being distinct.	The software is significantly customized. Within the context of the contract, the promise to transfer the software license is not separately identifiable, distinct, from the customization. The software license and the customization are not distinct from each other. However, the software is separately identifiable from the other goods and services in the contract. The customer's ability to use and benefit from the software is not affected by the help desk support or the updates. Product is distinct.
Help desk support	Help desk support services are sold separately. Services are capable of being distinct.	Support is separately identifiable from other goods and services in the contract. Services are distinct from the other promises in the contract.
Any available software update and any needed customization	The updates are not available separately, but the customer can benefit from them with other resources readily available (the software license and services previously delivered). Services are capable of being distinct.	Upgrades are separately identifiable from other goods and services in the contract. They do not significantly modify or customize the software, and the software is not highly dependent or integrated with the upgrade. The software remains functional without the upgrades. The updates do not significantly affect the customer's ability to use and benefit from the software. Services are distinct.

The entity concludes that the contract includes three performance obligations:

- the software and its customization;
- the help desk support, which is distinct because the customer can benefit from it on its own;
- the software updates and resources for customization that are readily available to the customer.

All these are distinct within the context of the contract and, applying the indicators, are separately identifiable performance obligations.

It is expected that the new standard may lead to entities identifying more performance obligations than under previous guidance. For example, free products or services or service-type warranties might be separate performance obligations under the new guidance.

Example 2.7: Highly Independent or Highly Interrelated

Fabricator agrees to design a new type of wine bottle opener for Inventor and to produce ten prototypes. The specifications provided by Inventor include untested functionality. As part of the contract, Fabricator will be required to test the product and revise the design while making and testing the prototypes, modifying the prototypes as necessary. As the design changes during the production process, Fabricator expects that all prototypes will need to be reworked. The customer cannot purchase either the design service or the manufacturing service. Because of the iterative process used, the two services are highly dependent and highly related to each other. Within the context of the contract, the two services are not separately identifiable.

Example 2.8: Multiple Performance Obligations

Mobile Telephone enters into a contract with a customer to deliver a cell phone and 24 months of voice and data services. The cell phone cannot be used on another telecom company's network. However, certain functions can be used outside the network: playing music and accessing calendars, contacts, emails, and the Internet.

In addition, customers have sold the cell phone to third-party resellers for a portion of the original purchase price. Mobile Telephone also sells the voice and data services to customers through renewals and to customers who purchased the handset at a retailer.

At first glance, it might appear that the cell phone and services are one performance obligation. However, after further analysis, Mobile Telephone concludes that the cell phone and services are two separate performance obligations. The cell phone is

- capable of being distinct because the customer can benefit from the phone on its own by selling it for more than scrap value, and it has functionality that the customer can benefit from without Mobile Telephone's network with the readily available resource of the cell phone either on its own or with services sold separately by Mobile Telephone *and*
- distinct within the context of the contract because the phone and the wireless services are not inputs to a single asset, indicating that Mobile Telephone is not providing significant integration services, the products of the phone and services separately indicating that they are not highly dependent on or interrelated with each other.

Promised Good or Service is Not Distinct

Once an entity determines that a promised good or service is not distinct, it must combine it with other promises in the contract until it identifies a bundle of goods or services that is distinct. The result may be that all the promises in a contract are accounted for as a single purchase obligation.

Example 2.9: Bundling Goods and Services that are Not Distinct

In this scenario, assume that all goods and services are sold separately. LMS provides hosting services to Publishing Company. In addition to the hosting service, LMS sells a hosted inventory management software system that requires the customer to purchase hardware sold by LMS. LMS also offers a technology team to migrate existing data and create interfaces and reports. LMS delivers the hardware, then the technology team, and finally provides the hosting services.

LMS analyzes the contract and LMS's business practices and determines that LMS regularly sells all the goods and services separately. Therefore, all of the goods and services are capable of being distinct. LMS also determines that the goods and services in the contract are distinct within the context of the contract because

- LMS is not providing a significant integration service,
- there is no significant level of customization, and
- the customer can purchase each good or service without significantly affecting the other goods or services purchased—therefore, the goods and services are not highly dependent on or highly interrelated with each other.

SERIES OF DISTINCT GOODS OR SERVICES THAT ARE SUBSTANTIALLY THE SAME AND HAVE THE SAME PATTERN OF TRANSFER

There are two ways an entity may determine that two or more goods or services are a single performance obligation. The first is if the entity determines that the goods or services are not distinct from each other. The second involves the goods or services that meet the criteria for being distinct, but may still be a single performance obligation. (Refer to the definition of performance obligation at the beginning of this chapter.)

The Series Provision

The second category of performance obligation requires the entity to assess whether the performance obligations are a series of distinct goods or services that are "substantially the same or have the same pattern of transfer to the customer." Without this part of the definition, some entities would face significant operational challenges. For example, services provided on an hourly or daily basis, like a cleaning service, might meet the criteria for a single performance obligation and the entity would be faced with accounting separately for numerous repetitive services. The service provision is a concept that is introduced by the Standard and does not exist in the legacy standards. This series provision guidance is intended to simplify the application of the revenue recognition model and promote consistency. (ASC-606-10-25-15; IFRS 15.23)

The Standard provides guidance to assess patterns of transfer. To have the same pattern of transfer, both of the following criteria must be met.

- Each distinct good or service in the series that the entity promises to transfer consecutively represents a performance obligation satisfied over time if it were accounted for separately.
- The entity uses the same method of progress to measure the transfer of each distinct good or service in the same series to the customer.

(ASC 606-10-25-15; IFRS 15.23)

If the criteria are met, the series of goods or services must be treated as a single performance obligation, the so-called "series requirement." The accounting treatment may vary for this application when accounting for contract modifications, variable consideration, and changes in transaction price.

Tip: The series requirement may be applied when there is a gap or an overlap in the transfer. In considering whether the service requirement should be applied, entities should consider the length of the gap.

The box on the left, in Exhibit 2.3, is similar to the principles in legacy U.S. GAAP (ASC 605-10-25-13) for multiple-element arrangements. The second is a new requirement, and for some entities this may result in a change in practice.

Example 2.10: Series of Distinct Goods or Services Treated as a Single Performance Obligation

File Manufacturer signs a contract with Office Suites to deliver 500 customized filing cabinets over time. If Office Suites terminates the contract for convenience, the contract requires Office

Exhibit 2.3 Series of distinct goods or services—criteria for same pattern of transfer

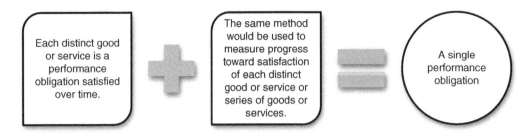

Suites to pay File Manufacturer for any finished or in-process cabinets, including a reasonable margin.

Each of the cabinets is distinct because each can be used on its own, and each is separately identifiable from the others because it does not affect, modify, or customize another.

Although each cabinet is distinct, File Manufacturer accounts for 500 units as a single performance obligation because

- each cabinet transfers to Office Suites over time, and
- File Manufacturer uses the same method to measure progress toward completion.

COMPARISON WITH LEGACY STANDARDS

IFRS

Legacy IFRS does not provide specific guidance for multiple deliverables. Consequently, many IFRS preparers have looked to U.S. GAAP for guidance on multiple deliverables. IFRS 15 provides guidance on the types of items that may be goods or services in the contract and defines which goods or services, such as administrative tasks, are not promised goods or services under the Standard.

U.S. GAAP. Legacy U.S. GAAP requires entities to identify "deliverables" in a contract, but does not provide specific guidance on that term. The Standard makes clear how to identify which items are promised goods or services and which are not.

3 STEP 3—DETERMINE THE TRANSACTION PRICE

Technical Alert

Subsequent to issuance of the Standard, the TRG surfaced issues related to noncash consideration:

- when noncash consideration should be measured, and
- under what circumstances to apply the constraint on variable consideration related to the fair value or noncash consideration when it varies both because of the form of consideration and for other reasons.

The FASB decided to make clarifying changes. However, the IASB decided that the guidance is clear and is not making changes. The changes are discussed further at the end of this chapter in the "Noncash Consideration" section.

As a purchaser of this book, you have exclusive access to a companion website, with the latest technical developments and other useful information. The website will contain updated information about exposure drafts and other technical guidance from the standards' setters. See the back of the book for information on how to access the site.

OVERVIEW

Transaction price: The amount of consideration to which an entity expects to be entitled in exchange for transferring promised goods or services to a customer, excluding amounts collected on behalf of third parties (for example, some sales taxes).
(ASC 606-10-20; IFRS 15.47)

Step 3 of the revenue recognition model requires entities to consider the terms of the contract and the entity's customary business practices to determine the transaction price. Transaction price is a new term. Entities will have to understand the term conceptually and in practice compared with the extant term "contract values." The transaction price only includes amounts to which the entity has rights and does *not* include

- amounts collected on behalf of another, such as sales taxes, and
- estimates of options on and future change orders for additional goods and services.

Determining the transaction price is critical, because it is the amount ultimately recognized as revenue. The objective of the guidance in Step 3 is to predict at the end of the reporting period the total amount of consideration to which the entity is entitled. Some believe that this step has the potential to create the most changes in practice, because it is farthest away from legacy standards. Entities not experienced in making these estimates based on the tenets of legacy standards, specifically the fixed and determinable criteria, will be challenged.

The transaction price should be determined at the inception of the contract. As with other steps of the revenue recognition model, when determining the transaction price, the entity should look more widely than the contract terms and examine the entity's customary business practices, published policies, and specific statements. Also, the entity should assume that the terms of the contract will be fulfilled, that is, the goods or services will be transferred as promised and that the contract will not be canceled, renewed, or modified. (ASC 606-10-32-4; IFRS 15.49)

Exhibit 3.1 gives an overview of the process involved in determining the transaction price.

A contract may include fixed amounts, variable amounts, or both. Determining the transaction price can be straightforward or complex. For example, sales to a customer in a retail store are relatively simple. In other situations, for example where noncash consideration is included or the consideration varies depending on circumstances, determination of the transaction price can be more complex. Exhibit 3.2 shows the factors that should be considered when determining the transaction price.

Exhibit 3.1 Overview

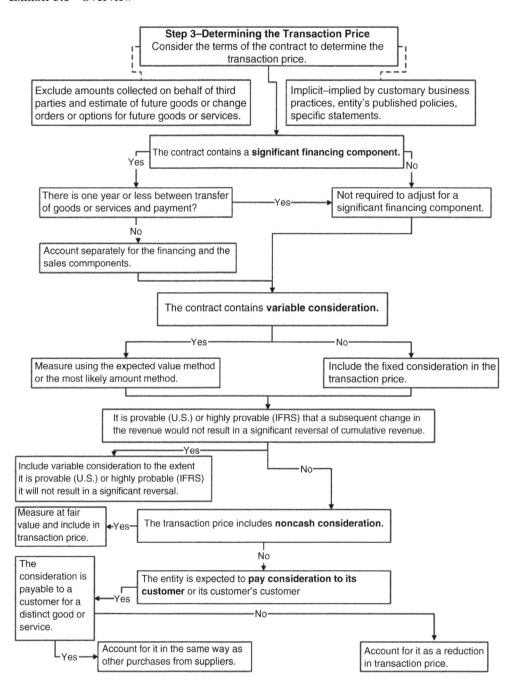

Exhibit 3.2   Factors to consider when determining transaction price (ASC 606-10-32-3; IFRS 15.48)

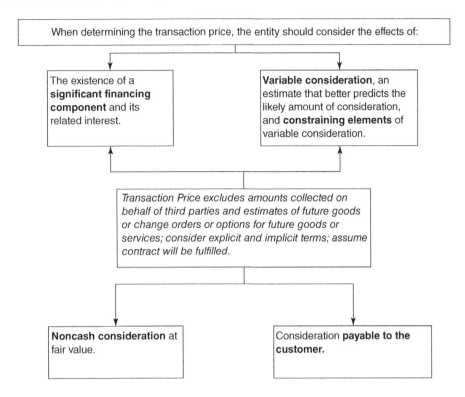

As one can infer from Exhibit 3.2, the factors that determine the transaction price may well lead to a transaction price that is significantly different from the contractual price. Each of the above elements will be discussed in depth in this chapter.

SIGNIFICANT FINANCING COMPONENT

Under some arrangements, there is a difference in timing—the timing of the payment does not match the timing of the transfer of goods or services. It is not uncommon for an entity to enter into a contract that includes, either explicitly or implicitly, payments over time.

Practical Expedient: The Standard includes a practical expedient for significant financing components. The amount of consideration does not have to be adjusted if, at contract inception, the entity expects that there will be one year or less between

1. transfer of goods or services, and
2. payment.
(ASC-606-10-32-18; IFRS 15.63)

When assessing whether the practical expedient can be applied, the entity must focus on the timing of the two events (transfer and payment) rather than the length of the contract. If an entity chooses to apply the practical expedient, it should apply it consistently to similar contracts under similar circumstances.

It is expected that this practical expedient will provide relief and will have limited effect on the pattern of revenue recognition.

Through the agreed-upon payment terms, the timing may provide the customer or the entity with a significant financing benefit. If the customer pays in advance, the entity has received financing from the customer. If the entity transfers the goods or services in advance of payment, the entity has provided financing to the customer. If one of these is the case, the entity must then examine the facts and circumstances to determine if a significant financing component exists that must be accounted for. See Exhibits 3.3 and 3.4 for more detail.

Exhibit 3.3   Timing of payment does not match timing of transfer of goods or services

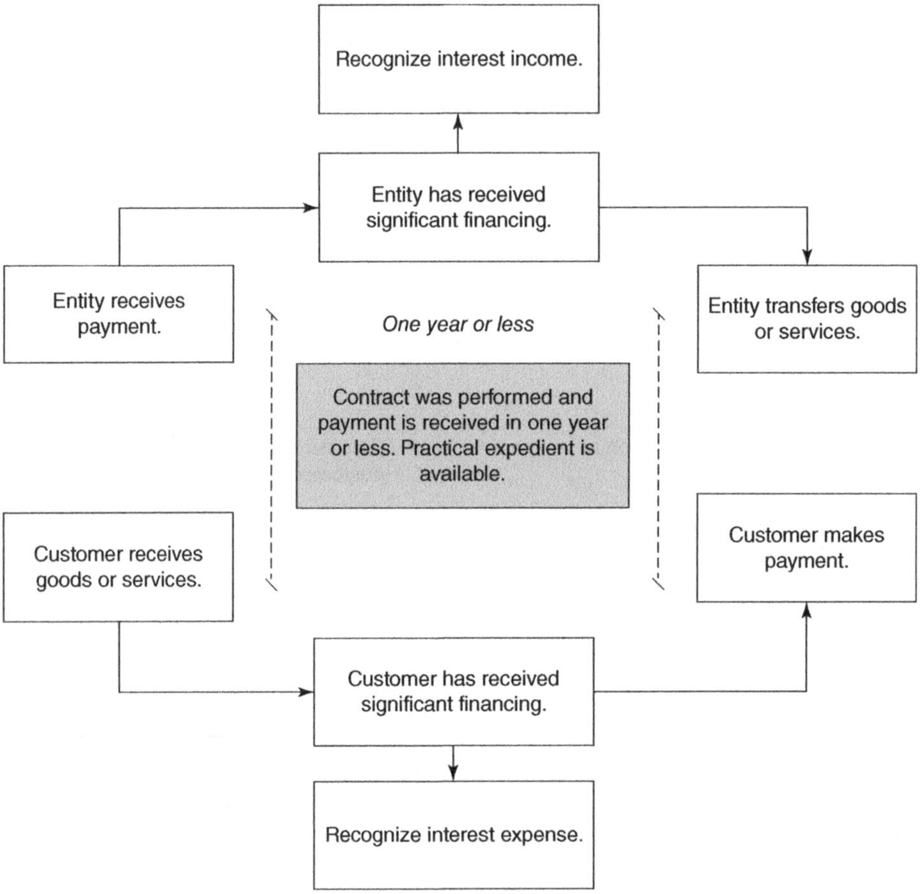

Determining Whether there is a Financing Component

Conceptually, the Standard recognizes that a contract with a financing component has two transactions—a sale and a financing. If a contract has a significant financing component, the entity should account for the financing component and adjust the transaction price. (ASC 606-10-32-15; IFRS 15.60) Determining what a "significant" component is may require considerable judgment. Companies that have contracts with a significant financing component may have operational challenges connected to measuring and tracking the time value of money. However, the practical expedient explained earlier should provide some relief.

Exhibit 3.4   Determining if there is a significant financing component—process flow

Determine if there is a significant financing component:
- Assess at contract level.
- One year or less between payments and transfer of goods or services–practical expedient available.
- Timing of payment matches timing of transfer–no significant financing component.

Consider all the facts and circumstances, including:
- Differences between promised consideration, explicit and implicit, and the cash selling price upon transfer of product.
- Combined effects of:
  - Expected length of time between transfer of goods or services and payment.
  - Prevailing interest rate.

(ASC 606-10-32-16; IFRS 15.61)

Consider factors contra indicative of a significant financing compoent:
- Customer paid in advance and timing of transfer of goods or services is in hands of customer.
- Substantial amount of consideration is variable and varies based on a future event not substantially in control of customer or entity.
- Timing difference arises for reasons other than providing financing.

(ASC 606-10-32-17; IFRS 15.62)

Determine discount rate:
- Should reflect discount rate that would be reflected in a separate financing transaction between entity and customer at inception of contract.
- Should reflect:
  - Inflation.
  - Credit risks of financing party.
  - Credit characteristics of the party receiving the financing.
  - Any collateral or security provided.

(ASC 606-10-32-19; IFRS 15.64)

Recognize interest or expense only to extent contract asset or liability is recognized.

Present financing and sales components separately.

The consideration recorded should reflect the price the customer would have paid if the customer paid cash when (or as) the goods or services transferred to the customer, that is, the objective is to reflect the cash selling price. The standard factors in the effects of a significant financing component because excluding it could result in two economically similar transactions recording substantially different revenue amounts.

The determination of whether a contract contains a significant financing component occurs at the contract level, not the contract portfolio level or the performance obligation level. In assessing whether a contract contains a significant financing component, the entity should take into consideration all the facts and circumstances, including both of the following.

- The difference between the amount of promised consideration and the cash selling price upon transfer of the goods or services.
- The combined effects of both
  - the expected length of time between the transfer of goods or services and when the customer pays, and
  - the prevailing interest rates in the relevant market.

(ASC 606-10-32-16; IFRS 15.61)

And, as with other assessments in the model, it is necessary to look at implicit and explicit contract terms.

Significant Financing Component—Contra Indicative Factors

A time difference between payment of consideration and transfer of goods and services to the customer does not always mean there is a significant financing component. If *any* of the factors listed in Exhibit 3.5 exist, then a contract with a customer would *not* have a significant financing component.

Exhibit 3.5   Significant financing component—contra indicative factors

Contra Indicative Factors	Examples
The customer paid in advance, and the timing of the transfer of goods and services is in the hands of the customer.	Customer loyalty points usable in the future, prepaid phone cards, gift cards.
A substantial amount of the consideration promised by the customer is variable, and the timing of that consideration varies on the basis of the occurrence or nonoccurrence of a future event not substantially within the control of the customer or entity.	Sales-based royalty.
The timing difference between the promised consideration and the cash selling price is justified for reasons not related to financing and the difference between those amounts is proportional to the reason for the difference. (ASC 606-10-32-17; IFRS 15.62)	Payment terms might provide the customer with protection if the other party fails to adequately complete some or all of its obligations under the contract, for example, retention payments in construction contracts.

These factors are explored in detail below.

Timing is at the Discretion of the Customer. When timing is at the discretion of the customer, a significant financing component may not exist because the objective in these situations is not to provide financing.

Example 3.1: Timing is at the Discretion of the Customer

At the beginning of the school year in September, Elizabeth's Art Supplies offers "Lizzie's Loot" with each purchase over CU 50. "Lizzie's Loot" entitles the customer to 20% off the purchase price for any supplies purchased in the future. Elizabeth's Art Supplies determines that "Lizzie's Loot" does not represent a significant financing component because the timing is at the discretion of the customer.

Substantial Amount of the Consideration is Variable and Based on a Future Event Not Substantially within Control of the Customer or Entity. An example of this is legal services where the attorney is paid only upon a successful outcome. The substance of the timing difference is not a financing, but the resolution of uncertainties. In addition, the outcome is substantially outside the control of the parties to the contract.

Example 3.2: Substantial Amount of the Consideration is Variable and Based on a Future Event

Eustace Medical Publishing enters into a contract with an author to write a reference book on anatomy. The author will receive 10% of net sales. Eustace Medical Publishing determines that there is no significant financing because

- the consideration is variable and the purpose is to pay when uncertainties are resolved, and
- the consideration varies based on factors that are outside the control of the entity.

The Timing Difference Arises for Reasons Other than Providing Financing. A timing difference might not be related to financing. For instance, the intent of the parties might not be to provide financing but to secure the rights to a product or the future supply of a good or service, or to ensure that the entity performs as specified. This type of arrangement requires careful analysis and judgment on the part of the entity. If the primary intent of payment timing is for reasons other than providing a significant financing benefit to the entity or the customer, then the effects of the financing component need not be considered. The difference between the contract price and the cash selling price should be reasonably reflective of a financing motive.

Example 3.3: The Timing Difference Arises for Reasons Other than Providing Financing

St. Nick Ornaments creates handcrafted holiday ornaments and each year produces a highly successful line of collectible ornaments. St. Nick Ornaments contracts with The Holiday Store, giving it exclusive rights to the annual collectible ornaments. To secure these exclusive rights, The Holiday Store pays 30% of the contract price of the product in advance. St. Nick Ornaments examines the arrangement and determines that there is no significant financing component because the intent of the advance payment is not financing, but for The Holiday Store to secure exclusive rights.

Determining the Discount Rate for a Significant Financing Component

The entity should use the discount rate that would be reflected in a separate financing transaction between the entity and its customers at the time of the inception of the contract. (ASC 606-10-32-19; IFRS 15.64) That rate should reflect

- inflation,
- the credit risk of the financing party,
- the credit characteristics of the party receiving the financing, and
- any collateral or security provided, including assets transferred in the contract.

The entity needs to have access to enough information to determine the discount rate.

The rate may be determined by identifying the interest rate that discounts the nominal amount of the promised consideration to the cash the customer would pay when (or as) the goods or services transfer to the customer. If the contract contains an explicit rate, then the entity should consider whether that rate reflects the market rate. In some cases the contract may contain a low rate as a marketing incentive. If the contract does not reflect the market rate, then the entity should impute a more representative rate. The rate determined at the inception of the contract is the rate used throughout the terms of the contract.

Example 3.4: Discount Rate for a Significant Financing Component

Ace Appliances has a promotion to sell refrigerators to customers. The customers will not be charged interest if minimum monthly payments are made over a 36-month period. If the customers do not pay the minimum amount, they must pay the interest accrued. The interest is accruing at a rate of 9.875%. Ace Appliances concludes that

- there is a significant financing component in the agreement with the customers,
- the 9.875% reflects the market rate, and
- the 0% rate reflects the marketing incentive and not the credit profile of the customer.

Ace Appliances uses the discount rate of 9.875% to determine the transaction price. It recognizes revenue and a loan receivable for the discounted transaction price.

Customer's Credit Risk. Generally, under the Standard, the transaction price is not adjusted for a customer's credit risk, that is, the risk that a customer will not pay the entity. However, there is an exception when the contract includes a significant financing component. The *only* time the transaction price is adjusted for credit risk is if there is a significant financing component. Note that the discount rate is not adjusted *after* contract inception for changes in interest rates or other circumstances, including a change in the customer's credit risk.

Based on the facts and circumstances, management needs to decide whether billing adjustments are

- a modification of the transaction price that reduces revenue, or
- a credit adjustment, write-off of an uncollectible amount that impairs a contract asset, or receivable and is assessed under ASC 310, *Receivables* or IFRS 9, *Financial Instruments*.

Implied Price Concession. If the customer's credit risk is known at the inception of the contract, then the entity must determine if there is an implied price concession. If so, it is not included in the estimated transaction price. This may be difficult to determine: has the entity offered an implied price concession or has the entity chosen the risk of the customer defaulting? The Standard does not provide detailed application guidance to help distinguish between price concessions (reduction of revenue) and customer credit risk (bad debt expense). Entities will have to exercise significant judgment and will need to have clear policies in place. (See also the "Variable Consideration" section in this chapter.)

Impairment. If a customer's credit risk is impaired, resulting in an impairment of a contract asset or receivable, then the entity should measure the impairment based on the guidance in ASC 310 or IFRS 9, *Financial Instruments*.[1]

Presentation of a Significant Financing Component

The entity should separate the loan component from the revenue component. Interest income or expense resulting from a financing should be presented separately from the revenue component. Once a performance obligation is satisfied, the entity recognizes the present value of the

---

[1] IFRS 9 was issued in 2014 as a replacement of IAS 39. It is effective for periods beginning after January 1, 2018.

consideration as revenue. The financing component (interest income or expense) is recognized over the financing period. The income or expense is recognized only to the extent that a contract asset, receivable, or contract liability, such as deferred revenue, is recognized for the customer contract. When accounting for the financing component, the entity should look to the relevant guidance on the effective interest method in IFRS 9 or IAS 39, or in ASC 835-30, *Interest—Imputation of Interest*:

- subsequent measurement guidance in ASC 835-30-45-1A through 45-3;
- application of the interest method in ASC 835-30-55-2 and 55-3.
(ASC 606-10-32-20; IFRS 15.65)

VARIABLE CONSIDERATION

Variable consideration in contracts is common, and the guidance applies to a wide variety of fact patterns. The entity must examine the explicit and implicit terms of the contract to identify variable consideration. Variability in the consideration could affect

- whether the entity is entitled to the consideration—an example of this is a requirement to meet a deadline for a performance bonus, or
- the specific amount of consideration—this might come into play when the quantity of customer purchases is tied to a volume discount.

Types and Sources of Variable Consideration

Variable consideration comes in two types:

- pricing adjustments for transactions that have already been completed, for instance, refunds;
- incentive and performance-based fees, for example, licenses and royalties.

Exhibit 3.6   Sources of variable consideration

Common Examples of Consideration that Cause Variable Consideration		
Discounts	Rebates	Refunds
Credits	Price concessions	Incentives
Performance bonuses	Penalties	Returns
Market-based fees	Money-back guarantees	Service-level agreements
Liquidating damages	Price protection plans	Price matching plans

(ASC 606-10-32-6; IFRS 15.51)

Under legacy guidance, some of these items caused entities to delay revenue recognition. Under the revenue model in the Standard, entities will now have to estimate their effect because the model focuses on when control transfers. Even if a contract has a stated fixed price, the consideration may still be variable. This happens when the consideration is contingent on the occurrence or nonoccurrence of an event.

Exception. If a contract is for a license of intellectual property for which the consideration is based on the customer's subsequent sales or usage, then the entity should *not* recognize revenue for uncertain amounts.

Determining if Variable Consideration Exists

Variable consideration may be explicitly stated in the contract or may be variable if either of the following exists.

a. The customer has a valid expectation arising from an entity's customary business practices, published policies, or specific statements that the entity will accept an amount of consideration that is less than the price stated in the contract. That is, it is expected that the entity will offer a price concession. Depending on the jurisdiction, industry, or customer, this offer may be referred to as a discount, rebate, refund, or credit.
b. Other facts and circumstances indicate that the entity's intention, when entering into the contract with the customer, is to offer a price concession to the customer.
(ASC 606-10-32-7; IFRS 15.52)

Price Concessions. Price concessions are reductions in the contract price that are commonly made outside the initial contract terms. Price concessions may be made for a variety of reasons, such as

- increasing the chances of securing other contracts,
- appeasing a dissatisfied customer, or
- encouraging the customer to make payments.

An entity that has a practice of making price concessions or expects to do so for a specific contract needs to reduce the transaction price to reflect the consideration it expects to be entitled to. Determining whether the contract contains an implicit price concession may be difficult, and the entity must take into account all the facts and circumstances.

Example 3.5: Implicit Price Concession

Learning Solutions has no past history of entering into price concessions. Learning Solutions enters into a contract to provide Mega Corporation with training for new hires. Learning Solutions sees the potential for significant additional contracts with Mega Corporation. To develop the long-term, potentially highly lucrative client relationship, Learning Solutions is willing to accept a price lower than the stated contract price. The contract does not explicitly state that the consideration is variable, but the facts and circumstances indicate that the entity's intention at contract inception is to offer a price concession. Therefore, the consideration is variable.

Discounts. Entities often give discounts based on volume or for prompt payment. Prompt payment discounts are variable, and management needs to estimate the discount based on its experience with the customer, similar customers, and/or similar transactions. Volume discounts are an incentive to order larger amounts of a product and to encourage future purchases and customer loyalty. These arrangements may involve variable consideration if the total amount to be purchased is not known at contract inception. Entities should estimate the total expected sales and include in the transaction price at least the minimum. Note that volume discounts may give the customer a material right to a free or discounted product in the future. If so, see guidance on material rights in Chapter 6.

Example 3.6: Volume Discounts

Road Cover has a one-year contract to deliver paving supplies to Village. The price per unit will decrease as the quantities ordered increase.

Price/Unit	Volume
CU 1000	0–10,000 units
CU 900	10,001–20,000 units
CU 800	20,001+ units

Volume is based on calendar year sales. Based on Village's street paving plan and past experience, Road Cover believes the total sales volume for the calendar year will be 25,000 units. The transaction price is calculated as follows:

CU 1000 per unit	× Units 1–10,000	=	CU 10,000,000
CU 900 per unit	× Units 10,001–20,000	=	9,000,000
CU 800 per unit	× Units 20,001–25,000	=	4,000,000
Total estimated sales			CU 23,000,000
Total volume		÷	25,000 units
Average price per unit		=	CU 920

Road Cover determines that it is probable (U.S. GAAP) or highly probable (IFRS) that a significant reversal of cumulated recognized revenue will not occur. Road Cover, therefore, recognizes CU 920 in revenue as each unit is sold.

Example 3.7: Variable Consideration—Reassessment of Volume Discount

Road Cover sold 2000 units in the first quarter of the contract. At the end of the first quarter, Road Cover learns that Village has cut back 20% in the number of streets it plans to repair in the calendar year. Road Cover now anticipates selling a total number of 20,000 units in the year. Road Cover updates its estimate of the transaction price as follows:

CU 1000 per unit	× Units 1–10,000	=	CU 10,000,000
CU 900 per unit	× Units 10,001–20,000	=	9,000,000
Total estimated sales			CU 19,000,000
Total volume		÷	20,000 units
Average price per unit		=	CU 950

Road Cover should recognize revenue of CU 950 per unit for sales after the first quarter. In addition, assuming the performance obligation is satisfied, Road Cover should recognize an additional CU 60,000 for the units sold in the first quarter:

$$CU\ 950 - 920 = CU\ 30 \times 2000\ units = CU\ 60,000$$

This cumulative catchup adjustment reflects the new estimate per unit based on the new information.

Rebates. Rebates are a commonly used sales incentive. Some rebates are based on reaching a certain volume; others are based on a single sale. Most depend on the customer requesting the rebate.

As with other forms of variable consideration, management should estimate the amount based on experience either with its own rebates or through the marketplace. If management cannot reasonably estimate the amount of consideration related to the rebates that need to be constrained, management needs to estimate a minimum amount of revenue that should be recognized.

Pricing Based on an Index. A contract price may be tied to an index, such as

- the consumer price index,
- a commodity index, or
- a financial index.

For example, a sale involving gold might be based on the market price on a specific date.

Price Protection and Price Matching Plans. An agreement may have a price protection clause that allows a customer to request a refund if other customers are offered a lower price during a specific time period. Price matching plans extend that concept to the vendor's competition.

Example 3.8: Price Protection

Laptop Manufacturer enters into an agreement with Ace Office to sell laptops to Ace Office for CU 500 each. The contract includes price protection whereby Laptop Manufacturer will reimburse Ace Office for the difference between CU 500 and the lowest price offered to any customer of Laptop Manufacturer during the six-month period of the contract. Laptop Manufacturer has offered similar price protection clauses in the past and has experience to predict the outcome.

Laptop Manufacturer expects to offer a 10% price decrease during the term of the contract and concludes that it is probable (U.S. GAAP) or highly probable (IFRS) that a significant reversal of revenue will not occur.

Laptop Manufacturer determines that the transaction price is CU 450 (contract price of CU 500 less the expected 10% reimbursement). Laptop Manufacturer recognizes a liability for the CU 50 it expects to refund to Ace Office.

The process of determining the effects of variable consideration is illustrated in Exhibit 3.7, and discussed in the next section.

Estimating Total Variable Consideration

If the contract's consideration includes a variable amount, then the entity must go through a process to determine the effect of that variability on the transaction price. It must

- determine the method for estimating the consideration
- measure the consideration
- determine if the variable consideration should be constrained, and
- account for subsequent changes in transaction price.

Determining the Method for Estimating Variable Consideration. To determine the amount of variable consideration to include in the transaction price, the entity must first estimate the amount by using one of two methods. This is not a free policy choice. The entity is required to choose one of two methods it expects to better predict the amount of variable consideration under the specific facts and circumstances and must apply that method consistently for similar contracts. The two methods that the entity must choose from are

- the expected value method and
- the most likely amount method.

Measuring the Variable Consideration. Whichever method an entity chooses to estimate the consideration, it should be applied consistently throughout the contract when estimating the

Exhibit 3.7   Assessing variable consideration—process flow

The entity determines that the contract contains variable consideration because:
- It is explicitly stated in the contract.
- Customer has a valid expectation based on customary business practices, etc., that client will accept less consideration.
- Other facts suggest the entity intends to offer a price concession.

Determine the method for estimating the consideration. Use either the:
- Expected value method or
- Most likely amount method.

Measure the consideration at fair value.

Determine if variable consideration should be constrained. Consider the following indicators that it is probable or highly probable that the variable consideration will result in a significant reversal of cumulative revenue:

- The amount is high susceptibility to factors outside the entity's influence.
- The uncertainty will not be resolved for a long period of time.
- The entity's experience with similar contracts is limited or that experience has low predictive value.
- With similar contracts under similar circumstances, the entity has a history of offering a broad range of price concessions or changing the payment terms or conditions.
- The contract has a large number and broad range of possible consideration amounts.

Include some or all of the variable consideration in the tran saction price to the extent that it is probable (U.S. GAAP) or highly probable (IFRS) that a subsequent change in the estimate would not result in a significant reversal of cumulative revenue recognized.

Exhibit 3.8   The two methods for estimating variable consideration

The Expected Value Method: The sum of probability weighted amounts within a range of possible consideration amounts.	This method may be most predictive when the entity has a large number of contracts with similar characteristics. This method reflects all the uncertainties—the probability of receiving greater amounts and lesser amounts. However, it may not always be the best predictor.
The Most Likely Amount Method: Identifies the single most likely amount in the range of possible consideration amounts. (ASC 606-10-32-8; IFRS 15.53)	This method may be appropriate when the contract has only two or a small number of possible outcomes, because the expected value method might not result in one of the possible outcomes. This method would be appropriate, for example, when a performance bonus is either met or not, that is, it is binary.

effects and uncertainty of an amount of variable consideration. All reasonably available information should be considered, including historical, current, and forecast data. The entity would normally use the same information it used during the proposal process and when it set prices. Note that the entity does not need to use every outcome in its analysis. A few discrete outcomes may provide a valid estimate. (ASC 606-10-32-9; IFRS 15.54)

Example 3.9: Estimating Variable Consideration—Performance Bonus

Ace Contractors enters into a contract to build a small office building for CU 500,000. The contract includes a performance bonus of CU 100,000. The bonus decreases 20% for every week beyond the agreed-upon completion date. Ace Contractors has performed similar contracts in the past and believes that its experience is predictive of the outcome. Ace Contractors decides that because no one amount is more likely to be received than another, the expected value method is most predictive for the variable consideration in this contract. Ace Contractors estimates probabilities for completion of the contract at

70%—agreed-upon completion date
20%—completed one week late
10%—completed two weeks late.

To determine the variable part of the transaction price, Ace Contractors makes the following probability-weighted calculation:

		Base Price + On Time Bonus	**Probability**	
On time:	70%	600,000 [500,000 + (100,000 × 1)]	× 70% =	420,000
1 week late:	20%	580,000 [500,000 + (100,000 × 1−20%)]	× 20% =	116,000
2 weeks late:	10%	560,000 [500,000 + (100,000 × 1−40%)]	× 10% =	56,000
				592,000

To arrive at the expected value, Ace Contractors adjust for the on time bonus and bases the transaction price on the probability weighted estimate. They must reassess the estimate at the end of each reporting date. Ace Contractors might have decided to use the most likely outcome method if the performance bonus were binary—they would either receive the bonus or not, depending on whether completion was on time. If management believed that this method were more predictive, Ace Contractors would use the most likely outcome and the total transaction price would be CU 600,000—the outcome with 70% probability. (This example does not include the constraints in variable consideration discussed later in this chapter.)

A contract may include two different variable amounts based on the resolution of different circumstances. In that case, the entity may use different methods to estimate the variable consideration—different methods for different uncertainties.

Example 3.10: Measuring Variable Consideration with Two Methods

Home Developer, Inc. contracts with the Flynn family to construct a home in Boca Raton, FL. The price of the home is CU 1.5 million. For each week the project is late, the Flynns will deduct CU 5000 from the selling price. In addition, the Flynns' architect will review the finished home. Based on meeting agreed-upon parameters, the Flynns will pay a 10% bonus to Home Developers, that is, the variable is binary. The contract contains two different variables. Home Developers decides to use two different methods to estimate the two variables—the expected value method for the late penalty and the most likely amount method for the bonus based on the architect's assessment.

Refund Liability

If an entity receives consideration from the customer and expects to refund some or all of that consideration, then the entity must recognize a refund liability. The liability is measured at the amount of consideration received (or receivable) for which the entity does not expect to be entitled. The refund liability should be updated at the end of each reporting period for changes in circumstances. (ASC 606-10-32-10; IFRS 15.55) See Chapter 6 for information on rights of return.

Constraining Estimates of Variable Consideration

Because revenue is a critical metric, it is important to include estimates of consideration that are robust and give useful information. Some estimates of variable consideration are too uncertain and should not be included in the transaction price. After estimating the amount of variable consideration, the entity should then apply the following constraint focused on the probability of a significant reversal of cumulative revenue recognized:

> *The entity should include some or all of the variable consideration in the transaction price to the extent that it is probable (U.S. GAAP) or highly probable (IFRS) that a subsequent change in the estimate would not result in a significant reversal of cumulative revenue recognized.*
> (ASC 606-10-32-11; IFRS 15.56)

The constraint of variable consideration addresses concerns about premature recognition of revenue, that is, recognizing revenue based in the future before there is sufficient certainty that the amount will be realized. Focusing on the potential for significant reversals of revenue helps lower the risk that revenue will be overstated. Revenue that would not reverse significantly in a subsequent period is more predictive of future revenues.

Application to Fixed Fees. The significance of the reversal is assessed compared with the cumulative amount of revenue recognized. So, in its analysis, the entity should consider not only variable consideration but factor in fixed consideration as well. The constraint applies to contracts with a fixed price if it is uncertain whether the entity will be entitled to all the consideration even after the performance obligation is satisfied. An example of this is a legal service provided for a fixed fee that is only payable if the customer wins the case. The revenue might still be recognized before the court rules if the entity considers it probable (U.S. GAAP) or highly probable (IFRS) that the fee is not subject to significant reversal of cumulative revenue recognized.

Assessing Probability of a Reversal. "Significant" is relative to the amount of total revenue in the contract (total variable and fixed consideration), not just the possible variable consideration. Determining the probability of a reversal of revenue requires considerable judgment, and it is good practice for the entity to document its basis of conclusion. It may be particularly difficult to assess the probability under certain situations. These include

- payments contingent on regulatory approval—for example, of a new drug
- long-term commodity supply arrangements dependent on market prices at a future delivery date
- contingency fees based on the outcome of litigation or the settlement of claims with government agencies.

To assess the probability of a reversal, the entity takes into account two elements:

- the likelihood of a reversal, and
- the magnitude of a reversal.

Indicators that Significant Revenue Reversal Will Occur. The Standard includes indicators to help assess whether it is probable that a significant reversal of cumulative revenue recognized will occur. The presence of one of these indicators does not necessarily mean that the constraint applies, but might be an indicator that could increase the likelihood or the magnitude of a revenue reversal. Note that these are factors to consider rather than criteria.

When making the assessment, the entity should evaluate, among others, the factors in Exhibit 3.9.

Exhibit 3.9   Factors that increase the likelihood or magnitude of a significant reversal

---

- The high susceptibility to factors outside the entity's influence. Such factors might be
  - the volatility of the market,
  - third-party judgment or actions,
  - weather conditions, or
  - the promised goods' high risk of obsolescence.
- The uncertainty will not be resolved for a long period of time.
- The entity's experience with similar contracts is limited or that experience has low predictive value.
- With similar contracts under similar circumstances, the entity has a history of offering a broad range of price concessions or changing the payment terms or conditions.
- The contract has a large number and broad range of possible consideration amounts.

(ASC 606-10-32-12; IFRS 15.57)

These factors are explored in more depth below.

The Amount is Highly Susceptible to Factors Outside the Entity's Influence. Factors outside the entity's influence include consideration that is based, in whole or in part, on a market, such as a stock exchange or an index. It is difficult to make an estimate on where a market might go. These factors could also include the actions of a third party, such as a customer's subsequent sale of products. In assessing these factors, the entity would take into account the reliability of any predictive information. That information might lead the entity to conclude that the variable consideration is not constrained.

The Uncertainty is Not Expected to Be Resolved for a Long Period of Time. Naturally, a long period of time between contract inception and resolution opens up the possibility of more variables being introduced. This makes it more difficult for the entity to conclude that it is probable (U.S. GAAP) or highly probable (IFRS) that a significant reversal of cumulative revenue recognized will not occur. In contrast, some performance bonuses tied to goals, such as cumulative sales, might become more probable over a longer period of time.

The Entity's Experience is Limited or has Limited Predictive Value. If an entity's experience with a particular situation is limited or nonexistent, its ability to predict the likelihood and magnitude of a revenue reversal is limited or has little predictive value. The entity might be able to rely on other evidence, but it must carefully assess the predictive value of that evidence.

The Entity has a Practice of Offering Price Concessions. An entity that has a consistent track record of the types and amounts of price concessions it offers subsequently may have a better predictive experience than an entity that does not. For example, say a contractor offers 20% discounts on flooring upgrades that the clients request. Having been in the business for 20 years, the contractor has a track record on which to base its probability assessment.

The Contract has a Large Number and Broad Range of Possible Consideration Amounts. An entity that entered into a contract with many possible outcomes over a broad range may find it difficult to predict the likelihood of the revenue reversal. In contrast, a contract with limited possibilities may be more predictive, especially if management has experience with the arrangement in question.

Example 3.11: Variable Consideration is Constrained

XYZ Land sells a parcel of undeveloped land to Acme Development. XYZ Land receives a fixed amount of CU 2,000,000 and 10% of any future sale of the land in excess of 10 million. XYZ Land has no experience with real estate sales and the market has been volatile. Because of market conditions, Acme Development does not expect a sale in the near future.

When assessing how to record the transaction, XYZ Land considers the following factors:

- the entity has no predictive experience in the real estate industry;
- the variable amount is highly susceptible to factors outside the entity's influence;
- the uncertainty is not expected to be resolved in a short period of time.

XYZ Land concludes that it is not probable (U.S. GAAP) or highly probable (IFRS) that a significant reversal of cumulative revenue recognized will not occur. No amount of variable consideration will be included in the transaction price. The transaction price at contract inception is, therefore, CU 2,000,000. XYZ Land will reassess at the end of the reporting period.

Again, the constraint dictates that to include variable consideration in the transaction price, the entity must

- have experience with similar contracts,
- be able to estimate the variable consideration, and
- based on that experienced judgment conclude that it is probable or highly probable that there will *not* be a significant reversal when the associated uncertainty is resolved. (ASC 606-10-32-11; IFRS 15.56)

Reassessing the Transaction Price for Variable Consideration

The estimated transaction price should be reassessed and updated at the end of each reporting period until the underlying uncertainty is resolved. Included in this update is an assessment of whether an estimate of variable consideration is constrained. Changes in the estimate are treated the same way as any other changes in the transaction price. These updates will then represent faithfully at the end of the reporting period the circumstances present at that time and a change in circumstance during that period. (ASC 606-10-32-14; IFRS 15.59) (See Chapter 5 for more information about updating changes in transaction price.)

Example 3.12: Variable Consideration—Subsequent Reassessment

Assume the same facts as in Example 3.11. Three years after the initial transaction, the following emerge:

- Acme Development is actively marketing the land;
- land prices have bounced back and are significantly higher;
- XYZ Land reassesses the situation and determines based on sales of similar parcels of land in the area that it is probable (U.S. GAAP) or highly probable (IFRS) that a significant reversal of cumulative revenue recognized will not occur related to CU 200,000 of variable consideration.

XYZ Land adjusts the transaction price to include CU 200,000 of variable consideration. It will continue to update its estimate until the uncertainty is resolved.

Example 3.13: Increase in Transaction Price

An entity determines that the transaction price should include CU 100 of variable consideration. At the end of the subsequent reporting period, the entity believes the variable amount is CU 200. To increase the transaction price, the entity must conclude that it is probable (U.S. GAAP) or highly probable (IFRS) that the change will not result in a significant revenue reversal.

Sales-Based or Usage-Based Royalty Exception to Variable Constraint Guidance

A narrow exception to the guidance on constraints in variable consideration involves sales-based or usage-based royalty consideration promised in exchange for a license of intellectual property only. For those types of consideration, the entity should recognize only when (or as) the later of the following events occurs:

- the subsequent sale or usage, or
- the performance obligation to which some or all of the sales-based or usage-based royalty has been allocated is satisfied (or partially satisfied).

(ASC 606-10-55-65; IFRS 15.B63)

Subsequent to the release of the Standard, the IASB in its Clarifications to IFRS 15 and the FASB in ASU 2016-10 clarified this guidance to delineate that the royalty in its entirety should be either within or not within the scope of the royalties exception. The Boards further clarified that the royalties exception applies when the license of intellectual property is the predominant item to which the royalty relates. Determining when a license is the predominant item requires judgment on the part of the entity. In making this judgment, the entity may want to consider the value the customer places on the license in comparison with the other goods or services in the bundle. (ASC 606-10-55-65A–65B; IFRS 15.B63A–63B)

Example 3.14: Sales-Based Royalty in Exchange for License of Intellectual Property and Other Goods and Services

TV Distributor licenses to Megasite the right for Megasite's viewers to view its popular TV series *Enemies* for six months for a 20% royalty on sales. The royalty is variable consideration. As part of the agreement, TV Distributor agrees to promote the series through TV and radio advertisements. TV Distributor determines that the license to show the series is the predominant element to which the royalty relates, and TV Distributor will recognize revenue when the later of the following events occurs:

- a customer views the series, or
- the performance obligation to which some or all of the sales-based royalty has been allocated is satisfied.

Comparison with Legacy Guidance

Under legacy U.S. guidance

- accounting for variable consideration is inconsistent and
- the entity does not include variable consideration until the variability is resolved.

Under legacy IFRS guidance, an entity recognizes revenue if it can estimate it reliably and preparers often defer revenue until the variable consideration can be measured reliably. Uncertainty may preclude recognition.

The new guidance improves upon the legacy guidance by

- creating a single model

- including an estimate of variable consideration in the transaction price to the extent it is probable (U.S. GAAP) or highly probable (IFRS) that a significant reversal will not occur
- if the entire amount does not meet the requirement then the entity can consider recognizing the portion that does meet the criterion
- allowing variable consideration to be estimated for recognition purposes.

The last bullet is expected to accelerate revenue recognition upon implementation.

The statement of financial position classification of amounts related to the right of return asset may be a change from current practice. Under legacy guidance, entities may not recognize a return asset. In the Standard, the carrying value of the asset is subject to impairment testing separate from the testing of inventory on hand. Also, the refund liability must be presented separately on a gross basis from the corresponding asset.

NONCASH CONSIDERATION

To determine the transaction price, at contract inception, any noncash consideration promised by the customer should be measured at fair value. Entities should look to determine the fair value of the noncash consideration first. This is the opposite of legacy guidance, where entities first look at what was given up. If the fair value cannot be reasonably estimated, then the entity should measure the consideration indirectly by reference to the standalone selling price of the goods or services promised to the customer. (ASC 606-10-32-21 and 32-22; IFRS 15.66 and 67)

The fair value of a noncash contribution may vary because of

- the occurrence or nonoccurrence of a future event, or
- the form of the consideration—for example, a change in the price of stock the entity is entitled to receive.

If the fair value varies because of a reason other than the form of the consideration, then the entity should apply the guidance on constraining estimates of variable consideration. (ASC 606-10-32-23; IFRS 15.68)

Technical Alert

In response to concerns brought to the Boards, the FASB issued ASU 2016-12 and clarified, among other things, that the measurement date for noncash consideration is contract inception. The IASB believed the guidance was clear and chose not to issue a similar clarification. The difference in the Boards' decisions may lead to divergence in practice if an entity chooses a measurement date other than contract inception.

The FASB responded to concerns about how to apply the constraint in situations where consideration varies because of both the form of consideration and for reasons other than the form of consideration. The ASU clarifies that the guidance on constraining the estimate of variable consideration applies to variability resulting from reasons other than the form of consideration. Changes in fair value after contract inception because of the form of the consideration are not included in the transaction price. Therefore, the variable consideration guidance would not apply, for example, to variability related to changes in stock price when consideration is in the form of equity instruments. If the fair value of the noncash consideration varies for reasons other than form, entities should apply the guidance only to the variability resulting for reason other than the form of the consideration. (ASC 606-10-32-23)

The FASB also clarified that subsequent changes to transaction price due to its form are recorded not as revenue but as a gain or loss, in accordance with other standards.

Exhibit 3.10   Assessing noncash consideration—process flow

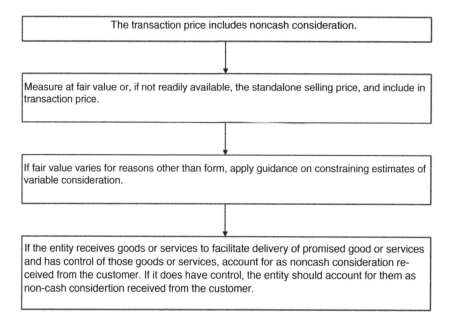

In some cases the entity may receive goods or services, like materials, equipment, or labor, from the customer in order to facilitate delivery of the promised goods or services. In that case, the entity should assess whether it has control of those goods or services. If it does have control, the entity should account for them as noncash consideration received from the customer. (ASC 606-10-32-24; IFRS 15.69)

Example 3.15: Noncash Consideration

Tech Support enters into a contract with New Company to provide weekly technology support and web services for one year beginning January 1, 20X1. Tech Support determines that the service is a single performance obligation because Tech Support is providing New Company with a series of distinct services that are substantially the same and have the same pattern of transfer. New Company agrees to pay Tech Support 5,200 shares of its common stock, paid upon successful completion of each week of service. The contract requires that the shares be paid after each week of service.

To determine the transaction price and, thus, the amount of revenue to be recognized, Tech Support measures the fair value of 5,200 shares at contract inception on January 1, 20X1. Tech Support does not reflect in revenue any changes in the fair value of the shares after contract inception. Rather, Tech Support should reference the guidance related to the form of the noncash consideration received in order to determine whether and how any subsequent changes in fair value should be recognized. Tech Support measures its progress toward complete satisfaction of the performance obligation and recognizes revenue (on the basis of the 1/1/X1 fair value of 5,200 shares) as each week of service is complete.

CONSIDERATION PAYABLE TO THE CUSTOMER

Customer contracts may include provisions where the entity is expected to pay consideration to its customers or its customer's customers. Consideration payable to a customer includes

- amounts the entity expects to pay to the customer,
- amounts the entity expects to pay to other parties that purchase the entity's goods or services from the customer, and
- credit, coupons, vouchers, or other items that can be applied against amounts owed. (ASC 606-10-32-25; IFRS 15.70)

Measurement

Unless consideration payable to a customer is for distinct goods or services received in return, it should be accounted for as a reduction of the transaction price. "Distinct" in this context is consistent with the guidance in Step 2. If the amount is variable, then the entity should estimate the amount in accordance with the guidance on variable consideration. (ASC 610-10-32-25)

Exhibit 3.11 Examples of consideration payable to the customer

Example	Description	Treatment
Slotting fees	Entity pays retailer fees for product placement—either physically or virtually.	Generally not a distinct good or service, therefore, treated as a reduction in transaction price.
Cooperative advertising arrangements	Vendor agrees to reimburse a reseller for advertising costs.	Needs careful analysis of facts and circumstances to determine if the payment is for distinct goods or services.
Coupons and rebates	Customer's customers may receive a partial refund of the purchase price.	Generally, not a distinct good or service and are treated as a reduction in the transaction price.
Purchase of goods or services	Entity purchases a distinct good or service from customer.	Entity must determine whether part of the payment is a reduction of the transaction price.
Pay-to-play arrangements	Entity pays a fee to the customer in order to obtain a new contract.	Generally, such payments are not associated with distinct goods or services and are treated as a reduction in transaction price.
Price protection	Agreement calls for the entity to reimburse a retailer up to a certain amount for shortfalls in the sales price over a specified period of time.	Does not normally provide a distinct good or service and are treated as a reduction in the transaction price. (See section earlier in this chapter.)

Exhibit 3.12   Consideration payable to the customer—process flow

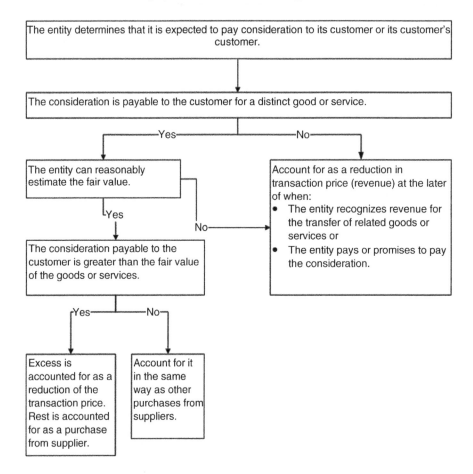

If consideration payable to the customer is for a distinct good or service, the entity should account for it in the same way it accounts for other purchases from suppliers. (ASC 606-10-32-26; IFRS 15.71)

If consideration payable to the customer is not for a distinct good or service, the consideration should be treated as a reduction in transaction price. The consideration payable to the customer may be greater than the fair value of the good or service received. In that case, to depict revenue faithfully, the entity should account for the excess as a reduction of the transaction price.

If the fair value of the goods or services is not reasonably estimable, the entity should account for all the consideration payable to the customer as a reduction of the transaction price. (ASC 610-10-32-26)

Recognition

For recognition of consideration payable to a customer accounted for as a reduction in transaction price, the Standard provides the following guidance:

. . . the entity shall recognize the reduction when (or as) the later of either of the following events occurs:

- The entity recognizes revenue for the transfer of the related goods or services to the customer.
- The entity pays or promises to pay the consideration of (even if payment is conditional on a future event). That promise may be implied by the entity's customary business practices.
 (ASC 606-10-32-27; IFRS 15.72)

The TRG brought an issue to the boards related to variable consideration payable to a customer and the timing of recognition. Some stakeholders questioned whether the guidance above is inconsistent with that on variable consideration, which might be interpreted to require earlier recognition under some circumstances. The staff view that the Board members deemed reasonable was that entities should consider both areas of guidance and record the reduction in revenue at the earlier of when it would be required under the variable consideration guidance as a change in transaction price and when the consideration is payable to a customer—when a promise is made or implied.

Example 3.16: Consideration Payable to Customer—Slotting Fees

Artisanal Soap sells its products to specialty stores and pays those stores a fee to ensure prominent product placement. Artisanal should reduce the transaction price by the amount of the slotting fees. Artisanal is not receiving a distinct good or service in exchange for the slotting fees.

Example 3.17: Consideration Payable to Customer for a Distinct Service

Everlasting Beauty sells its make-up line to Retailer for CU 500,000. Retailer also agrees in the contract to provide specific advertising in its promotions in exchange for an additional CU 100,000. Everlasting Beauty determines that it could get similar advertising at a cost of CU 100,000. Everlasting Beauty should account for the payment to Retailer consistent with purchases of similar advertising. The payment is consideration for a distinct service and reflects fair value. The transaction price of CU 500,000 is not reduced for the advertising services.

Example 3.18: Consideration Payable to Customer—Payment in Excess of Fair Value

Assume the same facts as in Example 3.17, except that the fair value of the advertising costs is CU 80,000. Everlasting Beauty should record CU 80,000 in advertising costs. The remaining CU 20,000 excess over fair value should reduce the transaction price, making the transaction price for the beauty products CU 480,000. In effect, the CU 20,000 is a sales incentive.

4 STEP 4—ALLOCATE THE TRANSACTION PRICE

OVERVIEW

In Steps 1 and 2, entities identify contracts and distinct performance obligations that form the units of account. In Step 3, the transaction price is determined by factoring in significant financing components, variable consideration, noncash consideration, and payments to customers. In Step 4, the entity allocates the transaction price to each of the performance obligations (units of account). This is usually done in proportion to the standalone selling price, that is, on a relative standalone selling price basis. With some exceptions, discounts are allocated proportionately to the separate performance obligations.

The Standard articulates the objective of Step 4. This objective is key to understanding the guidance related to Step 4.

> The objective when allocating the transaction price is for an entity to allocate the transaction price to each performance obligation (or distinct good or service) in an amount that depicts the amount of consideration to which the entity expects to be entitled in exchange for transferring the promised goods or services to the customer.
> (ASC 606-10-32-28; IFRS 15.73)

Exhibit 4.1 Overview of Step 4

This step is actually a two-part process:

1. *Determine the standalone selling price.* In some situations, the standalone selling price may not be observable. For example, the entity may not sell the good or service separately. If a standalone selling price is not observable, the entity must estimate it. (ASC 606-10-30-31; IFRS 15.78)

2. *Allocate the transaction price to the performance obligations.* The transaction price must be allocated proportionately to each performance obligation on a relative standalone selling price basis with some limited exceptions. However, when specific criteria are met, there are exceptions to the relative standalone selling price basis, and those exceptions relate to one or more (but less than all) performance obligations involving

- discounts, and
- variable consideration.

The Standard specifies the situations where the discounts or variable consideration should be allocated to a specific part of the contract rather than to all the performance obligations. These exceptions are discussed later in this chapter.

Example 4.1: Relative Standalone Selling Price Application

Here's a simple example of the basic price allocation premise. In a special promotion, Global Telecom sells a phone with services package for CU 920 for the first year. The standalone selling prices are CU 400 for the phone and CU 840 for the services. The discount is allocated to each performance obligation based on the relative standalone selling prices of each performance obligation, as allocated below.

Performance Obligation	Standalone Selling Price	Allocation Percentage	Relative Standalone Selling Price
Phone	CU 400	$400 \div 1240 = 32\%$	$CU\ 920 \times 0.32 = 297$
Service	840	$840 \div 1240 = 68\%$	$CU\ 920 \times 0.68 = 623$
Total	CU 1240		CU 920

Revenue is recognized as each performance obligation is satisfied.

DETERMINING STANDALONE SELLING PRICE

Standalone selling price: The price at which an entity would sell a promised good or service separately to a customer.
   (ASC 606-10-20; IFRS 15.A39)

The standalone selling price is determined at contract inception and is *not updated* for changes in selling prices between contract inception and when the performance under the contract is complete. If the entity enters into a *new* contract for the same good or service, it would reassess the standalone selling price and use the changed price for the new arrangement. A new contract may occur when

- the entity enters into a new arrangement in the future, or
- as a result of a contract modification.

If the contract is modified and the modification is not treated as a separate contract, the entity updates the estimate of the standalone selling price at the time of the modification. (See the "Changes in the Transaction Price" section later in this chapter, and the section "Contract Modifications" in Chapter 6.)

Exhibit 4.2   Process chart—determining standalone selling price

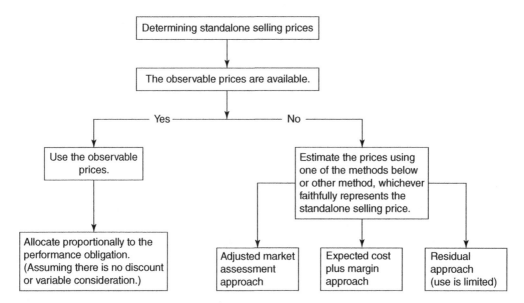

Unlike the standalone selling price, the transaction price may be updated. It must be reassessed, and if necessary updated, at the end of each reporting period. Resulting changes to the transaction price should be allocated on the same basis as at contract inception.

Standalone Selling Price Directly Observable

The best evidence of the standalone selling price is the *observable* price charged by the entity when the entity sells those goods or services separately in similar circumstances to similar customers. However, goods or services are not always sold separately. If the standalone selling price is not directly observable, the entity must estimate it.

> **Tip:** The contract price or the list price might be the standalone price; however, the entity should not presume that is the case. (ASC 606-10-32-32; IFRS 15.77) As in other steps in the process, the entity should consider customary business practices when determining the standalone selling price. For instance, the entity may regularly provide discounts to customers and these should be considered.

Example 4.2: Standalone Selling Prices Directly Observable

Home Safety sells a home alarm system. Customers pay CU 1,000 for the bundle of the alarm and one year of monitoring. Home Safety sells the alarm and the monitoring service separately, and concludes that the alarm and the monitoring service are distinct performance obligations. Home Safety further concludes that the standalone selling prices are CU 800 for the alarm system and CU 480 for the year of monitoring services. This information is observable evidence of standalone selling prices. Home Safety allocates the transaction price of CU 1,280 to the alarm and the monitoring services on a relative standalone selling price basis, as follows.

Performance Obligation	Transaction Price × Selling Price Ratios	Price Allocation
Alarm	[CU 1,000 × (800/1,280)] =	CU 625
Monitoring System	[CU 1,000 × (480/1,280)] =	CU 375
		CU 1,000

The standalone selling price is allocated proportionately to the two performance obligations.

Estimating a Standalone Selling Price that is Not Directly Observable

If the product or service is not sold separately, the entity must use another method to determine the standalone selling price. The Standard does not allow for postponement of revenue recognition because of a lack of reliable evidence. If the standalone selling price is not directly observable, it must be estimated. When estimating the standalone selling price, entities need to exercise judgment. Some entities may have robust procedures in place to estimate prices; others may need to put procedures in place. In estimating the standalone selling prices, the entity should *maximize the use of observable inputs* and consider all reasonably available and relevant information, including the following.

- Reasonably available data points, such as

  - standalone prices,
  - manufacturing costs,
  - margins,
  - price listings, and
  - third-party pricing.

- Market conditions, such as

  - demand,
  - competition,
  - constraints, and
  - trends.

- Entity-specific factors, such as

  - pricing strategies,
  - objectives, and
  - market share.

- Information about the customer or class of customer, such as

  - geographical distribution,
  - type, and
  - distribution channels.

The entity must apply estimation methods *consistently* for similar circumstances. The Standard does not prescribe or preclude any one method. It indicates that the method used to estimate the standalone selling prices should result in an estimate that represents faithfully the price an entity would charge for the goods or services if they were sold separately. The Standard does describe three estimation methods, listed in Exhibit 4.3 and described in more detail in the following sections. (ASC 606-10-32-33; IFRS 15.78)

Exhibit 4.3   Estimation methods

Estimation Method	Description
Adjusted market assessment approach	The entity evaluates the market in which it sells goods or services and estimates the price that a customer in the market would be willing to pay.
Expected cost plus a margin approach	The entity builds up a standalone selling price using costs and an appropriate margin.
Residual approach	The entity estimates the standalone selling price by deducting from the total transaction price the sum of the observable standalone selling prices of other goods or services promised in the contract. (See below for restrictions on the use of the residual approach.)

(ASC 606-10-32-34; IFRS 15.79)

Other approaches may be appropriate, as long as the objective of those approaches is to identify the amount the entity would charge if selling the underlying goods or services on their own.

The Adjusted Market Assessment Approach. Under this method, the entity looks to the market. The entity gathers external data and references prices from the competitors for similar goods or services and adjusts those prices, if needed, to reflect the entity's costs, margins, distribution channels, customer or geographic segments, etc.

The price may also be affected by market conditions, such as

- completion
- supply
- demand
- perceived value to the customer
- trends, etc.

A good or service may be sold in different markets for different amounts. For example, an entity may sell a good in an urban area near a distribution center for a lower amount than in a rural area. Competitors in a particular geographic area may drive down prices. Price concessions offered by sales representatives and other discounts may affect the range of prices at which the product is offered.

The Expected Costs Plus a Margin Approach. This approach starts more internally. The entity begins with forecasting its expected costs of satisfying a performance obligation. It then looks externally and factors in market information, assesses how much the market can bear, and adds to the costs an appropriate, reasonable margin for that good or service. In applying this method, costs should be consistent with those the entity would normally consider when pricing a product. Direct and indirect costs should be included. The entity may also need to factor in research and development costs it expects to recover. As with other inputs to the estimate, the entity needs to exercise judgment when assessing whether a margin is reasonable. In making that judgment, the entity should look at margins for similar products, industry averages and historical data, current market conditions, etc.

Example 4.3: Determining the Transaction Price when Standalone Selling Prices are Not Directly Observable

Technology Systems enters into a contract to sell computers, a new software program, and support systems to Small Business at a total cost of CU 1000. The performance obligations will be satisfied at different points in time. Technology Systems regularly sells the computers separately, giving it a directly observable standalone selling price. The prices of the software and support services are not directly observable. To estimate the standalone selling price of the software, Technology Systems uses the adjusted market assessment approach. To estimate the price of the software license, Technology Systems uses the expected cost plus a margin approach.

Product	Standalone Selling Price	Approach
Computer	CU 500	Directly observable
Software	250	Adjusted market assessment
Support services	750	Expected cost plus a margin
Total	CU 1,500	

Because the promised consideration (CU 1,000) is less than the sum of the standalone selling prices, the customer has received a discount. Technology Systems determines that it does not have observable evidence as to which performance obligation the discount applies. Therefore, the discount is allocated on a proportional basis.

Product	Allocated Transaction Price
Computer	(CU 500 ÷ 1,500) × 1,000 = CU 333
Software	(CU 250 ÷ 1,500) × 1,000 = CU 167
Support services	(CU 750 ÷ 1,500) × 1,000 = CU 500
Total	CU 1,000

The Residual Approach. The use of this approach is restricted. Entities may use this approach *only* if the standalone selling price is *uncertain* or *highly variable*.

- Uncertain. A standalone selling price is uncertain if the entity has not yet established a price for the good or service and the good or service has not previously been sold on a standalone basis.
- Highly variable. A standalone selling price is highly variable if the entity sells the same good or service to different customers, at or near the same time, for a broad range of amounts. (ASC 606-10-32-34(c); IFR 15.79(c))

The use of the residual approach is intentionally limited. The entity should not use the residual approach in cases where, for example,

- there is no remaining transaction price to allocate to the remaining performance obligations, or
- the allocated amount is not within a range of the entity's observable selling prices for the good or service.

The entity should be wary if applying the residual approach results in consideration of zero or very little consideration. Such an outcome may not be reasonable unless other GAAP applies, for instance, in cases where the obligation is partially out of scope of ASC 606 and IFRS 15.

Some arrangements may include a discount that specifically relates to only certain performance obligations that are typically sold together as a bundle. In those cases, when using the residual approach, the discount must be allocated to those performance obligations before deducting the standalone selling price from the total transaction price. (ASC 606-10-32-38; IFRS 15.83)

In arrangements where price can be highly variable because there is little incremental cost in order for the entity to provide the goods or services, the residual approach may be the most reliable approach to determine the standalone selling price. This may be especially relevant to intellectual property and other intangible assets. In addition, determining standalone selling prices for intangible property, including intellectual property, can be especially challenging because those items may often be sold as part of a widely priced bundle. For example, an entity may license software using a wide price band. Using the residual approach allows entities to bring in elements of the arrangement where prices are more reliable and to use the remainder to price the intangibles.

If the residual approach is used, the entity should be comfortable that the residual approach results in a faithful representation of the standalone selling price.

Example 4.4: Estimating the Standalone Selling Price Using the Residual Approach

Computer Solutions enters into a contract with a customer to provide three separate performance obligations: computers, services, and a license for newly developed software. The total transaction price is CU 30,000. Computer Solutions regularly sells the computers for CU 10,000 and the services for CU 12,000. The license has not been sold previously, there is no established price, and there is no comparable product sold by competitors. The computers, services, and license are not regularly sold at a discount.

Computer Solutions meets the requirements to use the residual approach to estimate the standalone selling price for the license because the standalone selling price is uncertain—a price has not been established and it has not been sold previously. Computer Solutions also determines that another method would not be appropriate.

Calculation of standalone selling price using the residual approach:

Total transaction price:	CU 30,000	
Less: Computers	<10,000>	Directly observable price
Servicing	<12,000>	Directly observable price
= License	CU 8,000	Residual price

Combination of Methods

Entities may use the residual approach if more than one good or service in the contract has a highly variable or uncertain standalone selling price. However, in this situation, an entity may have to use a combination of methods to estimate the selling prices. To use a combination of methods, entities should use this process.

1. Apply the residual approach to estimate the aggregate of the standalone selling price for all the goods or services with highly variable or uncertain selling prices.
2. Use another technique to estimate the standalone selling price of each promised good or service with highly variable or uncertain selling prices.

If the entity uses a combination of methods, it needs to evaluate whether allocating the transaction price at those estimated standalone selling prices is consistent with the Standard's allocation objectives and the guidance on estimating standalone selling prices. (ASC 606-10-32-35; IFRS 15.80)

Example 4.5: Estimating the Standalone Selling Price Using a Combination of Methods

Assume the same facts as in Example 4.3, except that the contract includes two licenses transferred at different points in time. To arrive at the standalone selling price for the two licenses,

Computer Solutions uses the two-step process above and applies the residual approach to estimate the price for the bundle of goods with highly variable selling prices.

Total transaction price	CU 30,000
Less: Directly observable prices	
Computers	< 10,000>
Servicing	≤ 12,000≥
Residual for licenses	CU 8,000

Then, Computer Solutions allocates the residual CU 8,000 to each license based on its best available information—the average selling price for those licenses that it is negotiating with other customers.

Item	Average Price Under Negotiation	Ratio	Allocations
License 1	CU 3,000	30%	CU 2,400 (8,000 × 30%)
License 2	CU 7,000	70%	CU 5,600 (8,000 × 70%)
	CU 10,000	100%	CU 8,000

ALLOCATING THE TRANSACTION PRICE

If there is one performance obligation in a contract, there are usually no issues with allocation. However, it is not unusual for a contract to have more than one performance obligation. Performance obligations may include multiple goods, initial services, and ongoing services. In cases with more than one performance obligation, the entity must allocate, at contract inception, the transaction price to the performance obligations so that revenue is recognized at the right time for the proper amount.

The allocation is based on the fair value of each performance obligation. The best indicator of the fair value of the performance obligation is the observable, standalone selling price of the underlying good or service, sold in similar circumstances to similar customers. The transaction price, generally, should be allocated in proportion to the standalone selling prices. (ASC 606-10-30-31; IFRS 15.74)

Allocating the transaction price on the relative standalone selling price basis is the default method to achieve the objectives of Step 4. It has the advantages of bringing rigor and discipline to the process and should enhance impartiality, but it is not an allocation principle.

Exhibit 4.4　Allocating the transaction price

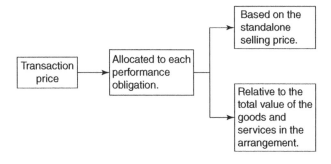

Allocation of a Discount

If an entity sells a bundle of goods or services for an amount less than the total of the standalone selling prices of the individual goods or services, the entity should treat the difference as a discount. The entity generally allocates the discount proportionally based on relative standalone selling prices. There is significant judgment involved in allocating a discount, and entities will need to have robust policies in place. For instance, the entity will need to have a policy that defines "regularly sells." (ASC 606-10-32-36; IFRS 15.81)

Example 4.6: Allocating a Discount—Proportional Allocation

Furniture Company regularly sells a set of six dining room chairs and a table for CU 1,400. Furniture Company also regularly sells the table and chairs individually. The company sells the bundle and agrees to satisfy the performance obligations at different points in time, delivering the tables on November 15 and the chairs on December 10, thereby establishing standalone selling prices of

Table:　　　CU 800
Chairs:　　CU 900

The difference between the total of the standalone selling price of CU 1,700 and the transaction price of CU 1,400 is treated as a discount and allocated proportionally between the table and chairs as follows.

Performance Obligation	Discount × Selling Price Ratios	Price Allocation
Tables	[CU 300 × (800/1700)] =	CU 141
Chairs	[CU 300 × (900/1700)] =	CU 159
		CU 300

If Furniture Company had delivered the tables and chairs at the same point in time, it could have accounted for the tables and chairs at a single performance obligation.

Exception to Proportional Allocation of a Discount. Generally, proportional allocation of a discount achieves the objective of Step 4 and reflects the economic substance of the transaction. However, there is an exception to proportional allocation of a discount. The entity may have observable evidence that the discount relates specifically to only some, but not all, performance obligations in the contracts. In that case, the entity should allocate the discounts to those performance obligations causing the discount if *all* of the following criteria are met.

a. The entity regularly sells each distinct good or service (or each bundle of distinct goods or services) in the contract on a standalone selling basis.
b. The entity also regularly sells, on a standalone basis, a bundle (or bundles) of some of those distinct goods or services at a discount to the standalone selling prices of the goods or services in each bundle.
c. The discount attributable to each bundle of goods or services in (b) is substantially the same as the discount in the contracts, and an analysis of the goods or services in each bundle provides observable evidence of the performance obligation (or performance obligations) to which the entire discount in the contract belongs.

(ASC 606-10-32-37; IFRS 15.82)

The criteria above are fairly restrictive, and the exception may not be common. As mentioned earlier in this chapter (in "The Residual Approach" section), if the entity meets the above criteria for allocating the discount entirely to one or more performance obligations in the contract, the entity must allocate the discount *before* using the residual approach to estimate the standalone selling price of a remaining performance obligation. (ASC 606-10-32-38; IFRS 15.83)

Example 4.7: Allocating a Discount—Exception to Proportional Allocation

Furniture Company arranges with a customer to sell a dining room table, six dining room chairs, and a buffet cabinet. The table and chairs will be delivered on November 15, and the buffet will be delivered on December 10. The total transaction price is CU 2,000. Furniture Company regularly sells the product on a standalone basis at

Table	CU	800
Chairs	CU	900
Buffet	CU	600
Total	CU 2,300	

Furniture Company also regularly bundles the table and chairs and sells the bundle for CU 1,400, or a discount of CU 300. The buffet is not sold as part of a bundle and is not discounted. Furniture Company has observable evidence that the CU 300 discount should be allocated to the table and chairs. Furniture Company allocates the discount before using the residual approach to estimate the standalone selling price of the remaining performance obligation transaction price as follows:

Table and chairs	CU 1,400 (800 + 600 − 300 discount)
Buffet	CU 600
Total transaction price	CU 2,000

If the buffet was also regularly discounted, then the discount would be allocated to all three products.

Allocation of Variable Consideration

As discussed in Chapter 3, some contracts contain consideration that is variable based on achievement of certain thresholds or goals being met, such as on-time completion of a project. Variable consideration is measured using one of two methods—probability weighted or most likely amount—and is subject to constraint. Variable consideration adds a layer of complexity to allocating the transaction price and may be subject to change over time.

Variable Consideration—Exception to Proportional Allocation

The Standard provides that the entity allocates total transaction consideration to the performance obligations based on the standalone selling price of those performance obligations. There are some situations where proportional allocation to all transactions does not represent the economic substance of the transaction, and so its use may not be appropriate. For example, the contract may call for an entity to produce two products at different times with a bonus contingent on and related to the timely delivery of only the second product. In another instance, the entity may be obligated to provide two products at different times, with a fixed amount for the first product that represents the product's standalone selling price and a variable amount contingent on the delivery of the second product. The variable amount might be excluded because of the requirements for constraining estimates of the transaction price. Therefore, it might be inappropriate to attribute the fixed consideration to both products.

To accommodate such situations, the Standard provides another exception to proportional allocation of the selling price. The first, discussed previously, relates to discounts; the second exception relates to variable consideration. Variable consideration in the contract may be attributable to the entire contract or to a specific part of the contract. The variable consideration may be attributable to a specific part of the contract, for example, in cases where the variable consideration relates to

- one or more, but not all, performance obligations, as in the case of a bonus contingent on the entity transferring a good or service in a specified timeframe, or
- one or more, but not all, of the distinct goods or services of a single performance obligation, as in the case of consideration increasing based on the consumer price index in the second year of a two-year contract.

(ASC 606-10-32-39; IFRS 15.84)

This exception may be applied to

- a single performance obligation,
- a combination of performance obligations, or
- distinct goods or services that make up part of a performance obligation.

Note that a relative standalone selling price allocation is not required to meet the allocation objective when it relates to the allocation of variable consideration to a specific part of a contract, such as a distinct good or service or a series.

Example 4.8: Variable Consideration Allocated to One of the Performance Obligations

LMS agrees to deploy a product management system for Publishing Company. The deployment of the system is for a fixed amount of CU 50,000. The contract also includes ongoing maintenance services for one year for consideration of 15% of publication sales to third-party customers. The standalone selling prices are CU 50,000 for system deployment and CU 100,000 for maintenance services. Using the expected value method, LMS estimates the sales-based royalty at CU 100,000.

The variable outcome, the sales-based royalty, relates specifically to the performance obligation to provide ongoing system maintenance. Therefore, the royalties should be allocated entirely to the ongoing maintenance services. This is consistent with the allocation objective of Step 4, because the entity's estimate of royalties approximates the standalone selling price of the maintenance service.

When the system is deployed, LMS recognizes revenue of CU 50,000. LMS recognizes revenue for the sales-based royalties when those sales occur.

Applying the Variable Consideration Exception to a Single Performance Obligation

The entity is required to allocate a variable amount entirely to a single performance obligation or to distinct goods or services that form part of a single performance obligation *only* when *both* of the following criteria are met.

a. The variable consideration relates specifically to the entity's efforts to satisfy the performance obligation or transfer the distinct good or service.

b. The allocation is consistent with the overall objective for allocating the transaction price.

(ASC 606-10-32-40; IFRS 15.85)

This fact pattern may commonly be found in long-term service contracts that include a bonus.

Example 4.9: Allocating Variable Consideration to a Single Performance Obligation Involving a Performance Bonus

HVAC Company enters into a three-year contract to provide HVAC services using a new, energy-efficient system. HVAC is paid based on the customer's usage per month. HVAC Company is also entitled to a 10% bonus if the customer's costs are reduced 10% on a quarterly basis. HVAC Company accounts for the distinct services as a single performance obligation satisfied over time.

HVAC Company has no experience with the performance of the new HVAC system in this area of the country. Therefore, HVAC Company concludes that it is not probable (U.S. GAAP) or highly probable (IFRS) that a significant reversal of cumulative revenue recognized will not occur. At the end of the first quarter, the customer experiences a decrease of 13% in costs.

HVAC Company recognizes the performance bonus—the change in the estimate of variable consideration—immediately because the work has been performed. The amount is not allocated to the entire three-year contract.

Series Not Accounted For as a Single Performance Obligation. In other instances, the variable consideration may *not* be allocated entirely to a performance obligation or to a distinct good or service that forms part of a single performance obligation. At times, variable consideration might be attributable to some, but not all, performance obligations. If that is the case, to reflect the economic substance of the transaction, the entity should allocate the remaining amount of the transaction price based on the allocation requirements for standalone selling prices and allocation of a discount discussed earlier in this chapter.

Interaction between the Two Allocation Exceptions—Variable Discount

A discount may meet the definition of variable consideration if it is variable in amount or contingent on the occurrence or nonoccurrence of future events. The question becomes which exception would apply—the variable consideration exception or the discount exception. Responding to this issue, the TRG generally agreed that the entity should first determine whether the variable discount meets the variable consideration exception. If not, the entity should then consider whether it meets the discount exception.[1]

RECOGNITION

The amount the entity allocates to an unsatisfied performance obligation should be recognized in the period in which the transaction changes as

- revenue, or
- reduction in revenue.

---

[1] IFRS.org; March 2015 Meeting—Summary of Issues Discussed and Next Steps, July 13, 2015. Available at: www.ifrs. org/Meetings/MeetingDocs/Other%20Meeting/2015/June/RTRG-34-March-Meeting-Summary.pdf.

CHANGES IN THE TRANSACTION PRICE

As uncertainties are resolved or new information becomes available, the entity should revise the amount of consideration it expects to receive. Revising the expectation gives the financial statement users better information than ignoring changes and retaining original estimates, especially for long-term contracts. Transaction prices, including variable consideration and the related constraints, are updated at each reporting date. The update may result in changes in the transaction price after inception of the contract. Changes in the transaction price may be related to

- contract modifications, or
- changes in one or more of the factors used in estimating the transaction price, such as the resolution of uncertain events.

Except for changes resulting from modifications where the modification is treated as the end of the existing contract and the start of a new contract, entities should recognize a change in the transaction price by allocating it to performance obligations on the same basis as at contract inception. This should ensure that the changes in the estimate of variable consideration are allocated to the performance obligations to which that variable consideration relates. These changes should be recognized in the period in which they change. Changes in transaction price related to contract modification are discussed in detail in Chapter 6. Note that the treatment of changes in standalone selling prices differs from changes in transaction price. Entities should not reallocate the transaction price for changes in the standalone selling prices. That is, the entity should use the same proportionality of the transaction price as at contract inception and *not reallocate* the transaction price to reflect changes in standalone selling prices after contract inception.

Change in Transaction Price Not Related to Modification

The change in transaction price should be recognized as revenue or as a reduction in revenue in the period in which the change takes place. (ASC 606-10-32-43; IFRS 15.88) The cumulative recognized revenue will then represent faithfully the revenue the entity would have recognized at the end of the subsequent reporting period as though the entity had that information at contract inception.

Variable Consideration Exception. There is an exception to this allocation approach. The exception occurs when the changes in transaction price

- are shown to be related to one or more, but less than all, performance obligations or distinct goods or services in a series of distinct goods or services that are appropriately accounted for as a single performance obligation *and*
- meet the requirements for variable consideration to be allocated entirely to a performance obligation or to a distinct performance obligation that forms part of a single performance obligation.

(ASC 606-10-32-44; IFRS 15.89)

Where the exception applies, the entity should allocate the change in transaction price entirely to one or more, but not all, performance obligations or a series that meets the requirements to be treated as a single performance obligation. The allocated adjustment amount should be reflected as an increase or decrease to revenue in the period of adjustment.

Subsequent Information Related to Variable Consideration

In cases where information related to variable consideration comes to the entity's attention between the end of the reporting period and the release of the financial statements, the entity should follow the guidance in Topic 855, *Subsequent Events* and IAS 10, *Events after the Reporting Period.*

Exhibit 4.5   Changes in transaction price not related to contract modifications

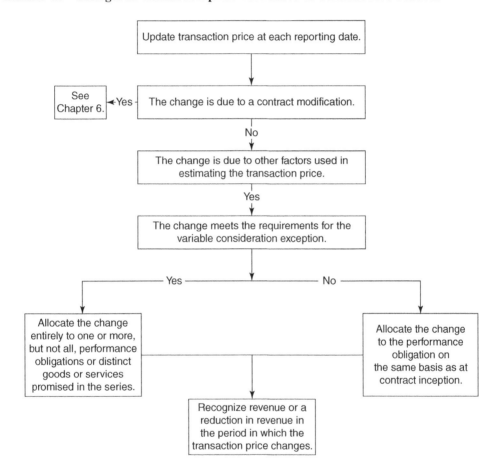

COMPARISON WITH LEGACY GUIDANCE

The allocation approach in the new Standard applies to all industries, including the software industry. The Boards chose not to include in the new Standard any special allocation rules for "bundled arrangements." Legacy U.S. guidance in ASC 605-25, *Software Revenue Recognition – Multiple Element Arrangements* requires entities to

- demonstrate vendor-specific objective evidence of fair value in order to separate elements, and

- where there is a lack of vendor-specific evidence, combine elements into a single unit of accounting.

Entities that have applied the guidance in ASC 605-25 are not required under the new Standard to demonstrate vendor-specific objective evidence of fair value to separate elements. In addition, the new Standard does not specify a hierarchy of evidence and instead emphasizes the use of maximum observable inputs when developing estimates of standalone selling prices.

Vendor-specific objective evidence is no longer required in order to avoid revenue deferral or multiple-element software arrangements. If available, it can be used. If not, the price can be estimated. It is expected that this change may accelerate revenue in cases where entities have had to defer revenue because of lack of vendor-specific objective evidence. It is also expected that companies may identify more performance obligations than they had previously because they do not have to combine elements into a single unit of accounting where there is a lack of vendor-specific objective evidence.

The Standard has some similarities with legacy guidance. However, there are some differences, which may result in entities allocating a different amount to a unit of account. For instance, legacy U.S. guidance does not provide exceptions in the multiple-element-arrangements model for allocating discounts or variable consideration.

Legacy IFRS guidance in IAS 18, *Revenue* does not address accounting for multiple-element arrangements. IFRIC 13, *Customer Loyalty Programmes*, describes two allocation methods but does not prescribe a hierarchy. Entities have had to use their judgment, resulting in diversity in practice. Given the limited guidance, some entities, especially those in the software and technology industries, applied U.S. guidance on multiple-element arrangements. IFRS 15 brings a substantial change in approach.

5 STEP 5—RECOGNIZE REVENUE WHEN (OR AS) THE ENTITY SATISFIES A PERFORMANCE OBLIGATION

OVERVIEW

> An entity shall recognize revenue when (or as) the entity satisfies a performance obligation by transferring a promised good or service (that is, an asset) to a customer. An asset is transferred when (or as) the customer obtains control of the asset.
>   (ASC 606-10-25-23; IFRS 15.31)

Step 5 addresses when to recognize revenue. At this point in the process, entities have determined the transaction price, allocated it, and are ready to record revenue.

According to the Standard, revenue is recognized when control is transferred. So, the critical question is: when is control transferred? A performance obligation is satisfied when the customer obtains control of the good or service (asset).

> **Tip:** Revenue recognition in the Standard's model is based on when control of an asset transfers. This is fundamentally different from most models used in the legacy standards, where the focus is on the transfer of risks and rewards. The Boards believe that with the risks and rewards model, it can be difficult for an entity to assess when an appropriate level of risks and rewards transfer, particularly if the entity retains some level of risks and rewards. The Boards believe that the control-based model may result in more consistency in the timing of revenue recognition. Risks and rewards remain an indicator of whether control has transferred, but it is just one of several indicators. Thus, the new model may change the timing of revenue recognition for many entities.

To implement Step 5, the entity must determine at contract inception whether it will satisfy its performance obligation over time or at a point in time. This key part of the model requires the entity first to determine if the obligation is satisfied over time. If not, it is, by default, satisfied at a point in time. (ASC 610-10-25-24; IFRS 15.32) This decision is also important because whether an entity transfers an asset over time also affects whether the sale meets the series requirement discussed in Chapter 2 and, consequently, the allocation of variable consideration, change in transaction price (Chapter 4), and contract modification (Chapter 6).

Exhibit 5.1   Overview of Step 5

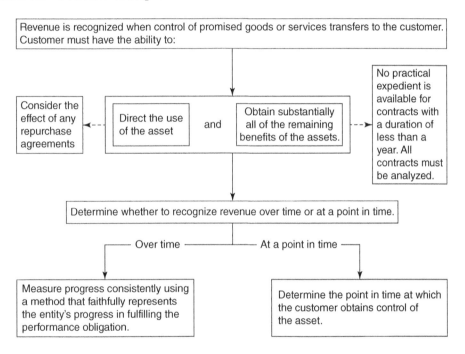

CONTROL OF AN ASSET

The Standard applies a single model, based on control, to allow entities to determine when revenue should be recognized. (ASC 610-10-25-25; IFRS 15.33) The concept of control is not only applicable to goods, but services as well. At some point, goods and services are assets when they are received or used. Services are an asset as they are consumed, even if only briefly, and even though they may not be recognized as an asset. Transfer of control aligns with the Boards' definitions of an asset, which include the use of control to determine recognition of an asset.[1] The asset can be tangible or intangible.

---

[1]   U.S. Standards definition: Assets are "probable future economic benefits obtained or controlled by a particular entity as a result of past transactions or events." FASB Statement of Financial Accounting Concepts No. 6, para. 25.

IFRS Standards definition: "An asset is a resource controlled by the entity as a result of past events and from which future economic benefits are expected to flow to the entity." IFRS Conceptual Framework, Section 2, para. 2.6.

Determining whether the customer obtains control may require judgment. To have control of an asset, entities must have the ability to

- direct the use of the asset, and
- obtain substantially all of the remaining benefits of the asset.

Direct the Use of an Asset

A customer may have the future right to direct the use of an asset. However, the customer must have actually obtained that right for control to have transferred. Transfer of control may occur during production or afterwards. Directing the use of an asset means the customer has the right to

- deploy the asset,
- allow another entity to deploy it, or
- prevent other companies from having control of the asset.

Benefits of the Asset

Conceptually, the benefits of the asset are the potential cash flows—either inflows or savings in outflows. These benefits can be obtained directly or indirectly by, for example,

- using the asset to
  - produce goods
  - provide services
  - enhance the value of the assets
  - settle liabilities
  - reduce expenses
- selling the asset
- exchanging the asset
- pledging the asset
- holding the asset.

Tip: Notice that the assessment of controls is primarily from the customer's perspective. Recognition generally occurs when the customer obtains control, not when the entity surrenders control. In most cases, this would not alter the timing of recognition, but the Boards made clear their preference for assessment done from the customer's perspective. Evaluating control from the customer's perspective reduces the risk of recognizing revenue for activities that do not transfer control of an asset to a customer.

Other Considerations

When evaluating control, the entity must consider the effect of any agreement to repurchase the assets. (ASC 610-10-25-26; IFRS 15.34) Repurchase agreements are explored in detail in Chapter 6.

Note that, unlike other aspects of the Standard, Step 5 does not have a practical expedient for contracts with a duration of less than a year. The entity has to analyze all contracts to determine if the obligation is satisfied over time or at a point in time.

Exhibit 5.2   Control of an asset—summary of requirements

Direct the use of an asset	→	• Deploy the asset
		• Allow another entity to deploy the asset
		• Prevent another entity from deploying the asset
and		
Obtain the remaining benefits from an asset	→	• Use or consume the asset
		• Sell or exchange the asset
		• Pledge the asset
		• Hold the asset

Exhibit 5.3   When to recognize revenue

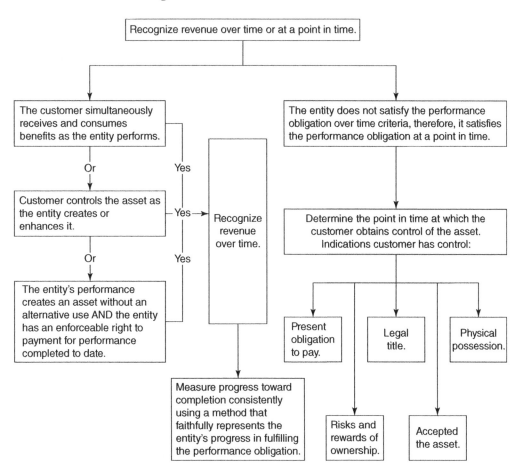

PERFORMANCE OBLIGATIONS SATISFIED OVER TIME

As the Standard developed, constituents, especially in the construction industry, were concerned that it might be difficult to determine when control transferred. The construction industry constituents were concerned that they would have to change to the completed contract method and that would not be a faithful depiction of the underlying economics. Therefore, the guidance includes criteria that focus on timing for assessing when performance obligations are satisfied over time.

Exhibit 5.4 Performance obligations satisfied over time—criteria

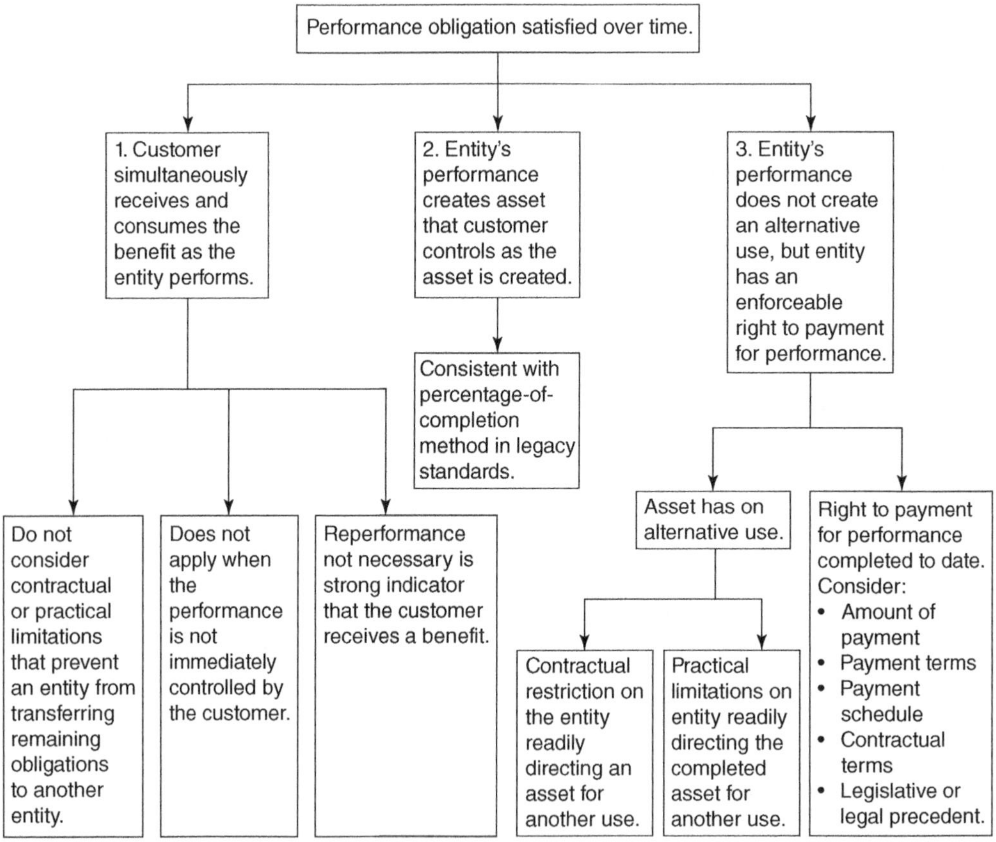

A performance obligation is satisfied over time if *any one* of the following three criteria is met (ASC 606-10-25-27; IFRS 15.35):

1. The customer simultaneously receives and consumes the benefits as the entity performs. Examples of this include a one-year gym membership or a recurring service, like a cleaning service or a monthly payroll-processing service. In those cases, the entity transfers the benefit of the services to the customer as the entity performs. An indication that the customer receives and consumes the benefits is if another entity would not need to substantially reperform the work completed to date.

2. The entity creates or enhances an asset that the customer controls as the asset is created or enhanced. Examples that fit this criterion might be a work-in-process asset that passes to the customer's control as the entity manufactures goods or a building under construction on the customer's land. It is common in government contracts for the customer (the governmental entity) to control work in process or other outputs. In contrast, a commercial contract may not give control of a work in process to a customer.

3. This criterion consists of two parts:

   - the asset created by the entity does not have an alternative use to the entity, and
   - the entity has an enforceable right to payment for performance completed to date.
   - For example, a plane built to the customer's specifications where the entity has a right to payment may fit this criterion.

Exhibit 5.5   Performance obligations satisfied over time—summary of criteria

Criterion	Example
1. The customer simultaneously receives and consumes the benefits provided by the entity's performance as the entity performs.	Recurring services
2. The entity creates or enhances an asset that the customer controls as the asset is created or enhanced.	Constructing a building on a customer's site
3. The entity's performance does not create an asset with an alternative use and the entity has an enforceable right to payment for performance completed to date.	Plane built to the customer's specifications

Criterion 1: Customer Simultaneously Receives and Consumes the Benefit as the Entity Performs

The Boards created this criterion to clarify that for pure service contracts, services are transferred over time even if the services are received and consumed at the same time. They specified that this criterion does not apply to an asset that is not consumed completely as the asset is received. (ASU 2014-09 BC125–128; IFRS 15.BC125–128)

Contractual or practical limitations that prevent an entity from transferring the remaining obligations to another entity are not part of this assessment. However, the entity should consider the implications of possible termination of the agreement.

Bear in mind that not all service contracts fit this criterion, particularly those that create a work-in-process asset. The criterion does not apply when the entity's performance is not immediately consumed by the customer. For example, an entity may have a contract to provide a professional opinion. During the course of the engagement the entity creates a work in process. These circumstances do not fit Criterion 1. For those cases, the entity must consider Criteria 2 and 3.

Example 5.1: Customer Simultaneously Receives and Consumes the Benefit as the Entity Performs

RVC Cleaning Services has a contract with Brower Pharmacy to clean the shop once a week. RVC Cleaning Services identifies the services as a single performance obligation consisting of a series of services that are substantially the same and have the same pattern of transfer to the customer. The customer simultaneously receives and consumes the benefits of the performance, and another entity does not have to reperform the work. RVC Cleaning Services assesses the contract and decides that Criterion 1 applies. RVC invoices once a week and recognize revenue when it invoices. RVC recognizes revenue by measuring its progress toward satisfaction of the performance obligation.

Customer Simultaneously Receives and Benefits from a Commodity. Subsequent to the issuance of the Standard, constituents raised an issue regarding the factors that an entity should consider when determining whether an entity simultaneously receives and consumes the benefits of a commodity, such as electricity, natural gas, heating oil, etc. As with other assessments, the TRG members and FASB and IASB staff believe that an entity, as with any agreement, should consider all facts and circumstances, including:

- inherent characteristics, for example, whether the commodity can be stored;
- contract terms, for example, whether it is a continuous supply contract or a contract to meet immediate demands;
- information about infrastructure or other delivery mechanisms.

Depending on the entity's assessment of the facts and circumstances of the contract, and whether the contract indicates that the customer will simultaneously receive and consume benefits, revenue related to the sale of a commodity may or may not be recognized over time.

Reperforming the Work. The customer receives and consumes the benefits if another entity would not need to substantially reperform the work completed to date. The assessment of benefit can be subjective. The fact that reperformance is not necessary is an objective basis for determining whether the customer receives a benefit. In determining whether another entity would need to substantially reperform the work completed to date, the vendor is required to

- disregard any contractual or practical barriers to the transfer of the remaining performance obligations to another entity, and
- presume that any replacement vendor would not benefit from an asset that it currently controls (such as work-in-process balance).

Example 5.2: Assessing Whether Another Entity Would Need to Reperform the Work Completed by the Entity to Date (Criterion 1)

TransportCo enters into an agreement with CarDealer to transport cars from the Port of Oakland to Philadelphia. TransportCo delivers the cars to Denver, where CarMoveCo picks up the cars and transports them to Philadelphia. CarMoveCo does not have to reperform TransportCo's work, that is, it does not have to take the cars back to the Port of Oakland in order to deliver them to Philadelphia. So, CarDealer receives a benefit. Therefore, Criterion 1 is met and transportation of the cars is satisfied over time.

Criterion 2: Entity's Performance Creates an Asset that the Customer Controls as the Asset is Created or Enhanced

The customer's control of an asset as it is being created or enhanced indicates that the customer is getting the benefits of the asset. Thus, the entity's performance transfers the assets to a customer over time. This criterion is consistent with the rationale for using the percentage-of-completion method in previous standards. In effect, the entity agrees to a continuous sale of assets as it performs.

Example 5.3: Customer Controls Work in Process

Builder enters into a contract with Medical Practice to build an office building on land Medical Practice owns. The building is built to Medical Practice's specifications, with Medical Practice having the right to change specifications as work progresses. Medical Practice makes progress payments throughout the construction period. Medical Practice can terminate the contract with penalty at any time. The work in process belongs to Medical Practice. The contract is accounted for as a single performance obligation. Medical Practice controls the work in process, because

- the work in process is owned by Medical Practice if the contract is terminated and
- Medical Practice can change the specifications.

Builder recognizes revenue as it constructs the office building, because the performance obligation is satisfied over time.

Example 5.4: Customer Does Not Control the Work in Process

Casework enters into a contract to build wooden bookcases for use in the new Medical Practice offices. Medical Practice makes a deposit upon signing the contract. The rest of the consideration is paid when the bookcases are completed. Medical Practice can terminate the contract at any time, but Casework retains ownership of the bookcases. If the contract is canceled, the bookcases can be completed and sold to another customer. Medical Practice takes title and possession upon completion of the contract.

An assessment of the terms of the contract indicates that

- Control of the bookcases is not transferred as they are built.
- Medical Practice does not retain the work in process if the contract is canceled.
- Casework can sell the bookcases to another customer.

None of the "over time" criteria apply. Casework should recognize revenue when it delivers the bookcases to Medical Practice. Delivery is the point at which control is transferred and the performance obligation is satisfied.

Criterion 3: Entity's Performance Does Not Create an Alternative Use, but Entity has an Enforceable Right to Payment for Performance Completed

In some situations, applying the first two criteria might be challenging, and it might be unclear whether the asset is controlled by the customer. So, the Boards developed Criterion 3 for entities that create assets with no alternative use, but where the entity has the right to payment. This criterion might be useful for goods or services that are specific to a customer.

Criterion 3 may be the criterion most relevant to long-term contracts accounted for under the percentage-of-completion method, although the Standard does not use that term. Instead, the Standard looks to the terms of the contract. Thus, a reporting entity may not be able to use the same measure of progress as under the percentage-of-completion method. The criterion also puts even greater importance on the way a contract is drafted.

In applying this criterion, entities should consider contractual restrictions and practical limitations, but not possible termination.

Alternative Use. What is meant in Criterion 3 by "alternative use"? An alternative use might be selling the asset to another customer. An asset is considered *not* to have an alternative use if there are

- contractual restrictions preventing the entity from readily directing the asset to another use during the creation or enhancement of the asset, or
- practical limitations to readily directing the completed asset to another use.

(ASC 610-10-25-28; IFRS 15.36-37)

Contractual Restrictions A contract may restrict the entity from readily directing the asset for another use, such as sale to a different customer, while creating or enhancing the asset. Another type of restriction might be where the entity has to deliver the first 100 items of an otherwise standard item to the customer. The contractual restriction has to be substantive—and the customer's right to the promised asset enforceable. The restriction is not substantive if the asset is interchangeable with other assets and could be transferred to another customer without breach of contract or significant incremental costs. The possibility of the customer terminating the contract is not relevant to the consideration of whether the entity could redirect the asset for another use.

Practical Limitations Practical limitations, such as incurring significant cost to repurpose the asset or the asset having specifications unique to the customer, preclude the entity from readily directing the completed asset for another use. Entities should consider the characteristics of the asset that will transfer. Customization might be a factor in assessing alternative use, but it is not determinative. Some goods, for example real estate, might be standardized, but not have an alternative use because the entity is legally obligated to transfer the asset to the customer.

The alternative use assessment requires judgment and is made at contract inception and not updated unless the parties agree to a contract modification that substantially alters the performance obligation.

> **Tip:** Contract restrictions and practical considerations require the entity to apply significant judgment. Entities must be careful to take into account all the facts and circumstances of the contract.

Example 5.5: No Alternative Use

Consultant enters into a contract to evaluate the effectiveness of Customer's service department. For reasons other than nonperformance, the customer cancels the engagement before the work is completed. The contract requires Customer to compensate Consultant for costs incurred to date plus a 20% margin. That margin approximates the margin Consultant earns on similar engagements. The entity has the right to payment for the work performed to date.

Consultant assesses the terms at contract inception against the "over time" criteria:

Criterion 1   This is not met because the new consulting firm hired would have to reperform work completed to date. Customer receives the benefit of Consultant's work only when it receives the professional's opinion. Therefore, Customer does not simultaneously receive and consume the benefits.

Criterion 2   This is not met because Consultant is not creating an asset that Customer controls as Consultant performs.

Criterion 3   This criterion is met. Consultant does not have an alternative use for the work performed for Customer because it is specific to Customer's service department. This creates a practical limitation on Consultant's ability to readily direct the asset to another customer. The contract terms give Consultant an enforceable right to payment for costs incurred to date plus a reasonable margin, which approximates the margin Consultant earns on similar engagements.

Because Criterion 3 is met, no alternative use is created, Consultant recognizes revenue over time.

Right to Payment for Performance Completed to Date. Alternative use is necessary, but it is not enough to demonstrate control. An entity must also have an enforceable right to payment for performance completed to date. The second part of Criterion 3 is the "enforceable right to payment for performance completed to date." The entity may have a contract to construct an asset with no alternative use, constructing at the direction of the customer. If the entity is also entitled to payment completed to date at all times during the term of the contract, and if the contract is terminated for reasons other than nonperformance, Criterion 3 is met. (ASC 606-10-25-29; IFRS 15.37) As with many aspects of the Standard, readers must be judicious in carefully considering the terms of the contract.

Exhibit 5.6   Factors to consider in assessing whether a right to payment exists

Factor	Comments
Amount of payment	Entity's right to payment should be for an amount that approximates the selling price of the goods or services transferred.
Payment terms	Enforceable right to demand or retain payment if the contract is terminated.
Payment schedule	A payment schedule does not necessarily indicate whether an entity has an enforceable right to payment for performance to date.
Contractual terms	If the customer terminates the contract without having that contractual right, the contract terms may entitle the entity to continue to transfer the goods or services and require the customer to pay the corresponding consideration.
Legislative or legal precedent	Legislation, administrative practices, or legal precedence may confer a right of payment even if the contract does not. Conversely, legal precedent may indicate right to payment in similar contracts has no binding effect. Business practice may result in the right to payment being unenforceable in that jurisdiction.

The Amount of Payment   To protect itself from the risk that the customer will terminate the contract and leave the entity with an asset of little or no value, the contract will often provide some compensation. Requirement to pay for performance suggests that the customer has obtained the benefits from the entity's performance. This payment does not need to be a fixed amount, but the amount

- at a minimum must compensate the entity for performance to date at any point if the contract is terminated for reasons other than failure to perform;
- should reflect the selling price of the items transferred to date, covering the entity's cost plus a reasonable profit margin.

The margin does not have to equal the margin the entity would have received if the contract was fulfilled. It should reflect the extent of the entity's effort or a reasonable return on the entity's capital costs if the contract's margin is higher than the return the entity usually generates.

In calculating a net amount that covers costs incurred and a reasonable profit, deposits and other upfront payments should be considered. (ASC 606-10-55-11; IFRS 15.B9)

If the entity is only entitled to reimbursement of costs, then the entity does not have a right to payment for the work to date.

Payment Terms   The Boards believe that a customer's obligation to pay for performance indicates that the customer obtained benefit from the performance. The right to payment does not have to be a present unconditional right, but the entity must have an enforceable right to demand or retain payment. For example, the payment may only be required at specified intervals or upon completion. The entity must assess whether it has the right to demand or retain payment if the customer cancels the contract for other than nonperformance. Even if the contract does not explicitly give the entity the right to payment, the entity would also have a right to payment if the customer does not have an explicit right to cancel the contract, but the contract entitles the entity to fulfill the contract and demand payment if the customer tries to terminate the contract.

Payment Schedule   A right to payment for performance to date in a contract is not the same as a payment schedule that specifies milestone or progress payments. A payment schedule may be based on milestones not related to performance.

A right to payment for performance schedule gives the entity a contractual right to demand payment if the customer terminates the contract prior to completion. These terms may not always align with the entity's rights to payment for performance obligation completed to date. For example, the contract might specify that consideration is refundable for reasons other than failure to perform.

Contractual Terms   A customer may terminate a contract without having the right to terminate at that point in time, for example, if the customer has failed to fulfill its obligations under the contract. In such cases, law or legal precedent may allow the entity to fulfill its performance obligation and require the customer to pay the appropriate consideration. The entity could also have an enforceable right to payment in a case where the customer might not have the right to terminate the contract or might have the right to terminate only at specified times.

Legislative or Legal Precedent and Customary Practices   In making the right to payment assessment, the entity should look at legal precedents and customary business practices. The entity may have the right to payment even if the right is not specified in the contract. On the other hand, relevant legal precedent for similar contracts may indicate that the entity has no right to payment. Because the entity has a customary business practice of not enforcing a right to payment, the right to payment may be unenforceable.

Example 5.6: Asset Does Not have Alternative Use and Entity has Enforceable Right to Payment for Work Completed to Date

Learning Management Pro Systems (LMPS) enters into a contract to develop and install a learning management system for the human resources department of International Resources Group (IRG). The system is built to IRG's specifications. In addition, LMPS has an enforceable right to payment for performance completed to date. The contract calls for progress payments at various steps of completion. If IRG terminates the contract, LMPS is not prohibited, under the contract, from selling the system to another customer. However, LMPS would incur significant costs to reconfigure the system for another entity. LMPS is creating an asset with no alternative use, because the specific design of the system limits LMPS's practical ability to sell the system to another customer. LMPS meets the criteria for recognizing revenue over time.

PERFORMANCE OBLIGATIONS SATISFIED AT A POINT IN TIME

By default, if the performance obligation is not satisfied over time, it is satisfied at a point in time. How does the entity determine the point in time?

Determining the Point in Time at Which a Performance Obligation is Satisfied

To determine the point in time, the entity must consider when control has transferred and the customer has control of the assets. (Control was discussed earlier in this chapter. Remember, control is determined from the customer's perspective.) Also, the Standard provides indicators (not conditions that must be met) that help the entity assess when the customer has the ability to direct the use of the asset, tangible or intangible, and obtain the benefits from the asset.

Exhibit 5.7 Indicators that control has passed to a customer

Customer has:

Present obligation to pay	Legal title	Physical possession	Risks and rewards of ownership	Accepted the asset

Not all of the indicators need to be met. These indicators are not hierarchical, and there is no suggestion that certain indicators should be weighted more heavily than others. (ASC 606-10-25-30; IFRS 15.38) Below is more information about the indicators.

The Entity has a Present Right to Payment. This may indicate that the customer has the ability to direct the use of, and obtain substantially all of the remaining benefits from, an asset.

The Entity has Transferred Legal Title to the Asset. The entity with legal title typically can direct the use of the asset and receive the benefits from an asset, such as selling/exchanging the asset or securing/settling debt. If the entity retains legal control only to protect against the customer's failure to pay, those rights would not mean that the customer does not have control of the asset.

Example 5.7: Legal Title Retained Solely as a Protective Right

TruckCo sells construction trucks and other equipment to ConstructionCo. TruckCo retains title to the equipment to protect itself from nonpayment. This is TruckCo's normal practice, and it enables TruckCo to more readily recover the equipment in the event of nonpayment.

There is only one performance obligation in the contract. The performance obligation is satisfied when control transfers. ConstructionCo has the ability to use the equipment. TruckCo analyzes the terms of the engagement and determines that it should recognize revenue upon delivery of the equipment. ConstructionCo has the benefit of the asset. So, the substance of the transaction is that control has transferred and the retention of legal title as a protection against nonpayment does not change the substance.

The Entity has Transferred Physical Possession. Physical possession does not always mean more control. For example, in a consignment arrangement or under a repurchase agreement, the entity may have control. In contrast, in some bill-and-hold arrangements where the entity has physical possession, the customer controls the assets.

The Customer has the Significant Risks and Rewards of Ownership. In considering the risks and rewards, the entity should exclude any risks that give rise to a separate performance obligation. For example, an entity may have transferred a computer to a customer, but has not performed an additional performance obligation to perform maintenance services. Notice that although the Standard is a control-based model rather than the legacy risks and rewards model, the Boards did include risks and rewards as one of the factors to consider.

The Customer has Accepted the Asset. Some contracts contain an acceptance clause that protects the customer, enabling the customer to force corrective actions for items that do not meet the contract's requirements. In some cases, the clause may be a mere formality. The entity must exercise judgment to determine if control has transferred. In making the assessment, the entity should look at its history of customer acceptance. The acceptance clause may be significant if the product is unique or there is no product history. An acceptance clause that includes a trial before payment does not indicate control. This, however, is different from a right of return, as discussed in Chapter 6.

Customer Acceptance As mentioned above, some contracts include customer acceptance clauses to protect the customer. They give customers the right to cancel a contract or demand remedial action if the good or service does not meet their specifications. The different types of acceptance clauses and their appropriate accounting treatment are summarized in Exhibit 5.8.

Exhibit 5.8   Customer acceptance clauses

Clause	Accounting Treatment
The entity can objectively verify that the goods or services comply with the contract. (ASC 610-10-55-86; IFRS 15.B84)	Customer acceptance is a formality. Revenue can be recognized.
The entity cannot objectively determine if specifications have been met. (ASC 610-10-55-87; IFRS 15.B85)	The entity would probably not be able to conclude that the customer has accepted the product or service before a formal acceptance, because the entity cannot determine if the customer can direct the use of the product and obtain substantially all the benefits from the asset.
The entity delivers a product for trial or evaluation, and the customer is not committed to pay until the trial period ends. (ASC 610-10-55-88; IFRS 15. B86)	The customer does not have control of the product until the customer accepts the product or the trial period has ended.

Example 5.8: Customer Acceptance Clause

St. Nick Collectibles delivers its new holiday ornaments to Collector Store on July 15. St. Nick Collectibles instructs Collector Store not to begin selling the items until the official August 15 release date. Collector Store does not have the ability to direct the use of and receive the benefits of the items. Even though Collector Store has physical possession of the items, St. Nick Collectibles cannot recognize revenue until its time-based restriction has expired.

MEASURING PROGRESS TOWARD COMPLETE SATISFACTION OF A PERFORMANCE OBLIGATION

For each performance obligation satisfied over time:

. . . the objective when measuring progress is to depict an entity's performance in transferring control of goods or services promised to a customer (that is satisfaction of an entity's performance obligation).
(ASC 606-10-25-31; IFRS 15.39)

Once the entity determines that a performance obligation is satisfied over time, it measures progress toward completion to determine the amount and timing of revenue recognition.

An entity cannot apply multiple measures of progress within a single performance obligation. The entity must apply a single method of measuring progress for each performance obligation that best reflects the transfer of control, that is, a measure that is consistent with the objective of depicting its performance. The entity should apply the method consistently to enhance comparability of revenue in different reporting periods. The entity must apply that method consistently to "similar performance obligations in similar circumstances," and the entity must be able to apply that method reliably. (ASC 606-10-25-32; IFRS 15.40)

Adjusting the Measure of Progress. Circumstances, like changes in costs, can affect the measure of progress. The progress toward completion must be measured at the end of each reporting period. (ASC 606-10-25-35; IFRS 15.40) If the measure of progress changes, the resulting changes should be accounted for as a change in accounting estimate per FASB ASC 250-10 or IAS 8.

Practical Expedient

If an entity has a right to consideration for an amount that corresponds directly to the value transferred to the customer of the entity's performance obligation completed to date, the entity may, as a practical expedient, recognize revenue for the amount the entity has a right to invoice. (ASC 606-10-55-18; IFRS 15.B16) A common example of this is a service contract where the entity bills a fixed amount for each block of time provided. Assessing whether an entity's right to consideration corresponds directly with the value to the customer requires judgment.

The TRG[2] examined a question regarding situations where an entity may change the price per unit transferred to the customer over the term of the contract. TRG members generally agreed that the resolution depends on the facts and circumstances of the arrangement. The TRG further opined that in contracts with changes in rates, it is possible to meet the practical expedient requirement as long as the rate changes reasonably represent the changes in value to the customer. For example, an IT support services contract where the level of service decreases as the level of effort decreases might qualify. The TRG gave another example: A contract to purchase electricity at prices that change each year based on the forward market price of electricity would qualify for the practical expedient if the rates per unit reflect the value of the provision of those units to the customer. *Note of caution to SEC reporters:* The SEC observer at the TRG meeting noted that entities need to have strong supporting evidence that variable prices represent value to the customer.

In assessing whether the practical expedient can be applied, entities should also evaluate significant upfront payments or retrospective adjustments to determine if they have a right to invoice for each incremental good or service that corresponds directly to the value to the customer.

---

2 IASB, July 2015 Meeting—Summary of Issues Discussed and Next Steps.

In addition, entities should be aware that the presence of an agreed-upon customer payment schedule does not mean that the amount an entity has the right to invoice corresponds directly with the value to the customer of the entity's performance completed to date. In addition, the existence of specific contract minimums or volume discounts does not necessarily preclude use of the practical expedients if those clauses are nonsubstantive.

Methods for Measuring Progress

To determine the best method, the entity should look at the nature of the promised goods and services and the nature of the entity's performance. The Standard does not prescribe any particular methods, but does present two broad methods to consider. Progress measures may be input or output methods.

Output methods are

- based on the value to the customer of the goods or services transferred,
- the results of the efforts expended, and
- directly measure the value to the customer relative to the total goods or services provided.

"Value to the customer" is an objective measure of the entity's performance. As seen below from the types of output method, value to the customer is not assessed on market prices or standalone selling prices.

Input methods use the entity's efforts, or inputs, devoted to satisfying performance obligation.

Two common methods are the cost-to-cost method (input) and units of delivery method (output).

Exhibit 5.9   Methods for measuring progress

Method	Description	Measures
Output	Based on the value to the customer of goods or services transferred to date, relative to the remaining goods or services.	• Surveys of work performed to date • Appraisals of results achieved • Contract milestones reached • Time elapsed • Units produced • Units delivered
Input	Based on the entity's efforts relative to the total expected inputs.	• Resources consumed • Labor hours expended • Costs incurred • Time elapsed • Machine hours

Output Methods. Output methods include

- surveys of work performed to date,
- appraisals of results achieved,
- contract milestones reached,
- time elapsed,
- units produced, and
- units delivered.

The Standard does not list all possible methods. Entities need to exercise judgment when choosing an output method. The entity should consider whether the method faithfully depicts progress toward complete satisfaction of the performance obligation. For example, an entity may choose to base its assessment on units delivered. However, if the entity has produced a material amount of work in process or finished goods that belong to the customer, those units are ignored and the method may result in units delivered or units produced that are not included in the measurement. The units-delivered method would then distort the entity's performance by not recognizing revenue for assets controlled by the customer but created before delivery or before production is complete. The units-delivered or units-produced methods would be acceptable if the value of any work in process, or units produced but not delivered at the end of the period, is immaterial to the contract or to the financial statements as a whole. (ASC 606-10-25-33; IFRS 15.42)

The units-of-delivery and units-of-production methods may not be appropriate where the contract includes design and production services. Each item transferred may not have an equal value to the customer. Items produced earlier in the process will probably have a higher value. However, in the case of a long-term manufacturing contract for standard items that individually transfer an equal amount of value to the customer, a units-of-delivery method might be appropriate.

Likewise, the contract milestone measure is not appropriate if material amounts of goods or services transferred between milestones would be excluded, even though the next milestone has not been met.

Example 5.9: Choosing the Measure of Progress

Ship Builder has entered into a contract to produce six ferries for a private ferry service in Stockholm. The customer provides significant input into the design of the ferry. As Ship Builder gains experience and takes advantage of the learning curve, it expects to build the last ferries in less time than the first ones. The entity considers the design and production services one performance obligation. The entity decides not to use a units-of-delivery method because that method would not faithfully depict the level of performance. The entity will use an input method based on costs incurred.

Example 5.10: Measuring Progress—Output Method

On March 1, 20X1, PaveCo enters into a contract to repave 3 miles of pavement in Rocksmith Village for a fixed fee of CU 3 million. All work in process belongs to the village.

As of July 1, 20X1, PaveCo has replaced 2 miles of the total 3 miles of pavement. The effort required for each mile of pavement is consistent. Because Rocksmith Village controls the work-in-process asset being created, PaveCo determines that the performance obligation is satisfied. PaveCo also determines that an output method would best depict the services performed, because the effort is consistent for each mile replaced. PaveCo measures the progress toward completion at 66 2/3% (2 miles/3 miles) and recognizes revenue for 2/3 of the contract price, or CU 2 million.

It is clear from the discussion above that the entity must be careful in its selection of measurement method. The Standard emphasizes the need for an entity to consider the contract's facts and circumstances, and select the best method to depict performance and transfer of control. For example, an output measure may be the most faithful depiction of an entity's performance. However, it may be difficult to directly observe the outputs used to measure, and it may be costly to gather the output information. In some circumstances, an entity may need to use an input method.

Input Methods. Inputs are measured relative to total inputs expected to be used. Inputs may include

- resources consumed
- labor hours expended
- costs incurred
- timing elapsed
- machine hours.

> **Tip:** Where the entity's inputs are expended evenly throughout the contract period, the entity may consider recognizing revenue on a straight-line basis.

Input methods that use costs incurred may not be proportionate to the entity's progress. For example, if the performance obligation includes goods or services, the customer may control the goods before the services are provided.

> **Tip:** The Standard may result in increased use of the cost-to-cost measure of progress.

A challenge with input methods is connecting the input to the transfer of control of goods or services to the customer, that is, making a direct relationship between inputs and the transfer of control. There may not be a direct relationship between inputs and the transfer of goods or services. Only those inputs that depict the entity's performance toward fulfilling the performance obligation should be used. Other inputs should be excluded. Judgment is needed in making these determinations. The entity may need to adjust the measure of progress and to exclude from the end inputs

- costs incurred that do not contribute to the entity's progress in satisfying the obligation, for example, setup costs (such costs may need to be capitalized as fulfillment costs—see Chapter 7 on contract costs)
- costs that are not proportionate to the entity's progress.

In the latter case, to achieve a faithful representation, the entity may recognize revenue to the extent of cost of goods incurred. This may be done at contract inception, if the entity expects all of the following conditions would be met:

- The good is not distinct.
- The customer is expected to obtain control significantly before receiving services related to the goods.
- The cost of the transferred good is significant relative to the total expected cost to completely satisfy the performance obligation.
- The entity procures the goods from the third party and is not significantly involved in designing and manufacturing the good, but the entity is acting as a principal.

(ASC 606-10-55-21; IFRS 15.B19)

Uninstalled Materials Because of diversity in practice, the Standard includes guidance related to uninstalled materials. To ensure that the input method faithfully measures progress toward completion of a performance obligation, the Standard clarifies the adjustment for uninstalled materials. If a customer obtains control of goods before they are installed, the entity should not continue to carry them as inventory. It would not be appropriate for the entity to include the uninstalled goods in a cost-to-cost calculation. That could overstate the entity's performance, and, therefore, revenue. The entity should recognize revenue for the transferred goods, but only for the cost of those goods. The goods should be excluded from the cost-to-cost calculation. This adjustment should generally apply to goods that have a relatively significant cost, and only if the entity is essentially providing a procurement service to the customer.

Example 5.11: Uninstalled Materials

On October 1, 20X1, Computer Data enters into a contract to deliver and install 500 computers in ABC's new office building for total consideration of CU 500,000. Computer Data delivers the computers to the storage area of the new building in December 20X1. The units will not be installed until the workspaces are built out in March 1, 20X2. Computer Data expects to incur total costs of CU 400,000, including CU 300,000 for the computers.

Transaction price	CU 500,000
Expected costs:	
Computers	CU 150,000
Other costs	CU 250,000
Total expected costs	CU 400,000

The customer controls the computers upon delivery. Computer Data uses an input method based on costs incurred to measure its progress toward completion of the performance obligation. In this case, Computer Data must assess whether the costs incurred are proportionate to the entity's progress.

Computer Data concludes that including the costs of the computers would overstate the extent of the entity's progress. In accordance with the guidance in the Standard, Computer Data adjusts the measure of progress to exclude the computer parts. Computer Data recognizes revenue for the procurement and delivery of the computers in an amount equal to the costs to procure the computers, that is, at zero margin.

As of 12/31/20X1:		
Other costs incurred:		CU 50,000
Performance complete:	(CU 50,000 for other costs ÷ 250,000 costs minus computers)	20%
At 12/31/20X1, Computer Data recognizes		
Revenue	[20% × (500,000 − 150,000) + 150,000]	CU 220,000
COGS	(50,000 other costs + 150,000 for computers)	CU 200,000

> **Tip:** When using an input method, adjust that measure of progress and exclude amounts related to activities that do not depict the transfer of control, for example, abnormal amounts of wasted materials or labor.

Cost-to-Cost Method. As mentioned previously, one common input method is the cost-to-cost method. Costs that might be included in the cost-to-cost method are

- direct labor
- direct materials
- subcontractor costs
- those allocation costs, directly related to contract activities, that depict the transfer of control to the customer
- costs chargeable to the customer under the contract
- costs incurred solely because of the contract.

Direct labor and direct materials are relatively straightforward to identify and associate with a contract. It may be more difficult to decide whether other costs contribute to the transfer of control to the customer. For example, the following would generally not depict progress toward satisfying a performance obligation:

- general and administrative expenses not related to the contract, unless the terms call for reimbursement;
- selling and marketing costs;
- research and development costs not specific to the contract;
- depreciation of idle plant and equipment;
- wasted materials, unless budgeted when negotiating the contract;
- abnormal costs, again unless budgeted when negotiating the contract.

The Standard does not provide guidance on how to identify unexpected costs. Entities must, therefore, exercise judgment to distinguish normal wasted materials or inefficiencies from those that do not dictate progress toward completion.

Example 5.12: Measuring Progress—Cost-to-Cost Input Method

Government Contractor enters into an agreement to build a lunar lander for CU 1 billion. Government Contractor estimates the cost at CU 750,000,000. These costs exclude wasted materials. In the first year, Government Contractor incurs costs of CU 75 million. Space Agency controls the lander as it is created. Government Contractor concludes that the cost-to-cost method most faithfully depicts the progress toward completion of the lunar lander, the single performance obligation in the contract. At the end of the first year, Government Contractor estimates progress toward completion, identifying costs incurred of CU 75,000,000 of total costs to complete of CU 750,000,000, or 10% of the total estimated cost. Therefore, Government Contractor recognizes

Revenue (1,000,000,000 × 0.10), or	CU 100,000,000
Costs	CU 75,000,000
Gross profit	CU 25,000,000

Example 5.13: Input Method—Prepaid Costs

Plumber contracts with Condo Developer to install kitchens in a new development. The contract is for CU 60,000 and covers a three-year period. Plumber expects to incur total costs of CU 40,000. In anticipation of supply needs, Plumber purchases CU 2,000 of piping that is generic and not specifically produced for the project. Plumber decides that the contract is a single performance obligation that will be satisfied over time, and to use an input method based on costs.

The Standard specifically excludes any inputs that do not depict the entity's performance in transferring control to the customer. (ASC 606-10-55-21; IFRS 15.42) The piping represents materials purchased that have yet to be used and were not fabricated specifically for the project. They are merely being held at the job site. To measure progress at the end of year 1, Plumber must back out the cost of the piping from the costs incurred to date.

Costs incurred to date	CU 10,000
Less: materials held at the job site	(2,000)
Costs incurred for work performed to date	8,000
Total estimated costs	40,000
Percentage completed at end of year 1	
(8,000 ÷ 40,000) =	20%

Therefore, in year 1, Plumber should recognize revenue of 20% × CU 60,000, or CU 12,000.

Inability to Estimate Progress

It may be possible that an entity cannot reasonably estimate its progress toward completion of a performance obligation, for example, if it does not have reliable information or is in the early stages of the contract. In that case, the entity may recognize revenue as the work is performed, but only to the extent of cost incurred if the entity expects to recover costs. However, no profit can be recognized. Once the entity is able to make a reasonable estimate of performance, it should make a cumulative catchup adjustment for any revenue not previously recognized. This adjustment should be made in the period of the change in the estimate. (ASC 606-10-25-36 and 25-37; IFRS 15.44 and 45)

Measuring Progress Toward Satisfaction of a Stand-Ready Obligation

The promise in a stand-ready obligation is the assurance that the customer will have access, not delivery, to a good or service. If the stand-ready obligation is satisfied over time, a time-based measure of progress, like a straight line, may be appropriate. Often, this might be the case for unspecified upgrade rights. However, entities should examine the contract and not automatically default to a straight-line attribution model. For example, straight-line attribution would not be appropriate if the benefits are not spread evenly over the life of the contract. An example of this is a contract with a snow-removal provision that obviously provides more benefit in winter.

Determining the Measure of Progress for a Combined Performance Obligation

For a performance obligation consisting of two or more goods or services that is satisfied over time, an entity must select a measure of progress that faithfully depicts the economics of the transfer. Such a determination may be difficult and require significant judgment. Entities should not merely default to an approach, like final deliverable, where revenue would be recognized over the performance period of the last promised goods or service. When choosing a method, entities should consider the reason why the goods or services were bundled in the first place. If a good or service was bundled because it was not capable of being distinct, it may not provide value on its own, and the entity may not want to consider that good or service when determining the pattern of transfer. If a measure of progress does not faithfully depict the economics of the transfer, the entity should consider whether there may actually be more than one performance obligation.

COMPARISON TO LEGACY GUIDANCE

IFRS

Under IFRS legacy guidance, the stage-of-completion method is used to account for

- construction contracts in the scope of IAS 11,
- the sale of goods under IAS 18, and
- the rendering of services.

When reliable estimates are available, revenue is recognized using the percentage-of-completion method. When reliable estimates cannot be made but there is assurance that no loss will be incurred, the percentage-of-completion method based on a zero profit margin is used until reliable estimates can be made. Contract costs that will probably not be recovered are recognized as an expense immediately. Legacy IFRS prohibits the completed-contract method.

The Standard is generally consistent with the legacy guidance. However, it does introduce new criteria to determine when revenue should be recognized over time. Consequently, some contracts currently recognizing revenue under the stage-of-completion method may now require revenue to be recognized on completion of the contract, while other contracts may now require recognition of revenue over time for the first time.

U.S. GAAP

Legacy U.S. GAAP applies the percentage-of-completion method, generally, to recognize revenue for long-term contracts when reliable estimates are available. When a reliable estimate cannot be made but there is an assurance that no loss will be incurred, the percentage-of-completion method based on a zero-profit method is used. When reliable estimates cannot be made, the completed-contract method is used. Under the Standard, the entity recognizes revenue when control of the asset is transferred to the customer. The focus is on analyzing control of the good or service.

The Standard also uses the right to payment as opposed to the milestone or progress method. Milestone or progress payments are an agreement to pay. The Standard's right to payment is the unconditional right to receive payment to the date of the assessment of the contract if the contract were to terminate prior to the completion of the contract, as long as the reason for early termination is not failure to perform by the reporting entity.

The Standard provides a model for determining whether revenue should be recognized at a point in time or over time. Such guidance does not exist in the legacy standards, and the Standard may change the entity's conclusion as to whether to recognize revenue over time or at a point in time. So, too, manufacturers currently out of scope of ASC 605-35 (which generally recognizes revenue at a point in time) may find that they need the requirements to recognize revenue over time. These changes may particularly affect service transactions where there is a lack of legacy guidance.

6 OTHER ISSUES

RIGHT OF RETURN

Rights of return affect the transaction price by creating variability in the transaction price. It is not uncommon for an entity to transfer control of a product while granting to the customer the right to return the product for reasons such as defective product or dissatisfaction with the product. The refund might include

- a full or partial refund,
- a credit that can be applied against amounts owed or which will be owed in the future to the vendor, or
- another product in exchange.

The Standard does not apply to exchanges for another product of the same type, quality, condition, and price. The guidance for warranties applies to returns of faulty goods or replacements.

> **Practice Pointer:** Manufacturers and retailers, not otherwise significantly affected by the Standard, need to assess whether new policies and procedures are needed for returns.

At the time of initial sale, when revenue is deferred for the amount of the anticipated return, the entity recognizes a refund liability and a return asset. The asset is measured at the carrying amount of the inventory less expected cost to recover the goods. If the realizable value of the item expected to be returned is expected to be less than the cost of the related inventory, then the entity makes an adjustment to cost of goods sold. The realizable value includes

- any adjustment (for example, costs of recovering the item), and
- any potential decrease in value.

At the end of the reporting period, the entity reassesses the measurement and adjusts for any changes in expected level of returns and decreases in the value of the returned products.

In summary, the entity should recognize all of the following for the transfer of products with right of return and the services subject to refund:

- revenue in the amount of consideration to which the entity expects to be entitled;
- a refund liability;
- a return asset and corresponding adjustment to cost of sales for its right of return products from customers upon settling the refund liability.

The entity applies the revenue recognition constraint and does not recognize the revenue until the constraint no longer applies, which could be at the end of the return period.
(ASC 606-10-55-25 through 27; IFRS 15.56-59)

Example 6.1: Right of Return

Ace sells 100 filing cabinets at a price of CU 120 each to Big Box Office Supplies. The entity's unit cost is CU 60. Big Box Office Supplies has the right to return the cabinets within 30 days. Thus, the consideration is variable. The entity decides that the expected value method is the better predictor of the amount of consideration. Using this method, the entity predicts that 93 cabinets will not be returned. Ace also decides that it has sufficient experience with this type of transaction with Big Box Office Supplies to conclude that it is probable that a significant reversal in the cumulative amount of revenue will not occur as the uncertainty is resolved over the return period. The cost of recovering the returned products will be CU 10 per unit.

Gross revenue (100 units × CU 120)	CU 12,000
Less: refund liability (7 units x CU 120)	CU 840
Net revenue to balance sheet	11,160
Inventory	6,000
Right to receive assets [7 units × (CU 60 − 10)]	350
Cost of sales	CU 5,650

Note that the expected return is recorded in topline revenue.

At contract inception, the entity records:

Cash	12,000	
Revenue		11,160
Refund liability		840

To recognize the sale less revenue on products expected to be returned.

Right to receive assets	350	
Cost of sales	5,650	
Inventory		6,000

To recognize the cost of sales and assets expected to be recovered.

In some cases, the entity may charge the customer a restocking fee to compensate for repackaging, shipping, or reselling the item at a lower price. At the March 2015 TRG meeting,[1]

---

[1] TRG Agenda Paper 34, March 2015 Meeting—Summary of Issues Discussed and Next Steps, dated July 13, 2015.

TRG members generally agreed that those costs should be recorded as a reduction in the amount of the return asset when or as control of the good transfers.

To recap, rights of return are not considered a performance obligation in the revenue model. They are a form of variable consideration. Entities must estimate rights of return using the guidance on estimating variable consideration and apply the variable constraint. Once the entity determines it has rights of return amounts, it records a liability (balance sheet) and net revenue (income statement) amount. In the revenue model, all variable consideration must be included in the top-line revenue number. In addition, the entity must record a returned asset outside of inventory and a contra amount against cost of sales. To measure the returned asset, the entity looks at the value of the inventory previously held and reduces it by the expected costs to recover that inventory. The entity must also test the returned asset for impairment, not as part of inventory, but as its own separate asset. This test must be done periodically, and estimates must be updated at each reporting period.

Comparison with Legacy Guidance

Legacy guidance in both U.S. GAAP and IFRS requires a provision for returns. The guidance in the Standard is similar, but the methodology for estimating revenue may differ from that which entities have used.

WARRANTIES

Overview

As any consumer knows, there are different types of warranty. Some warranties may simply provide assurance that the product will function as expected, in accordance with certain specifications—assurance-type warranties. Other warranties provide customers with additional protection—service-type warranties. The type of warranty and the benefits provided by the warranty dictate the accounting treatment. So, the entity must first assess the nature of the warranty.

Exhibit 6.1 Overview of warranty assessment

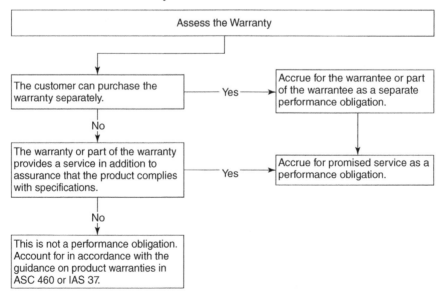

Warranties can be

- explicit—written in the contract, or
- implicit—as a result of customary business practices or law.

Warranties can also be standard or extended.

Assessing the Warranty

A warranty purchased separately is a separate performance obligation. Revenue allocated to the warranty is recognized over the warranty period. A warranty not sold separately may still be a performance obligation. Entities have to assess the terms of the warranty and determine under which category below the warranty falls.

- **Category 1.** These warranties, called assurance-type warranties, provide assurance that the product will function. A warranty that only covers the compliance of the product with agreed-upon specifications is termed "an assurance warranty." These warranties obligate the entity to repair or replace the product and are accounted for under the guidance in ASC 460, *Guarantees*, or IAS 37, *Provisions, Contingent Liabilities and Contingent Assets.*
- **Category 2.** These warranties, called service-type warranties, provide a service in addition to product assurance. For example, this category of warranty may offer additional protection against wear and tear or against certain types of damage. The additional service is accounted for as a separate performance obligation.

When assessing whether the warranty, in addition to product assurance, provides a service that should be accounted for as a separate performance obligation, an entity should consider factors such as the following.

a. Whether the warranty is required by law. If the entity is required by law to provide a warranty, the existence of the law indicates that the promised warranty is not a performance obligation because such requirements typically exist to protect customers from the risk of purchasing defective products.

b. The length of the warranty coverage. The longer the coverage period, the more likely it is that the promised warranty is a performance obligation because it is more likely to provide a service in addition to the assurance that the product complies with agreed-upon specifications.

c. The nature of the tasks that the entity promises to perform. If it is necessary for an entity to perform specific tasks to provide the assurance that the product complies with agreed-upon specifications (for example, a return shipping service for defective products), then those tasks likely do not give rise to a performance obligation.

(ASC 606-10-55-33; IFRS 15.B31)

Warranty is a Performance Obligation. If a warranty is determined to be a performance obligation, the entity applies Step 4 of the revenue recognition model and allocates a portion of the transaction price to the warranty. The entity will have to exercise judgment to determine the appropriate pattern of revenue recognition. For example, an entity may determine it is appropriate to recognize revenue on a straight-line basis over the term of the warranty, or, based on historical fact patterns, the entity may recognize revenue in the latter part of the term.

Contract Includes Both Types of Warranty. Some contracts may include both an assurance-type and a service-type warranty. If the entity cannot reasonably account for the service element separately from the assurance amount, it should account for the assurance and service elements as a single performance obligation. Revenue is allocated to the combined warranty and recognized over the warranty period. The guidance does not make clear how the entity should interpret the "reasonably account" threshold.

Example 6.2: Warranty—Sale of a Product with Warranty

CompuSafe provides a hard-drive storage system. The package includes a 2 TB hard drive and up to 10 hours of training on how to use the system. The package includes a standard warranty, and the customer can opt to purchase an extended warranty for three additional years.

CompuSafe analyzes the package and concludes that there are three performance obligations:

- transfer of the hard-drive products;
- training service—CompuSafe provides a distinct service;
- extended warranty—extended warranty can be purchased separately.

The transaction price for the storage system and the extended warranty is CU 4,800. The standalone selling price of the hard drive is CU 3,000, the training service is CU 1,000, and the extended warranty is CU 800. CompuSafe estimates that it will incur costs of CU 200 to make repairs under the standard warranty. CompuServe records the following entries.

Debit:		Credit:		
Cash	CU 4,800			
Warranty expense	CU 200			
		Accrued warranty costs	CU	200
		(for the standard, assurance-type warranty)		
		Contract liability	CU	800
		(for the service-type warranty)		
		Revenue	CU	4,000
Cost of goods sold	CU 1,200			
		Inventory	CU	1,200

The standard warranty is not a performance obligation. It provides assurance that the product complies with stated specifications. It is an assurance-type warranty, and, therefore, is not a performance obligation. CompuSafe accounts for it as a cost accrual, using the relevant guidance.

Comparison with Legacy Guidance

IFRS. Unlike legacy guidance, the Standard does not provide for deferral of revenue because of the presence of a warranty. This may cause earlier recognition of revenue.

U.S. GAAP. Under legacy guidance, warranties not separately priced are accounted for when goods are delivered. Revenue is recognized for the full price, and an accrual is made for the estimated cost of the warranty obligation. (ASC 605-20-25-1 to 25-6) Only if a warranty is separately priced, is it accounted for separately. The Standard also evaluates whether a warranty not separately priced provides a service. If it does, the warranty or part of it is treated as a separate performance obligation.

PRINCIPAL VERSUS AGENT

Technical Alert

Subsequent to issuance of the Standard, questions surfaced regarding its principal versus agent guidance. In response, the FASB issued ASU 2016-08 and the IASB clarified IFRS 15. The changes are reflected in the discussion below.

As a purchaser of this book, you have exclusive access to a companion website, with the latest technical developments and other useful information. The website will contain updated information about exposure drafts and other technical guidance from the standards' setters. See the back of the book for information on how to access the site.

Overview

More than one party may be involved in providing goods or services to a customer. In those situations, the Standard requires the entity to determine whether, for each specified good or service, it is a principal or an agent, whether the nature of its promise is a performance obligation

- to provide the specified goods or services (principal), or
- to arrange for another party to provide them (agent).

Exhibit 6.2   Principal versus agent—process flow

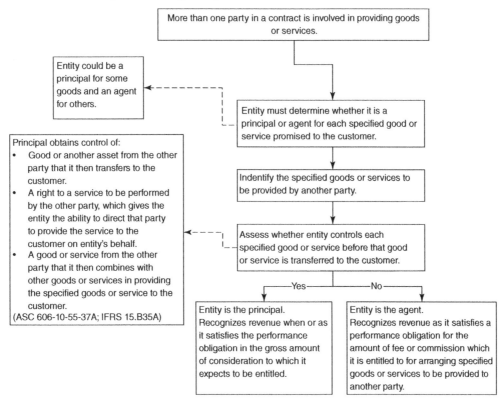

Exhibit 6.3   Principal versus Agent

	Performance Obligation	**Report**
Principal	Provide the specified goods or services	Gross, when or as the performance obligation is satisfied, for the consideration received from the customer.
Agent	Arrange for the specified goods or services to be provided by the other party	Net for the fee the entity expects.

(ASC 606-10-55-37B and 55-38; Clarifications of IFRS 15 B35B and B36)

As with other issues in the Standard, whether an entity is a principal or an agent depends on control. Before assessing control, the entity must *identify* the unit of account, that is, the specified good or service being provided to the customer. An entity may be a principal for one or more specified goods or services in a contract and an agent for others in the same contract. The entity must also determine the nature of each specified good or service:

- a good;
- a service;
- a right to a good or service from the other party that it then combines with other goods or services to provide a specified good or service to the customer.

(ASC 606-10-55-37A; Clarifications to IFRS 15 B35A)

The entity must determine whether it has *control* of the specified goods or services before they are transferred. If the entity has control before transfer to the customer, it is the principal. The Standard includes indicators to support the assessment of whether an entity controls the specified good or service before it is transferred. These include but are not limited to the following.

a. The entity is primarily responsible for fulfilling the promise to provide the specified good or service.

Exhibit 6.4   Principal versus agent control indicators

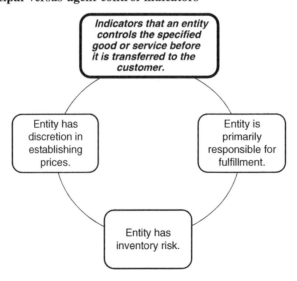

b. The entity has inventory risk before or after the goods have been transferred.

c. The entity has discretion in establishing prices for the specified goods or services.

(ASC 606-10-55-39; IFRS 15.B37)

These indicators are meant to support the entity's assessment. They should be considered in context and not be used as a checklist. The relevance of individual indicators to the control evaluation may vary from contract to contract.

Control of inventory is an indicator that one entity is the principal. Having substantive inventory risk may indicate that the entity is the principal. An entity may fulfill the specified good or service or it may engage another party to do so.

If control of the specified goods or services is unclear, the entity should recognize revenue net.

Example 6.3: Assessing Whether an Entity is a Principal or an Agent

Cat's Closet operates a website featuring the latest fashions for young working women. The site enables customers to click on an item and purchase it from the supplier. The supplier delivers the item directly to the customer. Cat's Closet receives a commission on all sales that result from click-throughs from the Cat's Closet site. Items are nonrefundable.

After analyzing the transactions, Cat's Closet's accountant determines that Cat's Closet does not control the specified goods before they are transferred to the customers who order from the website. In reaching that conclusion, the accountant looked to the indicators that an entity controls goods or services before transfer to the customer:

- Cat's Closet does not ship the goods;
- Cat's Closet does not have inventory risk;
- Cat's Closet does not establish prices.

Cat's Closet's performance obligation is to arrange the sale to the customer. Cat's Closet fulfills its specified service when it arranges the sale. Cat's Closet recognizes revenue for the amount of the commission.

Comparison with Legacy Guidance

U.S. GAAP. The Standard does not include all the detailed principal versus agent guidance that is in legacy guidance. Legacy guidance specifies that being the primary obligor is a strong indicator of the role of principal; the Standard has no such hierarchy. The Standard does not have specific principal versus agent guidance regarding shipping costs, whereas legacy guidance had specific guidance for shipping costs. Under the Standard, an entity may have to determine if shipping is a separate performance obligation.

IFRS. Because of the shift from a risk-and-reward approach model to the control model, determining whether an entity is the principal or an agent differs under the Standard.

CUSTOMER OPTIONS TO PURCHASE ADDITIONAL GOODS OR SERVICES

Some contracts give customers the option to purchase additional goods or services. These options may include

- sales incentives
- customer awards
- contract renewal options
- other discounts on future goods or services.

These options may be offered at a discount or for free. These options are separate performance obligations if they provide a *material right* to the customer. A right is material if it results in a discount that the customer would not receive if not for the entering into of the contract, that is, it must be incremental to the discounts typically given for the good or service, to that class of customer, in that geographical area. (ASC 606-10-55-42; IFRS 15.40) This provision acknowledges that customers are implicitly paying for the option as part of the transaction—the old accounting theory that there is no such thing as a free lunch.

Assessing Whether the Customer has a Material Right

This is a challenging area of the standard. In the October 2014 TRG meeting,[2] members generally agreed that when assessing whether a customer has a material right, the entity should consider quantitative and qualitative factors. Qualitative factors might be the following.

- What a new customer would pay for the same service.
- The availability and pricing of competitors' alternatives.
- Whether the average customer believes the fee is an incentive to stay beyond the stated contract term.

In addition, entities should consider not only the current transaction, but also accumulations in programs, such as loyalty programs.

Some contracts restrict customers from selling a good or service and that raised an issue with the Boards. The entity might, conclude that the customer cannot benefit from a good or service because it cannot resell the good or service for more than scrap value. On the contrary, the entity might conclude that the customer can benefit from the good together with other readily available resources. The Boards concluded that the assessment should be based on whether the customer could benefit from the good or service on its own, rather than on how the customer may actually use the good or service. Therefore, in making the assessment, the entity should disregard any contractual limitations.

In contrast, if the option price reflects the standalone selling price, then the entity is deemed to have made a marketing offer. (ASC 606-10-55-43; IFRS 15.B41)

Entities must carefully assess contract terms to distinguish between options and marketing offers.

> **Tip:** Even if the customer can only exercise the option because it entered into the earlier transaction, it is still a marketing offer if it reflects the standalone selling price. Determining whether the offer is an option or a marketing offer requires judgment.

Example 6.4: Option as a Separate Performance Obligation

Home Appliances sells a clothes washer to a customer and offers the customer a 40% discount if the customer buys a clothes dryer within 30 days. All customers are offered a 15% discount on clothes dryers. The incremental discount of 25% (40% − 15%) is the "material right." Home Appliances accounts for the 25% incremental discount as a separate performance obligation. Home Appliances further evaluates the estimated likelihood that the customer will use the incremental discount in the specified timeframe to arrive at a standalone selling

---

2 FASB/IASB Joint Transition Resource Group for Revenue Recognition, October 2014 Meeting—Summary of Issues Discussed and Next Steps.

price for the discount. Home Appliances defers recognition of that portion of the sale until the offer expires or the customer uses the discount and Home Appliances transfers control of the goods.

Recognition

Revenue is recognized when future goods and services are transferred or when the option expires. The transaction price is allocated to the performance obligations (including the option based on relative standalone selling prices). The estimate of the standalone selling price of an option reflects the discount a customer receives when exercising the option, adjusted for the discount a customer receives without exercising the option and the likelihood that the option will be executed.

Practical Alternative

Estimating the standalone selling price may be difficult, because the option may not be sold separately. The Standard provides a practical alternative. Instead of estimating the standalone selling price of the option, the entity can use the practical alternative and evaluate the transaction assuming that the option will be exercised. The transaction price is determined by including any consideration estimated to be received from the optional goods and services. The transaction price is then allocated to all goods and services, including those under option. The alternative can be applied if the additional goods or services meet both of the following conditions:

- they are similar to the original goods and services in the contract, *and*
- they were provided in accordance with the original contract's terms.
  (ASC 606-10-55-45; IFRS 15.B43)

Example 6.5: Discount Voucher that Gives the Customer a Material Right

Valentine's Day is approaching, and Vendor offers customers a 30% discount on any CU 100 purchase of jewelry. The discount can be used on any item up to CU 100 purchased in the next 30 days. Vendor is offering a 10% discount on all purchases in the next 30 days. The 10% discount cannot be combined with the 30% discount.

The customer has a material right of 20%—the 30% discount less the 10% discount offered to all customers.

Vendor accounts for the incremental discount as a performance obligation on the sale of jewelry. Based on historical experience, Vendor estimates an 80% likelihood that the discount will be used on CU of additional products. The estimated standalone selling price of the discount coupon is CU 9.60 (20% incremental discount × 80% likelihood of redemption × CU 60 average purchase). The allocation of the CU 100 transaction is calculated as follows.

Performance Obligations	Standalone Selling Price
	CU
Jewelry	100
Discount coupon	10
Total	110
	Allocated Transaction Price
Jewelry	90.91
Discount coupon	9.09
Total	100.00

Vendor allocates CU 90.91 to the jewelry purchase and recognizes the revenue. Vendor allocates CU 9.09 to the discount coupon and recognizes revenue when the customer uses the coupon or when it expires in 30 days.

CUSTOMER'S UNEXERCISED RIGHTS (BREAKAGE)

> Breakage are rights unexercised by the customer.

Under some arrangements, a customer may make a nonrefundable prepayment. For that prepayment, the customer has a right to a good or service in the future, and the entity stands ready to deliver goods or services in the future. However, the customer may not actually exercise those rights. The most common examples of this situation are gift cards or vouchers. These unexercised rights are known as breakage.

Recognition

Upon receipt of the customer's advance payment, the entity records a contract liability for the amount of the payment. When the contract performance obligations are satisfied, the entity recognizes revenue. A portion of the payment may relate to contractual rights that the entity does not expect the customer to exercise. The timing of revenue recognition related to breakage depends on whether the entity expects to be entitled to a breakage amount. To determine whether it expects to be entitled to a breakage amount, the entity should look to the guidance on constraining amounts of variable consideration found in Chapter 3. The entity should recognize revenue for breakage proportionately as other balances are redeemed. The assessment of estimated breakage should be updated at each reporting period. Any changes should be accounted for by adjusting the contract liability.

Exhibit 6.5   Breakage—overview

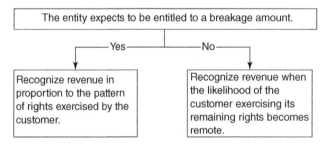

Example 6.6: Breakage—Gift Card Sale

Lucy's Pet Shoppe sells a gift card for CU 50. Based on past experience, they expect that 80% of the gift card will be redeemed. Lucy's Pet Shoppe is not legally bound to refund the unused 20% to the customer. Upon sale, they recognize cash and a contract liability for CU 50, but no revenue. The customer purchases CU 20 in pet toys. Lucy's Pet Shoppe recognizes revenue of CU 20 for the toy purchases. The purchase represents 50% of the expected redemption [20 ÷ (50 − 10)]. Therefore, following the redemption pattern, Lucy's Pet Shoppe recognizes CU 5 (50% × 10) for breakage.

Gift card amount	CU 50
Expected redemption (80% × CU 50) =	40

Expected breakage (20% × CU 50) =	10
Purchase = 50% of expected total redemption	20
Breakage recognized in proportion to purchases to date (50% × CU 10)	5

If Lucy's Pet Shoppe had no basis for estimating the breakage, then the breakage would have been fully constrained, and Lucy could not have recognized revenue until the likelihood of the customer exercising its right became remote.

Another common instance of breakage involves loyalty points.

Example 6.7: Breakage—Loyalty Points

QT Furniture sells baby furniture. Members of its loyalty program earn 10 loyalty points for every CU 100 spent. Loyalty points are redeemable for a discount of CU 1 for every point earned.

Customers spent CU 5,000,000 on baby furniture in 20X1 and earned CU 500,000 in loyalty points. The standalone selling price is CU 5,000,000, because the price to the customers is the same whether they belong to the loyalty program or not. QT Furniture expects 80% of the points to be redeemed, and, therefore, factoring in the likelihood of redemption, estimates a standalone selling price of CU 0.80 per point, or CU 400,000 in total.

The points provide a material right to the customers that they would not have without entering into the contract. Therefore, the loyalty points provided to the customers are separate performance obligations.

Technical Alert

In March 2016, the FASB issued ASU 2016-04, *Liabilities—Extinguishment of Liabilities (Subtopic 405-20) Recognition of Breakage for Certain Prepaid Stored-Value Products*, a consensus of the FASB's Emerging Issues Task Force. Prepaid stored-value products contain stored monetary value that can be redeemed for goods, services, or cash (e.g., gift cards). ASU 2016-04 requires entities that record financial liabilities related to prepaid stored-value products to follow the breakage model in the Standard. This ASU aligns the breakage model for financial and nonfinancial liabilities.

Unclaimed Property (Escheat) Laws

Legal rights related to unexercised rights vary by jurisdiction. Entities may be required to remit payment related to unexercised rights to a governmental entity. These requirements may fall under unclaimed property or "escheat" laws. If the entity must remit unclaimed property to a governmental entity, the entity should not recognize breakage as revenue. In these situations, it is important for the entity to understand its legal rights and obligations.

NONREFUNDABLE UPFRONT FEES

In some industries, it is common to charge an upfront fee. An upfront fee relates to an activity that the entity must undertake to fulfill the contract. The activity occurs at or near inception of the contract, and the upfront fee is an advance payment for future goods or services. Examples of upfront fees are

- joining—for example, gym membership
- activation—for example, a cell phone
- other initial setup fees.

Exhibit 6.6   Upfront fees—overview

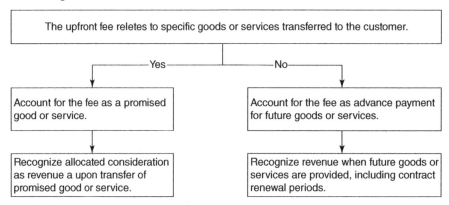

Recognition

Upon receipt of the fee, the entity should not recognize revenue, even if the fee is nonrefundable, if it does not relate to the performance obligation. Upfront fees are allocated to the transaction price and should be recognized as revenue when the related goods or services are provided. If there is an option to renew the contract and the option provides a material right, the entity should extend the revenue recognition period beyond the initial contract. (ASC 606-10-55-51; IFRS 15.B49)

Practical Alternative

If it is determined that the upfront fee should be accounted for as an advance payment for future goods or services, the entity may make use of the practical alternative mentioned in the previous section of this chapter: "Customer Options to Purchase Additional Goods or Services." (ASC 606-10-55-45; IFRS 15.B44)

Example 6.8: Upfront Fees Allocated to Separate Performance Obligations

InfoTech enters into a contract with PubCo to develop a platform to deliver PubCo content online to its customers. The contract requires InfoTech to develop specifications for the technology engine. PubCo expects to be able to sell the technology to other content providers. InfoTech receives an upfront fee of CU 250,000 for developing its proprietary technology, applying for the copyright, and deploying the platform for PubCo's content. InfoTech concludes that there are two separate performance obligations:

- copyrighting the software, and
- deploying the PubCo system.

InfoTech determines the transaction price at the inception of the contract, including the upfront fee and fees for the development of the technology and its deployment for PubCo. InfoTech allocates the transaction price to the two performance obligations.

Setup Costs

Some nonrefundable fees are intended to compensate an entity for costs incurred at the beginning of the contract. These costs may be, for example, for the hiring of additional personnel, systems setup, or moving assets to the service site. These efforts usually do not satisfy performance obligations because goods or services are not transferred to the customer. The fees are advance payment for future goods or services. The underlying costs should not be factored into the measure of progress used for performance obligations satisfied over time if they do not depict the transfer of services to the customer. Some setup costs might not meet the criteria for capitalization as fulfillment costs.

Renewal Options

In some situations, for instance, gym membership, a customer does not have to pay an additional upfront fee when the contract is renewed. Thus, the renewal option may give the customer a material right.

If a material right is not provided, the fee would be recognized over the contract term.[3] If a material right is provided, it is a performance obligation and the entity should allocate part of the transaction price to the material right. The entity has the option to apply the practical alternative for contract renewal if the criteria are met.

As with other aspects of the Standard, the entity has to exercise judgment when determining the amount to allocate to a material right. To make its assessment, the entity should look at historical data, expected renewal rates, marketing analysis, customer input, industry data, etc.

Example 6.9: Upfront Fee—Gym Membership

FizzFit operates health clubs that customers can join for an upfront fee of CU 100 and a monthly fee of CU 40. The upfront fee is compensation to FizzFit for registering and selecting classes for the customer. The customer can renew the contract without paying another upfront registration fee. The customer, therefore, has received a material right to renew the contract at a lower price than new customers.

FizzFit determines the performance obligations are

- access to the gym, and
- the option to renew the contract.

FizzFit includes the upfront fee in the transaction price and allocates it to the performance obligations based on their standalone selling prices. FizzFit recognizes the amount allocated to gym access over the initial period of the contract. It recognizes the amount allocated to the renewal right when the right is exercised or expires. For example, FizzFit may determine that customers can be expected to renew for two additional years, making consideration of CU 100 membership fee plus CU 40 per month for 36 months, or CU 1540. FizzFit could recognize CU 1540 ratably over the three years the services are provided. Alternatively, FizzFit could apply the practical alternative for contract renewal assuming the criteria are met.

Comparison with Legacy Guidance

IFRS. Currently, initial or entrance fees are recognized as revenue when

- there is no significant uncertainty over collection, and
- the entity has no obligation to perform continuing services.

The new Standard requires an entity to determine whether a nonrefundable upfront fee relates to a specific good or service transferred to the customer. If not, then the entity must determine whether the customer receives a material right.

---

[3] Ibid.

U.S. GAAP. Legacy guidance for the cable TV industry contains specific guidance for initial hookup fees. Because the Standard has no industry-specific guidance, those costs should be assessed for deferral under the Standard's new cost guidance. (See Chapter 7.)

LICENSES

Because of its challenging nature, the guidance in the Standard on licenses was one of the last items finalized. Experts had different views on the underlying economics of licensing issues, and those issues did not end with the release of the Standard in May 2014.

Technical Alert

After issuance of the Standard, the TRG brought concerns to the Boards about operability and consistency of application of the guidance in the Standard. Subsequent to the release of the Standard, the IASB through its *Clarifications of IFRS 15* and the FASB through ASU 2016-10 refined the implementation guidance for licenses. Those changes more clearly delineate when to recognize revenue from a license over time and when to recognize it at a point in time by changing the focus to the type of intellectual property (IP)—symbolic or functional. The changes are incorporated in this section. Below is an overview of some areas of board differences.

Areas of FASB/IASB Differences   The boards generally agreed on the changes. However, there were some differences. The FASB further clarified that when an entity grants a license to symbolic IP (IP that does not have significant standalone functionality), it is presumed that the entity's promise to the customer in granting a license includes undertaking activities that significantly affect the utility of the intellectual property.

In addition, the FASB decided to clarify that in some cases, the entity would need to determine the nature of a license that is not a separate performance obligation in order to appropriately apply the general guidance on whether a performance obligation is satisfied over time or at a point in time, and/or to determine the appropriate measure of progress for a combined performance obligation that includes a license. The IASB decided not to make that clarification, because the members believe that the guidance in IFRS 15 and its Basis of Conclusion is adequate.[4]

The Standard states that when determining whether a license provides a right to access or use the entity's IP, the entity should disregard restrictions of time, geographic region, or use, and guarantees provided by the entity that it has a valid patent on the IP and will defend the patent from unauthorized use. These restrictions and guarantees are disregarded because they are attributes of the license or protect the value of the IP. The FASB decided to clarify that they do not affect the identification of the promised goods or services in the contract. So, for instance, a contract for a license that grants unlimited rights to use would not identify a different number of promised licenses as would be the case in a contract that grants a license with a geographic restriction. The IASB decided that the guidance in IFRS 15 and the Basis of Conclusion is adequate.[5]

---

4   The analysis of the IASB's decision can be found in TRG Agenda Paper 7B, *Licenses of Intellectual Property—issues emerging from TRG discussions*, paragraphs 59–64.

5   The analysis of the IASB's decision can be found in TRG Agenda Paper 7B, *Licenses of Intellectual Property—issues emerging from TRG discussions*, paragraphs 68–73.

Sale of Intellectual Property

An agreement that calls for the transfer of control of all the worldwide rights, exclusively, in perpetuity, for all possible applications of the IP, may be considered a sale rather than a license. If the use of the IP is limited by, for instance, geographic area, term, or type of application, or substantial rights, then the transfer is probably a license. If the agreement represents a sale, the transaction is treated as a sale subject to the five-step model, including the guidance on variable constraint and the recognition constraint to any sale- or usage-based royalties.

Licenses of Intellectual Property

A license arrangement establishes a customer's right to an entity's IP and the entity's obligations to provide these rights. With the prevalence of technology in every business, accounting for IP licenses has become more critical than ever. In addition to the software industry, IP licenses are common in other industries, such as

- entertainment and media
- pharmaceuticals
- retail and consumer
- franchise.

Licenses may involve patents, trademarks, and copyrights. Licenses can

- be term-based or perpetual,
- be exclusive or nonexclusive,
- carry fixed to variable terms, or
- require upfront payments or over-time installments.

Assessing Whether a License is Distinct

As with other performance obligations, entities should assess if a license represents a distinct performance obligation, including whether the customer can benefit from the license on its own or together with other readily available resources, and whether the license is separately identifiable from other goods or services in the contract. Assessing whether a license is distinct may require significant judgment. (For more on determining whether a performance obligation is distinct, see Chapter 2.) The guidance in this section only relates to distinct licenses. Licenses that are not distinct include those that

- form a component of a tangible good and are integral to the functionality of the item, and
- the customer can benefit from only in conjunction with a related service.

(ASC 606-10-55-56; IFRS 15.B54)

If a license is not distinct, entities should account for the license and other goods and services as single performance obligation and look to the guidance in Chapter 5 to determine if the revenue should be recognized over time or at a point in time.

Example 6.10: License that is Not Distinct

A biotech company licenses intellectual property for a drug compound in development to a pharmaceutical company. The biotech company includes in the arrangement research and development services, services that only the biotech company can provide because of its specialized knowledge of the drug. The biotech company determines that the license and research and development are not distinct, because the pharmaceutical company cannot benefit from the license on its own or with resources readily available to it.

If another biotech company could provide research and development services, that would indicate that the pharmaceutical company could benefit from the license on its own and the license may be distinct.

Example 6.11: License that is Distinct

LMS licenses its software to Publishing Company to deploy its content to the Internet. LMS, as part of the arrangement, will also install the software. However, LMS sells the software to customers without installation services, and other vendors are able to install the software. The software license is distinct because Publishing Company can benefit from the license on its own together with resources readily available from other vendors, and the license is separable from other promises in the contract.

Nature of the Entity's Promise

Before identifying when the customer takes control of an asset, it is necessary to identify the nature of the entity's promise. Therefore, when accounting for a performance obligation that includes a license and other goods or services, the entity should consider the nature of its promise in granting a license. The Standard classifies all distinct licenses of intellectual property into two categories.

    a. *A right to access* the entity's intellectual property throughout the license period (or its remaining economic life, if shorter).[6]
    b. *A right to use* the entity's intellectual property as it exists at the point in time at which the license is granted.
(Emphasis added.)
(ASC 606-10-55-58; IFRS 15.B56)

When assessing whether a license is a right to use IP or a right to access IP, or when identifying the promises in a contract, the entity does not consider restrictions of time, geography, or use of the license and guarantees provided by the licensor that it has a valid patent to the industry IP and that it will maintain and defend the patent. Those attributes define the scope of the customer's rights and not whether the entity satisfies its performance obligation at a point in time or over time. (ASC 606-10-55-64; IFRS 15.B62)

The entity should assess whether the IP is expected to change during the term of the license. A customer does not meet the criteria for control if the IP is expected to change. If the entity is expected to be involved in the IP and undertake activities that significantly affect the licensed IP, this may be an indication that the IP is expected to change.

To determine if a customer could expect the entity to undertake activities that significantly affect the IP, the entity should consider

- customary business practices, published policies, or specific statements, and
- shared economic interest, such as a sales-based royalty.

FASB's Clarified Guidance

To determine whether a license is a right to use or a right to access IP, in ASU 2016-10, the FASB provides clarified guidance about the nature of the license. The FASB's approach looks to the

---

6 In ASU 2016-10, the FASB modified this item to: "A right to access the entity's intellectual property throughout the license period (or its remaining economic life, if shorter)."

Exhibit 6.7   Comparison of right to access and right to use

	Right to Access	**Right to Use**
Description	Customer simultaneously receives and consumes the benefit of the IP license as the entity performs. The entity undertakes activities that significantly affect the IP (required indirectly by the contract or the customer's reasonable expectation based on business practices, published policies, or specific statements). Those activities affect, positively or negatively, the customer. Those activities do not result in transfer of goods or services.	The license does not meet the criteria for a right to access license.
Examples	Brand, team, or trade names, logos, franchise rights.	Software, biological compounds, drug formulas, and completed media content (films, TV shows, music).
Recognition	Recognize over time, with an appropriate method, because the customer simultaneously receives and consumes the benefit of the IP.	Recognize at a point in time, because the customer has control: it can direct the use of and benefit from the license at the point in time at which the license transfers.

(ASC 606-10-58A and 55-58B; IFRS 15.B58-B61)

nature of the IP and focuses on whether activities undertaken by the entity significantly affect the IP. The license is either functional or symbolic, and that category determines whether the license is a right to access or a right to use. For both types of IP, the entity cannot recognize revenue before the beginning of the period in which the customer is able to use and benefit from the licenses.

Symbolic License. With a symbolic license, the IP may change over the course of time. This can occur because of the entity's continuing involvement with activities that affect its IP. Even if the right is unchanged, the benefit or value to the customer may be affected by the licensor's activities during the license period. With symbolic IP, the entity fulfills its obligation over time, as the entity

a. grants the customer rights to use and benefit from the entity's IP by making it available for the customer's use, and
b. supports or maintains the IP.
(ASC 606-10-55-60)

The customer has an expectation that the entity will undertake positive activities to maintain the value of the IP and avoid actions that would reduce the value of the IP.

Functional License. A functional IP license generally grants the customer the right to use the IP at a point of time. However, if both of the following criteria are met, then the license grants a right to access the IP.

a. The functionality of the IP to which the customer has rights is expected to substantively change during the license period as a result of activities of the entity that do not transfer a good or service to the customer, *and*

b. the customer is contractually or practically required to use the updated IP resulting from criterion (a).

(ASC 606-10-55-62)

The IP's utility may be significantly affected when

- the expected activities are expected to change the form or functionality of the IP, or
- the value for the customer of the IP is substantially derived from, or dependent on, the expected activities of the entity.

Examples of these might be when the ability to perform a function or the value of a logo changes.

Exhibit 6.8 Categories of distinct licenses of IP—FASB's alternative approach

	Symbolic IP	**Functional IP**
Description	This IP does not have significant standalone functionality. It represents something else. The lack of standalone functionality indicates that substantially all of the utility is derived from the entity's past or ongoing activities of the entity. It is assumed that the entity will continue to support and maintain the IP.	Customer derives a substantial portion of its benefit from standalone functionality. The licensor's ongoing activities do not significantly affect the utility of the IP.
Examples	Brand, team, or trade names, logos, franchise rights.	Software, biological compounds, drug formulas, and completed media content (films, TV shows, music).
Recognition	Over the license period using a measure of progress that reflects the licensor's pattern of performance.	At a point in time* when control of the IP transfers to the customer, that is, when the IP is available for the customer's use and benefit.

*Unless the functionality of the IP is expected to substantively change the form or functionality as a result of activities performed by the entity that are not separate performance obligations and the customer would be required or compelled to use the latest version of the IP. This would indicate that the customer has a right to access the IP. In such cases, the activities significantly affect the customer's ability to benefit from the IP and revenue would be recognized over time.

Sales- or Usage-Based Royalties

For related information on sales- and usage-based royalties, see Chapter 3.

Recognition

Revenue from a license of IP that is a right to access should be recognized over time using a method that reflects its progress toward completion of the performance obligation. Revenue from a license of IP that is a right to use should be recognized at a point in time. Once the entity determines that the revenue from the license should be recognized over time or at a point in time, the entity should apply the guidance in Step 5 to determine the point in time or select the appropriate method to measure the revenue over time.

In any case, revenue cannot be recognized from an IP license before

- the entity has made available a copy of the IP to the customer, and
- the license period has begun.

(ASC 610-10-55-58C)

Exhibit 6.9   Determining whether the nature of the promise is a right to access or a right to use

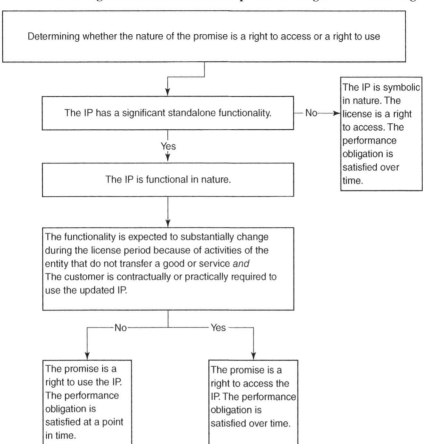

REPURCHASE AGREEMENTS

A repurchase agreement is a contract in which an entity sells an asset and also promises, or has the option (either in the same contract or another contract), to repurchase the asset. (ASC 606-10-55-66; IFRS 15.B64)

The repurchased asset may be

- the asset that was originally sold to the customer,
- an asset that is substantially the same as that asset, or
- another asset of which the asset that was originally sold is a component.

Agreements come in three forms.

1. Forward—the entity has an obligation to repurchase the asset.
2. Call option—the entity has a right to repurchase the asset.

Exhibit 6.10 Repurchased agreements—overview

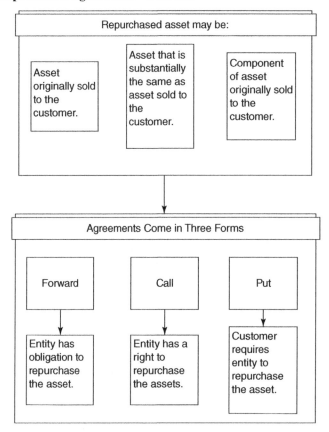

3. Put option—the customer has the option to require the entity to repurchase the asset at a price that is lower than the original selling price.
   (ASC 606-10-55-67; IFRS 15.B65)

A Forward or Call Option

When the entity has an obligation (forward option) or right (call option) to repurchase the asset, the customer may have physical possession, but is limited in its ability to

- direct the use of the asset, and
- obtain substantially all of the remaining benefits from the asset.

Therefore, the conditions as discussed in Chapter 5 for the customer to have control of the asset are not present, and the customer is deemed not to have control of the asset. The accounting treatment depends on the repurchase amount required. The entity should account for the contract as follows.

- A lease if the entity can or must repurchase the asset for a lower amount than the original selling price, unless the contract is part of a sale-leaseback transaction. If a sale-leaseback transaction, the entity should account for the contract as a financing transaction and not as a sale-leaseback in accordance with ASC 840-40.

Exhibit 6.11 Forward or call options

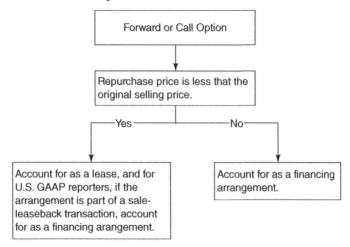

- • A financing arrangement if the entity can or must repurchase the asset for an amount equal to or more than the original selling price of the asset.
(ASC 606-10-55-68; IFRS 15.B66)

Recognition

When assessing the repurchase price, the entity should consider the time value of money. If the contract is accounted for as a financing arrangement, the entity should continue to recognize the asset, but the entity also recognizes a financial liability for any consideration received. Interest and processing and holding costs, if applicable, are recognized for the difference between the consideration received and the amount of consideration to be paid to the customer. The entity derecognizes the asset and recognizes revenue if the option is not exercised. (ASC 606-10-55-69 through 55-71; IFRS 15.B67-69)

Example 6.12: Call Option

On January 1, 20X1, Major Airline enters into an agreement to sell an X357 commuter jet to Puddle Jumper Air for CU 2,000,000. The agreement includes a call option whereby Major Airline has the right to repurchase the X357 for CU 2,200,000 on or before December 31, 20X1.

Because of the call option, Puddle Jumper is limited in its ability to direct the use of and obtain substantially all of the remaining benefits from that asset. Puddle Jumper has not obtained control of the X357. Major Airline accounts for the transaction as follows.

Recognition	Comment
As a financing arrangement	Exercise price of the option is more than the selling price.
Cash received	Cash is recognized not as revenue, but as financial liability.
Interest expense	For the difference between cash received and the exercise price of the option. This also increases the liability.

When the option expires unexercised on December 31, 20X7, Major Airline derecognizes the X357 and the liability and recognizes revenue of CU 2,200,000.

Put Options

A put option gives the customer the right to require the entity to repurchase the asset. If the repurchase price is lower than the original selling price of the asset, the entity must evaluate at contract inception whether the customer has a significant economic incentive to exercise the option. The entity makes that judgment by considering the relationship of the repurchase price to the expected market value of the asset, and the amount of time until the right expires.

If the entity concludes that the customer has a significant economic interest and anticipates that the option will be exercised, the option is accounted for as a lease, unless the agreement is part of a sale-leaseback transaction. (ASC 606-10-55-72; IFRS 15.B70-71) If not, the entity accounts for it as a sale with a right of return.

If the repurchase price is greater than or equal to the original selling price and is more than the expected market value of the asset, the entity accounts for the contract as a financing arrangement. The time value of money should be considered when comparing the repurchase price with the selling price. If the option expires unexercised, the entity derecognizes the liability and recognizes revenue.

Exhibit 6.12   Put options

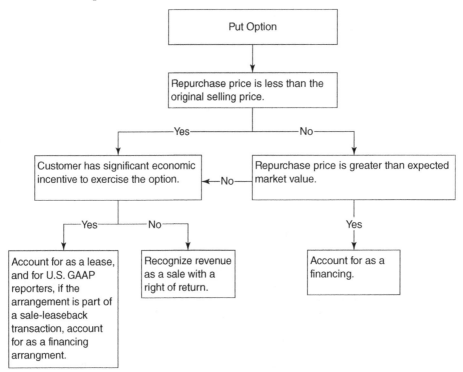

Example 6.13: Put Option

On January 1, 20X1, Major Airline enters into an agreement to sell an X357 commuter plane to Puddle Jumper Air for CU 2,000,000. The contract includes a put option that obliges Major Airline to repurchase the X357 at Puddle Jumper's request for CU 1,800,000 on or before December 31, 20X1. The market value at that date is expected to be CU 1,600,000.

At the inception of the contract, Major Airline determines that because the repurchase price significantly exceeds the expected market value of the X357 at the repurchase date, the customer has a significant economic incentive to exercise the put option.

Because the customer has limited ability to direct the use of and obtain substantially all of the remaining benefits from the asset, Major Airline concludes that as of January 1, 20X1, control of the X357 has not transferred to Puddle Jumper. Major Airline accounts for the transaction as a lease.

CONSIGNMENT ARRANGEMENTS

A consignment arrangement occurs when an entity ships goods to a distributor, but retains control of the goods until a predetermined event occurs. Because control has not passed, the entity does not recognize revenue upon shipment or delivery to the consignee. The Standard includes the following indicators to evaluate whether a consignment arrangement exists.

 a. The product is controlled by the entity until a specified event occurs, such as the sale of the product to a customer of the dealer, or until a specified period expires.

 b. The entity is able to require return of the products or transfer the product to a third party (such as another dealer).

 c. The dealer does not have an unconditional obligation to pay for the product (although it might be required to pay a deposit).

(ASC 606-10-55-80; IFRS 15.B78)

The Standard provides these indicators, but the entity is not limited to just them. Once control transfers, the entity recognizes revenue.

> **Practice Pointer:** A distributor may have physical control of the goods, but if the entity has enforceable rights to require return of the goods, the distributor may not have control.

Example 6.14: Consignment Arrangement

PubCo provides books to The Reading Store on a consignment basis. When The Reading Store scans the books at the register, it takes title to them. Up to that point, The Reading Store has no obligation to pay unless the books are lost or damaged while in the store's possession. Unsold, undamaged products can be returned to PubCo. PubCo also has the right to require return of the books. PubCo recognizes revenue when the books are

- scanned,
- lost, or
- damaged.

Comparison with Legacy Guidance

Legacy guidance uses the risk-and-rewards approach. The Standard shifts to a transfer-of-control approach, and that may change an entity's conclusion about when control has passed to the customer.

BILL-AND-HOLD ARRANGEMENTS

Bill-and-hold situations arise when

- the entity bills the customer for goods that are ready for shipment, but
- the entity does not ship the goods until a later date.

In these cases, the entity must determine if the customer has control of the goods. These arrangements may sometimes be used to manipulate revenue. The Standard provides four criteria, all of which an entity must meet in order to conclude that control has passed to the customer.

1. The reason for the bill-and-hold is substantive. For example, a customer may request that an entity holds a shipment because of a lack of warehouse space, or because the customer does not yet need the goods in its production process.
2. The product must be identified in some way as belonging to the customer.
3. The product must be ready for physical transfer upon request from the customer.
4. The entity cannot have the ability to use the product or to direct it to another customer. The goods cannot be used to fulfill orders for other contracts. Doing so may indicate that the goods are not controlled by the customer.

(ASC 606-10-55-83; IFRS 15.B81)

The entity needs to consider whether it meets those criteria and if it is providing custodial services. If the entity is providing custodial services, part of the transaction price should be allocated to that performance obligation.

Example 6.15: Bill-and-Hold Arrangements—Customer does Not Control the Goods

The entity's sales representatives contact their customers near the end of the fiscal year, encouraging them to place an order before fiscal year end. The sales representatives promise the customers that their payment period will be extended to 30 days after shipment, and the goods will not be shipped until the customer requests delivery. When the sales representatives receive orders, they request that the warehouse sets aside the products ordered. However, the fulfillment team has the option to use these goods to fulfill other orders. These orders do not meet the criteria required to demonstrate that the customer has control.

Example 6.16: Bill-and-Hold Arrangements—Customer Controls the Goods

Office Builder requests that Cabinet Company set aside cabinets for an office building that Office Builder is constructing. Office Builder anticipates needing the cabinets within two months, and wants to secure the cabinets so they can be shipped soon after approval is gained. Cabinet Company pulls the cabinets, puts them into a dedicated section of the warehouse, and packs them for shipment. The cabinets are not available for sale to another customer.

Cabinet Company concludes that the arrangement meets the criteria for recognizing revenue under the bill-and-hold arrangement.

- The reason is substantive—the customer has requested it.
- The cabinets are identified specifically as belonging to the customer.
- The cabinets are ready for physical transfer.
- Cabinet Company cannot use the cabinets to fulfill other orders.

In addition, Cabinet Company determines that the request by Office Builder to warehouse the goods represents a separate performance obligation. Cabinet Company needs to estimate the standalone selling price based on how long the service will be provided.

Comparison with Legacy Guidance

IFRS. The legacy guidance and the Standard's requirements are similar. However, the Standard does not require that the entity's usual payment terms apply. Also, legacy IFRS guidance takes into account whether the entity pays for the storage, shipment, and services of goods being held. Under the Standard, these are not directly relevant but may be part of the assessment of whether the terms are substantive.

U.S. GAAP. Current SEC guidance has two requirements that differ from the Standard's requirements. The Standard does not require that the bill-and-hold arrangement be explicitly requested by the customer, and the delivery schedule does not have to be specified.

CONTRACT MODIFICATIONS

> A contract modification is a change in the scope or price (or both) of a contract that is approved by the parties to the contract.
> (ASC 606-10-25-10; IFRS 15.18)

Parties to an arrangement frequently modify the scope or price or both of an ongoing contract. Such a change is sometimes called a change order, a variation, or an amendment.

Technical Alert

For an entity with a significant volume of contract modifications occurring over a long period of time, the Standard's guidance on accounting for modified contracts at times could be costly and complex. Subsequent to release of the Standard, in ASU 2016-12 and *Clarifications to IFRS 15*, the Boards clarified the guidance related to implementing contract modifications and provided for a practical expedient related to accounting for a modification that occurred before transition to the Standard.

For contracts modified before transition to the Standard, the practical expedient allows an entity to determine and allocate the transaction price on the basis of all satisfied and unsatisfied performance obligations as of the beginning of the earliest period presented. The entity may aggregate the effect of the modifications. This practical expedient relieves entities from having to separately evaluate the effects of each contract modification. Entities should note that the expedient, if used, must be applied consistently to similar types of contract.
    (ASC 606-10-65-1(f.4), IFRS 15.C5(c))

Approval

A contract modification must be approved by the parties. Like the original contract, the modification should be approved

- in writing,
- orally, or
- implied by customary business practice.

Practice Pointer: Entities must exercise judgment when assessing whether a change is a modification or should have been anticipated at the outset because of the entity's customary business practice.

Until the modification is approved, the entity should continue to apply the guidance to the existing contract. (ASC 606-10-25-10; IFRS 15.18)

Disputes. A modification may exist even if the parties have a dispute as to scope or price. The revenue standard focuses more on enforceability of the contract than on finalization of the modification. If the change in scope has been agreed to, but the price is not settled, the entity should estimate the change to the price in accordance with the guidance on estimating variable consideration and constraining estimates of variable consideration. (ASC 606-10-25-11; IFRS 15.19)

Example 6.17: Contract Modification—Unpriced Change Order

Contractor enters into an agreement with Homeowner to tear down a house and construct a new one. After an environmental inspection, Contractor determines that asbestos remediation related to the tear down is required. Homeowner agrees to go through with the remediation for a price to be determined in the future—an unpriced change order. After completion of the remediation, Contractor bills Homeowner for the cost charged by the environmental remediation specialist and a fee for Contractor consistent with Contractor's profit margin in the original agreement. Although Homeowner disputes the price, Contractor's legal counsel determines that Contractor has legally enforceable rights to the reasonable price charged.

Contractor's accountant determines that

- the contract modification is approved,
- the scope of work is approved, and
- Contractor can account for the modification and estimate the change in transaction price following the Standard's guidance on variable consideration.

Recognition

Recognition of contract modifications can be complex and require careful analysis. Exhibit 6.13 provides an overview of the recognition process, and the next sections explain the process in detail.

When a modification occurs, entities must determine

- if the modification has created a new contract and performance obligations, or
- if the existing contract has been modified.

If the entity determines that an existing, ongoing contract has been modified, then it must further analyze the modification to determine if the modification should be accounted for as a separate contract.

1. Effectively, a termination of the contract and execution of a new contract resulting in a prospective treatment.
2. Or, part of the original contract, which could result in a catchup adjustment.
3. Or, a combination of (2) and (3) above.

The accounting treatment depends on what was changed. Under the Standard, to faithfully depict the rights and obligations of a contract modification, entities must account for modifications on a

- prospective basis—when the additional goods or services are distinct, or
- cumulative catchup basis—when the additional goods or services are not distinct.

Contract Modification Represents a Separate Contract

The concept underlying accounting for a modification as a separate contract is that there is no substantive economic difference under the given set of circumstances between a new contract and a modification. Therefore, the entity must analyze the agreement and account for the modification as a separate contract if

1. the scope of the contract increases because of the addition of *distinct* promised goods or services, *and*

2. the price of the contract increases by an amount of consideration that reflects the entity's standalone selling prices of the additional promised goods or services and any appropriate adjustment to that price to reflect the circumstances of the particular contract. (ASC 606-10-25-12; IFRS 15.20)

Exhibit 6.13 Contract modification overview

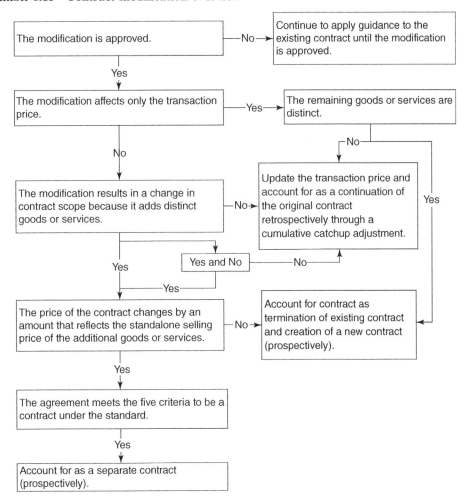

Exhibit 6.14 Contract modifications—accounting treatment

Treat as Separate Contract if:	Treat as Part of Contract if:
Scope of the contract changes because of the addition of distinct goods and services *and* the price of the contract increases by the standalone selling price of the additional goods and services.	All other modifications. Some modifications may be treated as though they are a termination of the contract and execution of a new contract.

Further, to be distinct, two criteria must be met:

1. the customer could benefit from the good or service;
2. the promise to transfer a good or service is separately identifiable from other promises in the contract.

(ASC 606-10-25-19; IFRS 15.27)

(See Chapter 2 for further information on determining whether performance obligations are "distinct.")

When these criteria are met, there is no economic difference between an entity entering into a separate contract for the additional goods or services and an entity modifying an existing contract.

Note that only modifications that *add* distinct goods or services can be treated as separate contracts. Modifications that reduce the amount of goods or services or change the scope, by their nature, cannot be considered separate contracts. They would be modifications of the original contract.

Practice Pointer: At the date of the modification, the entity must carefully evaluate whether the remaining goods or services are distinct. This assessment significantly affects the accounting treatment.

If the entity determines that the modification should be accounted for as a separate contract, the next step is to assess the agreement using the five contract criteria detailed in Chapter 1. If the contract meets the criteria, then the company should account for the change prospectively, accounting for the change in the current period and in any future period affected. Previously reported results are not changed.

Example 6.18: Contract Modification Represents a Separate Contract

On March 15, Acme Office Solutions enters into a contract to supply, for a price of CU 60,000 or 1,000 per unit, 60 desktop computers to XYZ Company over a six-month period beginning April 1. On May 15, XYZ modifies the contract to add another 30 identical computers at a price of CU 900 each for the additional 30 units, which is the standalone selling price at the date of modification.

Original contract (60 computers at CU 1000 each)	CU	60,000
Computers delivered at date of modification (20 × 1000)		<20,000>
Remaining obligation under original contract (40 × CU 1000)		40,000
New order for computers (at standalone selling price) 30 × 900		+ 27,000
Total revenue related to the modification	CU	67,000

This modification meets the criteria for treatment as a separate contract—the goods are distinct and Acme Office Solutions has a right to consideration that reflects the standalone selling price. They conclude that the modification is, in effect, a new contract. Therefore, the modification does not affect previous accounting under the original contract.

Total revenue of the modification is CU 67,000:

- CU 40,000 related to the original contract, and
- CU 27,000 related to the new guidance.

Acme Office Solutions recognizes revenue for the 40 remaining units under the original contract at CU 1,000 per unit. However, they recognize revenue at CU 900 per unit for the units requested under the modification. In effect, Acme Office Solutions treats the original contract and the modification as two separate contracts.

Contract Modification does Not Represent a Separate Contract

If the new goods or services are not distinct or not priced at the proper standalone selling price according to the criteria above, the changes are not treated as a separate contract. They are considered changes to the original contract, and the entity must then determine how to account for the remaining goods or services. That accounting depends on whether or not each of the remaining goods or services is distinct from the goods or services transferred on or before the date of the modification. The Standard describes three possible scenarios and the accounting under each.

- Scenario 1—Remaining goods or services are distinct.
- Scenario 2—Remaining goods or services are not distinct.
- Scenario 3—Remaining goods or services are a combination of distinct and not distinct goods or services.

Account for the remaining goods or services (that is, for the goods or services not transferred) as an adjustment to the existing contract as follows.

Scenario 1—Remaining Goods or Services are Distinct.

The remaining goods or services are distinct from the goods or services transferred on or before the date of the contract modification, but the consideration for those goods or services does not reflect the standalone selling price.

This type of modification is accounted for in the same way as a modification considered a new contract. In this scenario, the modification is negotiated after the original contract and is based on new facts and circumstances. Accounting for these changes using a cumulative catchup basis would be complex and might not reflect the economic substance of the modification. Entity should account for this type of modification prospectively as if it were effectively a termination of the existing contract and the creation of a new contract.

The amount of consideration already recognized under the contract is not adjusted. The amount of consideration allocated to the remaining performance obligations is the sum of the following.

1. The consideration promised by the customer under the original terms of the contract and included in the estimate of the transaction price and that has not yet been recognized as revenue. This amount includes amounts already received from customers and creates contract assets or receivables.
2. The consideration promised as part of the contract modification.
(ASC 606-10-25-13a; IFRS 15.21a)

Example 6.19: Contract Modification—New Price Not the Standalone Selling Price

Assume the same facts as in Example 6.18, except that the per unit price in the modification is CU 800. Acme Office Solutions determines that the new price is not the standalone selling price. Acme account for the modification prospectively and does not change previously reported units or amounts in the period of the change or in future periods. Acme Office Solutions recognizes revenue for the remaining products, those not fulfilled under the original contract and those ordered in the modification, at a blended price.

Remaining obligation under original contract

(40 units × CU 1000) =		CU 40,000

Products to be delivered under modification

(30 units × CU 900) =		27,000
		CU 67,000

New blended price per unit

(CU 67,000 ÷ 70 units) =		CU 957.14

Series of Distinct Goods or Services   The Scenario 1 accounting treatment also applies to situations where the entity determines that after the modification it has the same single performance obligation as before, but that the performance obligation represents a series of distinct goods or services. This situation typically may be found in energy contracts, mobile phone airtime services, or service contracts.

Example 6.20: Single Performance Obligation—Series of Distinct Goods or Services

RVC Cleaning Services enters into a two-year contract with Brower Pharmacy to clean the shop weekly for a fee of CU 100 per week. At the end of the first year, Brower Pharmacy negotiates a fee of CU 90 for the ongoing service. RVC Cleaning Services accounts for the modification prospectively.

Scenario 2—Remaining Goods or Services are Not Distinct.

The remaining goods or services are not distinct and, therefore, form part of a single performance obligation that is partially satisfied at the contract modification date.

Account for the modification as if it were a part of the existing contract:

- retrospectively, through a cumulative catchup adjustment.

Recognize the modification as an increase or decrease in revenue at the contract modification date, measured at the effect that the modification has on the transaction price and on the entity's measure of progress toward satisfaction of the performance obligation. (ASC 606-10-25-13b; IFRS 15.21b)

However, as explained above, modifications of contracts with a single performance obligation that is actually a series of distinct goods or services are accounted for prospectively, not by using a cumulative catchup adjustment. (See Example 6.4.)

Example 6.21: Contract Modification—Additional Goods or Services are Not Distinct

On July 1, Contractor enters into an agreement to build a home for Customer for CU 500,000. The home is to be built on Customer-owned land, and there is a CU 50,000 six-month completion bonus.

At inception:

Contract price	CU 500,000
Estimated costs	300,000
Estimated profit	200,000
Estimated profit percentage (200,000 ÷ 500,000)	40%

At contract inception, the entity expects a profit of 40% based on a transaction price of CU 500,000 and costs of CU 300,000. The entity excludes the bonus because it does not meet the collectibility threshold of "probable." The entity determines that costs incurred are the best measure of completion. On that basis, at the entity's August 31 fiscal year end, Contractor determines that the project is 60% complete based on incurred costs of CU 180,000. Contractor recognizes revenue of CU 300,000 and costs of CU 180,000. Contractor reassesses the bonus and determines that it is still constrained and does not recognize any revenue related to it.

In September, the parties agree to modify the floorplan. This increases the total costs to CU 320,000 and the total consideration to CU 530,000. Because of the modifications, Customer agrees to extend the completion date by two months. With the extra two months and the progress made to date, the entity determines that the collection of the completion bonus is now probable. The entity also concludes that the remaining goods and services are not distinct from the goods and services transferred before the date of the modification, and, therefore, the contract remains a single performance obligation. The modification should be accounted for as a cumulative catchup adjustment in the current period.

Calculation of catchup adjustment
Updated measure of progress: 180,000 cost to date ÷ 320,000 new total cost estimate = 56.25%

Original transaction price	CU 500,000
Bonus	50,000
Modification	30,000
New transaction price:	CU 580,000
Total to be recognized (580,000 × 56.25%)	326,250
Less amount recognized previously	<300,000>
Catchup adjustment	CU 26,250

Scenario 3—Remaining Goods or Services are a Combination of Distinct and Not Distinct Goods or Services.

The remaining goods or services are a combination of (a) and (b), that is, a combination of distinct and not distinct goods or services.

In this scenario, a change in the contract is treated as a combination of the first and second scenarios: a modification of the existing contract and the creation of a new contract. So, the entity does not adjust the accounting for completed performance obligations that are distinct from the modified goods or services, but adjusts revenue previously recognized for the effect of the modification on the transaction price allocated to performance obligations that are not distinct and the measure of progress. Account for the effects of the modification on the unsatisfied performance obligations following the guidelines above for (a) goods and services that are distinct and (b) goods and services that are not distinct. (ASC 606-10-25-13c; IFRS 15.21c)

Practice Pointer: The amount of consideration allocated to the remaining performance obligation includes amounts received but not yet recognized and amounts the customer has promised to pay that had not yet been recognized. There are situations where the entity may have recognized promised considerations but not yet received those amounts. The amounts create a contract asset or receivables. They have to be deducted from the consideration allocated to the remaining performance obligation. Otherwise, the entity would recognize revenue twice.

Exhibit 6.15 Summary of accounting treatment for contract modifications

Contract Modification Facts	In Effect	Account For
Contract modification represents a separate contract		
Goods or services not yet provided are distinct from the goods or services transferred and at the entity's standalone selling price	New, separate contract	Prospectively—only new goods or services
Contract modification does not represent a separate contract		
Scenario 1—Remaining goods or services distinct from goods or services transferred before modification	Termination of existing contract and creation of a new contract	Prospectively—both remaining and new goods at blended per unit amount No adjustment for performance obligations already satisfied
Scenario 2—Goods or services not distinct from existing contract	Continuation of contract	With a cumulative catchup adjustment, updating the transaction price and measure of progress
Scenario 3—Remaining goods or services are a combination of goods or services that are distinct and goods or services that are not distinct	Blend the approaches in Scenarios 1 and 2	Prospectively—those that are distinct Cumulative catchup adjustment—those that are not distinct

Change in Transaction Price Resulting from Modification

If a change in transaction price occurs as a *result* of a contract modification, the Standard takes an approach that is consistent with other modifications. That is, a contract modification that only affects the transaction price is accounted for like other contract modifications:

- prospectively if the remaining goods or services are distinct;
- as a cumulative catchup adjustment if the remaining goods or services are not distinct.

A change in transaction price may occur *after* a modification, but before fulfillment of performance obligations is complete. In that case, the Standard provides the following guidance.

   a. If the modification is accounted for as if it were a termination of the existing contract and the creation of a new contract, the entity allocates the change in the transaction price to the performance obligations identified in the contract before the modification if and to the extent that the change in transaction price is attributable to an amount of variable consideration promised before the modification.
   b. If the modification was not accounted for as a separate contract, the entity allocates the change in the transaction price to the performance obligations in the modified contract. These are the performance obligations that were not fully satisfied at the date of the modification.

(ASC 606-10-32-45; IFRS 15.90)

For more information on changes in transaction price, see Chapter 4.

Exhibit 6.16 Change in transaction price as a result of contract modification—overview

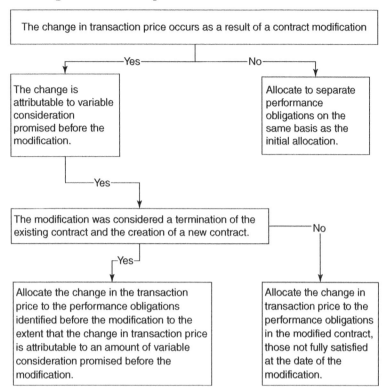

Comparison with Legacy Guidance

U.S. GAAP. In legacy guidance, contract modification guidance is currently limited to industry-specific guidance. Entities with long-term production and construction-type contracts generally account for contract modifications on a cumulative catchup basis. The accounting for contracts that fall under other subtopics may vary. The Standard focuses on types of modification and applies to all industries. It provides structure where practice was inconsistent. Evaluating modifications under the revenue standard requires significant judgment compared with the legacy, more prescriptive, guidance.

IFRS. IAS 18 does not include guidance on contract modification. IAS 11 on construction contracts includes guidance related to contract claims and variations. The standard brings guidance and consistency, and that guidance is relatively consistent with IAS 11's guidance on whether to treat a change as a separate contract or a modification to an existing contract. IFRS 15 may result in a change in practice for some entities.

ONEROUS CONTRACTS

Onerous obligations occur when the entity expects to incur a loss on a single performance obligation (onerous performance obligation) or on a contract (onerous contract). That is, the costs of the contract are higher than its economic benefit. The FASB and IASB discussed whether to include guidance on onerous contracts in the Standard, but ultimately decided against it. The current accounting treatment in U.S. GAAP and IFRS remains and is not converged.

IFRS guidance in IAS 37 applies to all contracts in the scope of IFRS 15. U.S. GAAP guidance contains no general authoritative standard that addresses onerous contracts. However, some industry-specific topics include guidance on this issue. This results in potential differences in practice.

7 CONTRACT COSTS

OVERVIEW

In addition to providing revenue recognition guidance for contracts with customers, the Standard also contains guidance for costs related to obtaining and fulfilling contracts with customers that are in the scope of the Standard. This guidance is codified in U.S. GAAP in a subtopic added by the Standard, ASC 340-40, *Contracts with Customers*, and can be found in IFRS 15.91-104.

The guidance on contract costs in ASC 340-40 and IFRS 15.91-104 covers

- incremental costs of obtaining a contract, and
- costs incurred to fulfill a contract.

It also covers

- amortization of assets arising from costs to obtain or fulfill a contract, and
- impairment of assets arising from costs to obtain or fulfill a contract.

Each of these topics is discussed in depth in this chapter. Exhibit 7.1 gives an overview of how the costs associated with customer contracts are treated.

Exhibit 7.1   Costs associated with customer contracts—overview

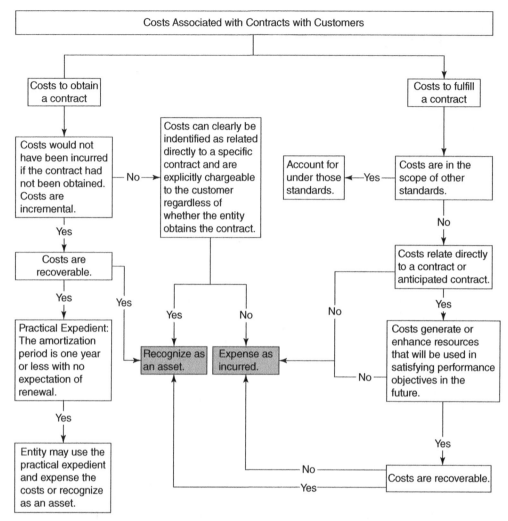

Practice Pointer: Applying the guidance on contract costs will likely result in the recognition of more assets than currently. For example, if recoverable, entities will have to capitalize and amortize costs related to sales commissions and startup costs. Applying the guidance may also require extra effort and changes to internal systems in order to track commissions on contracts. Likewise, entities that capitalize the bid costs of trying to obtain a contract will have to analyze whether those costs are incremental to obtaining a contract and, generally, will have to exclude nonincremental bid costs incurred regardless of whether the contract is obtained. See Costs That Are Not Incremental on the next page for limited exceptions to this guidance.

INCREMENTAL COSTS OF OBTAINING A CONTRACT

Incremental costs are those that an entity would not have incurred if the contract had not been obtained.
(ASC 340-40-25-2; IFRS 15.92)

An example of this type of cost is a sales commission. Such incremental costs should be recognized as assets if the entity expects to recover those costs. This is in line with the definition of an asset.[1]

Recoverability

Recoverable amounts are an asset, provided the entity's right to reimbursement is unconditional. Recovery may be

- direct, through explicit reimbursement under the contract, or
- indirect, through the margin in a contract.

Recoverability of costs is assessed on a contract-by-contract basis or for a group of contracts if the costs in question are associated with a group of contracts.

Determining when Costs are Incremental

Because the capitalization requirements only apply to incremental costs that are incurred to obtain a contract, it is important to understand what is meant by "incremental costs." Entities must distinguish between incremental costs to obtain a contract and other customer-related costs, such as those related to managing a customer relationship or costs incurred to grow sales in an existing contract. Entities and their systems must track these different types of cost.

Costs that are Not Incremental

Generally, costs that are not incremental, that would have been incurred trying to obtain a contract regardless of whether the contract was obtained, for example bid costs, should be expensed as incurred. However, those costs should be capitalized if they

- can clearly be identified as related directly to a specific contract, *and*
- are explicitly chargeable to the customer regardless of whether a contract is obtained.
  (ASC 340-40-25-3; IFRS 15.93)

Direct Response Advertising Costs. Under legacy standards, direct response advertising costs are capitalized if certain criteria are met (ASC 340-20-25). The Standard supersedes that legacy guidance and relocates some of it to industry-specific guidance on insurance contracts. (ASC 944-30-25-1AA) Under the Standard, these costs are not considered incremental to obtaining a contract and, therefore, are not subject to the capitalization rules and are expensed as incurred.

---

[1] U.S. definition: Assets are "probable future economic benefits obtained or controlled by a particular entity as a result of past transactions or events." FASB Statement of Financial Accounting Concepts No. 6, para. 25.
IFRS definition: "An asset is a resource controlled by the entity as a result of past events and from which future economic benefits are expected to flow to the entity." IFRS Conceptual Framework, Section 2, para. 2.6.

Other Marketing-Related Costs. Bid, proposal, selling, and marketing costs, including the advertising cost mentioned above, are not incremental. The entity incurs these costs whether or not it obtains the contract.

Fixed salaries for sales personnel, unlike sales commissions, are not considered incremental.

Practical Expedient

A practical expedient offers relief to entities with short-duration contracts without expectation of renewal. If the amortization period of the capitalizable incremental contract costs of obtaining a contract is one year or less, the entity may recognize it as an expense. (ASC 340-40-25-4; IFRS 15.94) When determining the amortization period, the entity should take into account renewals, amendments, and follow-on contracts.

Example 7.1: Costs of Obtaining a Contract—Commissions, Bonuses

Mary May, a sales representative for InfoTech, sells to MegaCo a one-year subscription to a database information system. Mary earns a 5% commission on the sale. The contract is not expected to be renewed, and InfoTech expects to recover the costs.

The commission is considered an incremental cost to obtain the contract. The commission would not have been incurred if the contract had not been obtained. Because InfoTech expects to recover the cost, under the Standard, it is allowed to record the commission as an asset and amortize it as revenue is recognized over the year. However, because the amortization period is one year or less and the entity does not expect the contract to be renewed, InfoTech has the option to use the practical expedient and expense the commission as incurred.

Mary's manager also earns a commission on Mary's sales. InfoTech determines that the manager's commission is incremental to obtaining the specific MegaCo contract.

Mary, as a member of the sales team, is also entitled to a bonus based on the "success" of InfoTech. The bonus is expensed because it is not directly attributable to obtaining a particular contract, the MegaCo contract. Bonuses based on quantitative and qualitative measures, such as profitability, EPS, or performance evaluations, are not directly related to the contract and, therefore, probably do not meet the capitalization criteria.

Example 7.2: Costs of Obtaining a Contract—Travel, Due Diligence

Mary incurs travel fees when meeting with the customer. InfoTech does not recognize those fees as assets, because they are costs associated with trying to obtain the contract and would have been incurred whether or not the contract was obtained.

Also, in preparation for offering the contract, InfoTech incurs external legal fees related to due diligence. The legal costs are associated with trying to obtain the contract, and they also would have been incurred even if the contract was not obtained. Therefore, the legal fees are expensed as incurred.

COSTS OF FULFILLING A CONTRACT

Before transferring goods or services, an entity often incurs costs to fulfill the contract's performance obligations. An entity may also incur such costs in anticipation of obtaining a specifically identified contract. Those costs can be capitalized.

To address how to recognize fulfillment costs, the entity must first determine whether these costs are addressed by other guidance. The cost to fulfill a contract required to be expensed by other standards cannot be capitalized under the Standard. That is, entities should first refer to the out-of-scope guidance listed below and then use the Standard's guidance to determine whether costs need to be capitalized. If the other standards preclude capitalization of a cost, then it cannot be capitalized under the Standard.

Scope Exceptions

In U.S. GAAP, the guidance on costs incurred in fulfilling a contract does not apply to costs included in the following.

- ASC 330 on inventory.
- ASC 340-10-25-1 through 25-4 on preproduction costs related to long-term supply arrangements. (In 2016, as part of its Technical Corrections and Improvements project, the FASB issued an exposure draft of an ASU[2] that will eliminate this scope exception by superseding the guidance on preproduction costs related to long-term supply arrangements within Subtopic 340-10. As a result, entities would apply the guidance in ASC 340-40.)
- ASC 350-40 on internal-use software.
- ASC 360 on property, plant, and equipment.
- ASC 985-20 on the cost of software to be sold, leased, or otherwise marketed.

(ASC 340-40-15-3)

IFRS 15 has similar scope limitations, and excludes costs that are in the scope of another contract and specifically mentions

- IAS 2, *Inventories*,
- IAS 16, *Property, Plant and Equipment*, and
- IAS 38, *Intangible Assets*.

(IFRS 15.95)

At the January 2015 TRG meeting, members generally agreed that the Standard does not amend the current standards on liabilities, such as ASC 405 and IAS 37.[3]

Three Criteria for Recognizing Assets for Costs of Fulfilling a Contract

Entities are required to recognize assets for the costs of fulfilling a contract, if not addressed by other standards, and if *all* of the following three criteria are met.

1. The costs relate directly to a contract or to an anticipated contract that the entity can specifically identify. An example of this would be costs relating to services to be provided under renewal of an existing contract, or the costs of designing an asset to be transferred under a specific contract that has not yet been approved.
2. The costs generate or enhance the resources of the entity that will be used in satisfying (or in continuing to satisfy) performance obligations in the future.
3. The costs are expected to be recovered.

(ASC 340-10-25-5; IFRS 15.95)

Notice that the criteria above align with the definition of an asset. If all three criteria above are met, the fulfillment costs must be capitalized. They cannot be expensed, and there is no practical expedient. More information on recoverability can be found earlier in this chapter.

---

[2] As a purchaser of this book, you have exclusive access to a companion website, with the latest technical developments and other useful information. The website will contain updated information about exposure drafts and other technical guidance from the standards' setters. See the back of the book for information on how to access the site.

[3] TRG Agenda Paper 25, *January 2015 Meeting—Summary of Issues Discussed and Next Steps*, dated March 30, 2015.

Categories of Fulfillment Costs

Determining which costs should be recognized requires judgment. Some costs are straightforward. Others are not as clear. There may be costs that relate to a contract, but that do not meet the definition of an asset, that is, they do not generate or enhance the resources of the entity or relate to the satisfaction or fulfillment of performance obligations. To help make these distinctions, the Standard divides contract fulfillment costs into two categories: costs to be capitalized and costs to be expensed as incurred. The Standard includes specific guidance on each type of contract-related cost. Exhibit 7.2 summarizes the guidance and list both types of contract-related cost—those that should be capitalized and those that should be expensed.

Exhibit 7.2 Treatment of costs of fulfilling a contract

Costs Required to be Capitalized Related Directly to a Contract or Specific Anticipated Contract if Other Criteria are Met (ASC 340-10-25-7; IFRS 15.97)	Costs Required to be Expensed as Incurred (ASC 340-10-25-8; IFRS 15.98)
Direct labor (salaries/wages of employees providing services directly to the customer, etc.).	General and administrative costs (unless they are explicitly chargeable to the customers under the contract, in which case an entity shall evaluate those costs in accordance with ASC 340-40-25-7 or IFRS 15.97).
Direct materials (e.g., supplies used in fulfilling the performance obligations).	Costs of wasted materials, labor, or other resources to fulfill the contract that were not reflected in the price of the contract.
Allocation of costs that relate directly to the contract or to contract activities (e.g., costs of contract management and supervision, insurance, and depreciation of tools and equipment used in fulfilling the contract).	Costs that relate to satisfied or partially satisfied performance obligations in the contract (i.e., costs that relate to past performance) even if the related revenue has not been recognized.
Costs that are explicitly chargeable to the customer under the contract.	Costs for which an entity cannot distinguish whether the costs relate to unsatisfied performance obligations or to satisfied or partially satisfied performance obligations.
Other costs that are incurred only because an entity entered into the contract (e.g., payments to subcontractors).	

Bear in mind that costs must be recoverable in order to be capitalized. (See discussion earlier in this chapter.)

If a cost cannot be capitalized under other guidance, and if an entity cannot determine whether a cost relates to past or future performance, it must be expensed as incurred.

Example 7.3: Costs that Create an Asset

Mary May, a sales representative for InfoTech, signed a five-year contract with MegaCo to provide a learning management system (LMS) to train MegaCo's 100,000 employees. InfoTech expects that MegaCo will renew the contract for one five-year period. Mary earns a CU 10,000 sales commission on the deal, which she receives before InfoTech begins work on the contract. Before InfoTech delivers the LMS, it works on the platform that will host the LMS and the technology that will connect the LMS to MegaCo's employees. InfoTech does not deliver the platform, but it will be used to deliver the training courses to MegaCo's employees, track results, and provide reports to MegaCo's human resources team. The costs incurred in setting up the technology and other costs are as follows.

Cost Item	Amount	Recognition
Mary's sales commission	10,000	Recognize as an asset under the Standard because the entity expects to recover the cost.
Consulting with MegaCo's LMS implementation team to create a statement of work (SOW)	40,000	If the costs meet the three criteria in the Standard for capitalization, record an asset.
Designing the interface	75,000	If the costs meet the three criteria in the Standard for capitalization, record an asset.
Hardware	10,000	Account for in accordance with ASC 360, *Property, Plant, and Equipment* or IAS 16, *Property, Plant and Equipment.*
Software	15,000	Account for in accordance with ASC 350-40, *Intangibles—Goodwill and Other—, Internal-Use Software* or IAS 38, *Intangible Assets.*
Migration and beta testing the LMS	60,000	Recognize as an asset under the Standard because the costs meet the three criteria for capitalization.
Final deployment of the system	30,000	Recognize as an asset under the Standard because the costs meet the three criteria for capitalization.
Two employees to provide service to MegaCo.		The entity concludes that the employees are responsible for providing customer services. However, they do not generate or enhance the resources of the entity, therefore, InfoTech recognizes payroll expenses as incurred.

InfoTech will amortize the assets over a ten-year period, the initial five years plus one five-year renewal period.

Setup Costs

Some of the costs in the previous example might be considered setup costs, costs incurred at the beginning of the contract that enable an entity to fulfill a contract. Such costs might include labor, travel, or overheads. If these costs do not fall into the scope of other standards, they should be assessed under the Standard.

Abnormal Costs

An entity, like InfoTech in the previous example, may incur learning-curve expenses. Such costs are usually anticipated and built into the price of the contract. These costs should be assessed to see if they meet the criteria for capitalization.

There may be other costs that are not anticipated. These may involve waste, spoiled goods, or unproductive labor costs. These "abnormal costs" should be expensed as incurred.

AMORTIZATION OF COSTS

The costs capitalized in connection with contracts with customers must be amortized. The amortization method selected must result in a systematic basis consistent with the contract's transfer of goods or services to the customer. (ASC 340-10-35-1; IFRS 15.99) For example, if the services are transferred continuously and evenly, then the straight-line method may be appropriate. In contrast, if, for instance, renewals are anticipated and no additional costs are expected, it may be appropriate for the amortization period to be longer than the initial contract period. Similarly, certain costs, like design costs, may relate to more than one contract and the amortization period could be longer than the term of just one contract. In determining the pattern of transfer, entities should analyze the specific terms of the contract and take into account their experience with the pattern of transfer and the timing of the transfer of control to the customer.

If there is a significant change in the timing of the contract, the entity should update the amortization schedule and account for any change as a change in accounting estimate. (ASC 340-10-35-2; IFRS 15.100)

Example 7.4: Costs—Recognition and Amortization

Alarm Systems enters into a contract and installs a security system at Condo Complex. The contract includes five years of monitoring the system for CU 40 per month. Alarm Systems determines that there is one performance obligation. They incur CU 750 to install the system. Alarm Systems recognizes an asset of CU 750 for installation costs and amortizes it over five years, consistent with the pattern of satisfaction of the performance obligation.

Example 7.5: Costs—Amortization and Contract Extension

Use the same set of facts as in Example 7.4. In year 3 of the contract, Alarm Systems extends the contract for two years beyond the five-year initial term. Condo Complex will benefit from the initial setup costs during the extension period. Alarm Systems amortizes the remaining setup costs over more years. The costs are adjusted in accordance with other guidance on changes in accounting estimates.

If the extension had been anticipated at the inception of the contract, Alarm Systems would initially have amortized the costs over seven years.

IMPAIRMENT LOSS

Assets must be tested for impairment at the end of each reporting period. Before recognizing an impairment loss related to contract costs, the entity should recognize impairment losses on contract assets in accordance with other guidance.

- U.S. GAAP:

  - FASB ASC 310-40-35-30 on inventory;
  - FASB ASC 985-20 on costs of software to be sold, leased, or otherwise marketed;
  - FASB ASC 360 on property, plant, and equipment;
  - FASB ASC 350 on goodwill and other intangibles.

- Under IFRS:

  - IAS 2, *Inventories*;
  - IAS 16, *Property, Plant and Equipment*;
  - IAS 38, *Intangible Assets*.

Entities can make their recoverability assessment contract by contract, or for a group of contracts if the costs are associated with a group of contracts. Entities will have to exercise considerable judgment when assessing the amortization pattern for a contract cost asset related to multiple performance obligations that are satisfied over different periods of time.

The objective of the recoverability assessment is to consider only the economic benefits in the contract. To do so, the entities must compare the carrying amount with the remaining amount of promised consideration. To calculate an impairment loss for an asset recognized in relation to contracts with customers, an entity uses the formula below.

Exhibit 7.3 Calculation of impairment loss (ASC 340-0-35-3; IFRS 15.101)

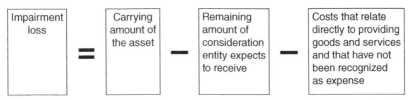

Practice Pointer: The amortization costs may include those related to anticipated contracts that are specifically identifiable. To determine which contracts are specifically identifiable, entities may want to look at past history with similar customers and the market beyond the initial contract term.

The entity should use the principles for determining the transaction price to determine the amount of consideration. For this purpose, though, the entity should not include the guidance on constraining estimates of variable consideration, but the entity should adjust the amount to reflect the customer's credit risk. When determining the transaction price, the Standard states than an entity should not anticipate that the contract will be "cancelled, renewed, or modified." This principle was raised with the TRG in relation to impairment at the July 2014 TRG meeting. The TRG generally agreed that an impairment test for capitalized costs should include cash flows for contract renewal periods.[4]

Under U.S. GAAP, an entity should not reverse an impairment loss previously recognized. However, IFRS requires an entity to reverse an impairment loss. This is consistent with the guidance in IFRS 36, *Impairment of Assets*.

COMPARISON WITH LEGACY GUIDANCE

The Standard makes changes to legacy guidance for contract-related costs. Some of the significant changes are highlighted below.

Cost of Obtaining a Contract

IFRS. The legacy guidance in IFRS on the treatment of the costs to obtain a contract with a customer is limited and found in IAS 38. The standard

- clarifies and brings specificity to this area,

---

[4] TRG Agenda Paper 5, *July 2014 Meeting—Summary of Issues Discussed and Next Steps*, revised March 18, 2015.

- introduces the new cost category of an asset arising from the capitalization of the incremental costs to obtain a contract, and
- moves the scope of IAS 38 to the new standard.

U.S. GAAP. The Standard requires capitalization of incremental costs to obtain a contract, like sales commissions, that were previously expensed. The Standard also changes the cost-capitalization guidance related to direct-response advertising costs and now requires those costs to be expensed.

Costs of Fulfilling a Contract

IFRS. The Standard affects those entities using the stage-of-completion method under IAS 11. The Standard withdraws IAS 11 and replaces its cost guidance. In addition, the Standard requires entities to capitalize the costs associated with fulfilling an anticipated contract if certain criteria are met. This is similar to IAS 11's guidance that such costs are recognized if it is "probable" that the contract will be obtained.

U.S. GAAP. In legacy guidance, fulfillment costs are generally expensed as incurred. Under SEC guidance, certain setup costs may either be expensed or capitalized by making an accounting policy election. Entities that expense these costs may be required to capitalize the costs under the Standard.

In legacy guidance, preproduction costs, such as those for design and development, are expensed as incurred. That treatment remains the same under the Standard, except if there is a contractual guarantee for reimbursement.

Amortization

U.S. GAAP. Under the Standard, the amortization period for contract cost assets is similar to legacy guidance. However, contract costs previously deferred without any corresponding deferred revenue may be amortized over a longer period of time under the Standard.

Impairment

IFRS and U.S. GAAP. The Standard introduces an impairment model that applies to assets recognized for costs to obtain or fulfill a contract. Entities apply the model in this order:

- existing guidance that applies;
- guidance for contract costs under the standard;
- impairment model for cash-generating units (IFRS) or for asset groups or reporting units (U.S. GAAP).

8 PRESENTATION AND DISCLOSURE

Technical Alert

In 2016, the FASB plans to issue a technical issues and corrections update related to revenue recognition. In the proposed ASU, the FASB will include guidance that allows entities to use a practical expedient for remaining performance obligations. In specific situations involving variable consideration, entities electing the expedient would not need to include the following types of variable consideration in the disclosure of remaining performance obligations:

1. sales-based or usage-based royalties provided in exchange for a license of intellectual property;
2. variable consideration allocated entirely to a wholly unsatisfied performance obligation or a wholly unsatisfied promise to transfer a distinct good or service that forms part of a single performance obligation and meets the criteria for that allocation. (See the "Applying Variable Consideration Exception to a Single Performance Obligation" section in Chapter 3.)

If an entity uses practical expedients, the proposed ASU requires it to disclose that use and

- the nature of performance obligations,
- the remaining duration, and
- a description of the variable consideration that has been excluded.

As a purchaser of this book, you have exclusive access to a companion website, with the latest technical developments and other useful information. The website will contain updated information about exposure drafts and other technical guidance from the standards' setters. See the back of the book for information on how to access the site.

PRESENTATION

When either party to a contract has performed, an entity presents the contract in the statement of financial position as a contract asset or a contract liability, depending on the relationship between the entity's performance and the customer's payment. An entity shall present any unconditional rights to consideration separately as a receivable.
(ASC 606-10-45-1; IFRS 15.105)

The Standard includes the following definitions of the three elements referred to above.

Contract asset: An entity's right to consideration in exchange for goods or services that the entity has transferred to a customer when that right is conditional on something other than the passage of time, for example, the entity's future performance.
    (ASC 606-10-20; IFRS 15.Appendix A)

Contract liability: An entity's obligation to transfer goods or services to a customer for which the entity has received consideration (or the amount is due) from the customer.
    (ASC 606-10-20; IFRS 15.Appendix A)

Receivable: An entity's right to consideration that is unconditional. The right to consideration is unconditional if only the passage of time is required before payment of the consideration is due.
(ASC 606-10-45-4; IFRS 15.108)

Overview

When either party performs, a contract asset or a contract liability is created. At the reporting date, the relationship between the entity's performance and the customer's performance under the contract determines the manner in which the entity presents the contract in the financial statements. The entity performs by transferring goods or services, and the customer performs by paying consideration. If either party has performed, the entity should present the event as a

- contract liability,
- contract asset, or
- receivable.

(ASC 606-10-45-1; 15.105)

For contracts with multiple performance obligations, contract assets and liabilities should be determined at the contract level, not the performance obligation level. So, an entity would not recognize an asset or liability for each performance obligation in the same contract, but would aggregate them into a single asset or liability for the contract.

If contracts are required to be combined, then the related contract asset or liabilities would be combined and presented net for different contracts with the same customer or related party of the customer. This may be operationally difficult for some entities, because their systems

Exhibit 8.1   Presentation—overview

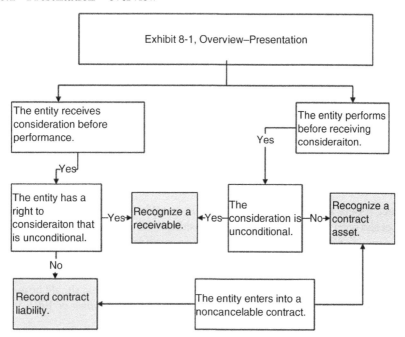

capture data at the performance obligation level to comply with the Standard's recognition and measurement requirements.

Presentation in the Statement of Financial Position

Exhibit 8.2   Rights and obligations—contract asset or contract liability

If one of the contract parties has performed before the other, an asset or liability must be recognized. While the Standard refers to "contract asset" and "contract liability," entities may use other terms as long as they provide information that makes the distinction between assets where rights are conditional and those that are unconditional. (ASC 610-10-45-5; IFRS 15.109) An unconditional right to consideration is presented separately as a receivable. Receivables are accounted for using existing guidance.

> **Practice Pointer:** The Standard recognizes the interdependencies of the rights and obligations in a contract and calls for presenting the remaining rights and obligations on a net basis.

Exhibit 8.3   Presentation of a contract in the statement of financial position

Circumstances as of the Reporting Date	Presentation
Entity has not satisfied its performance obligation by transferring goods or services. The customer has provided consideration or payment is due.	Contract liability, as of the earlier of when payment is made or payment is due.
Entity has transferred goods or services. The customer has not yet provided consideration, and payment is conditional on something other than the passage of time.	Contract asset, exclusive of any amounts presented as a receivable.
Entity has transferred goods or services. The customer has not yet paid, and payment is conditional on nothing but the passage of time.	Receivable.

Contract Assets and Receivables. Notice in Exhibit 8.3 that the distinction between a contract asset and receivable relies on whether consideration is based on something other than the passage of time. For example, an entity's right to consideration may be conditional on its fulfillment of another performance obligation in the contract. In that case, a contract asset should be recorded. Once the entity's right is based only on the passage of time, it is unconditional and the entity should reclassify the contract asset to a receivable. The receivable should be accounted for in accordance with other guidance, for example, ASC 310, *Receivables* or IFRS 9, *Financial Instruments*.

Example 8.1: Contract Assets and Receivables—Conditional on Another Performance Obligation

CaseCo enters into a contract with Big Box to deliver 100 bookcases at CU 80 each on December 15 and 500 filing cabinets at CU 200 each on December 31. Control is transferred upon delivery, and payment is due in 30 days, conditional on delivery of both products. No significant financing component is involved. The bookcases and filing cabinets are separate performance obligations.

When CaseCo delivers the bookcases on December 15 and, thus, transfers control to the customer, it should record a contract asset and revenue for the portion of revenue allocated to the bookcases. A receivable is not recognized because CaseCo does not have an unconditional right to consideration until both products are delivered. Payment is conditional on something other than the passage of time. When the filing cabinets are delivered CaseCo has an unconditional right to consideration based solely on the passage of time. Therefore, CaseCo should reclassify the contract asset related to the bookcases to a receivable. A receivable and revenue related to the filing cabinets should also be recorded.

CaseCo makes the following entries:

Upon transfer of bookcases		
Contract asset	8,000	
Revenue		8,000
Upon transfer of filing cabinets		
Receivable	108,000	
Contract asset		8,000
Revenue		100,000

Contract Liabilities. If a customer's payment precedes the entity's performance, the entity has a liability.

Example 8.2: Customer Pays Deposit—Cancellable Contract

On March 31, 20X1, CaseCo enters into a contract to make custom bookcases for OfficeBuilding, Inc. for a total consideration of CU 10,000. OfficeBuilding, Inc. gives CaseCo a deposit of CU 3,000 upon signing the contract. CaseCo records the cash and a contract liability for the deposit. This liability represents CaseCo's obligation to transfer the goods to OfficeBuilding, Inc. The liability will be reversed upon delivery of the bookcases, and revenue will be recognized.

CaseCo makes the following entries:

Upon signing the contract		
Cash	3,000	
Contract liability		3,000
Upon transfer of filing cabinets		
Contract liability	3,000	
Receivable	7,000	
Revenue		10,000

Unconditional Right to Receive Consideration

An entity could have an unconditional right to payment before invoicing. Whether or not the entity invoices does not dictate whether the entity has an unconditional right to consideration. The fact that an entity invoices a customer does not necessarily indicate that the entity has an unconditional right to consideration.

Noncancellable Contract. In the typical revenue contract with a customer, the entity has an unconditional right to payment when control has transferred. However, if the contract is non-cancellable, an entity has an unconditional right to payment on the date the payment is due, even if the entity has not performed. In that situation, on the date payment is due, a receivable and a contract liability are recorded. The payment must be nonrefundable, and the contract must be noncancellable. If refunds are a possibility, the entity should record a receivable and a refund liability. Revenue in these situations is not recorded. Revenue is only recognized when the entity performs.

Example 8.3: Customer Pays Deposit, Contract is Noncancellable

Assume the same facts as in Example 8.2, except that the contract is noncancellable and the deposit is due on April 30, 20X1. When the consideration is due (April 30, 20X1), CaseCo records

- a receivable for the amount of the deposit because it has an unconditional right to consideration, and
- a contract liability because it has an obligation to perform.

The entity records the cash when it is received and reverses the receivable. When the performance obligation is satisfied, revenue is recognized and the contract liability is reversed.

CaseCo makes the following entries:

At date consideration is due, *April 30, 20X1*		
Receivable	10,000	
Contract liability		10,000
Upon receipt of the cash deposit		
Cash	3,000	
Receivable		3,000
Upon satisfaction of the performance obligation		
Contract liability	10,000	
Revenue		10,000

Presentation in the Statement of Comprehensive Income

The Standard provides guidance on the presentation of revenue and related items in the statement of comprehensive income.

For IFRS preparers, IAS 1, *Presentation of the Financial Statements*, requires an entity to present or disclose revenue from contracts with customers separately from the entity's other sources of income.

Impairment. Receivables and contract assets are subject to an impairment assessment in accordance with IFRS 9 or IAS 39 for IASB reporters and ASC 310 for U.S. GAAP reporters. (ASC 601-10-45-4; IFRS 15.108) Any difference between the measurement of the receivable from a contract with a customer and the amount of revenue recognized is presented as an expense, for instance, as impairment loss. This is the case when the difference is caused by customer credit risk as opposed to an implied price concession. An implied price concession is deducted from the contract price to arrive at the transaction price. Entities will have to exercise judgment to distinguish between expenses due to customer credit risk and expenses due to implied price concession.

Presenting impairment losses adjacent to revenue might confuse investors about whether revenue is reported gross or net of recognized impairment losses. It also might be thought to be too prescriptive, because most companies have few impaired credit sales. Both boards were concerned that presenting revenue gross without a clear link to related impairment losses would not be useful to investors to assess the quality of revenue recognized. Therefore, the Boards decided to require entities to

- disclose impairment losses related to contracts with customers, and
- include a collectibility threshold.

In addition to contract assets, an entity may also have recorded other assets related to the contract, for example, capitalized costs. These assets must be presented separately from contract assets and contract liabilities. These costs are also assessed separately for impairment. (For more information on impairment, see Chapter 7.)

Other Presentation Considerations

Rights of Return. The carrying value of a return asset must be presented separately from inventory. The return asset is also subject to impairment testing separately from inventory. In addition, the refund liability must be presented separately, on a gross basis, from the related asset.

Significant Financing Component. The financing component should be presented separately from the revenue recognized. When the performance obligation is satisfied, the transaction price is recognized as revenue by applying an interest rate to the promised consideration. Entities should recognize the financing component as interest expense if the customer pays in advance, or as interest income if the customer pays in arrears. These amounts are recognized over the financing period using the interest method.

Note that receivables with a financing component are long-term receivables. On the income statement, the presentation of impairment losses on a long-term receivable is consistent with the presentation of other financial assets. Impairment losses on short-term receivables or contract assets are presented as a separate line item in operating expenses in the statement of comprehensive income.

DISCLOSURE

Under current U.S. GAAP, disclosures about revenue are limited and lack cohesion . . . the new disclosure package will improve the understandability of revenue, which is obviously a critical part of the analysis of an organization's performance and prospects.

—Marc Siegel, FASB Member

One of the main objectives of the revenue recognition project is to improve disclosures in order to provide more useful information to investors and other financial statement users. The objective of the disclosure requirements is for

an entity to disclose sufficient information to enable users of financial statements to understand the nature, amount, timing, and uncertainty of revenue and cash flows arising from contracts with customers.

(ASC 606-10-50-1; IFRS 15.110)

Exhibit 8.4 Disclosure categories

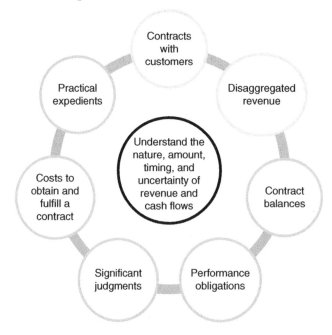

The Standard goes on to say that to achieve the objective, entities must disclose both qualitative and quantitative information about

- contracts with customers,
- significant judgments made in applying the Standard to the entity's contracts, including changes in those judgments, and
- assets recognized from the costs to obtain or fulfill a contract with the customer.

(ASC 606-10-50-1; IFRS 15.110)

Entities must disclose

- for contract balances:

  - the opening and closing balances of

    - receivables,
    - contract assets, and
    - contract liabilities;

- for performance obligations:

  - when the entity typically satisfies its performance obligations, including in bill-and-hold arrangements;
  - significant payment terms;
  - the nature of the goods or services, including those where the entity is acting as an agent;
  - obligations for returns, refunds, and similar obligations;
  - types of warranties and related obligations;
- the use of some practical expedients.

Level of Detail and Materiality

The level of detail may differ for each disclosure depending on the facts and circumstances. The assessment of how to disclose is made for each reporting period. The Boards did not want to create onerous disclosure requirements. The disclosures in the Standard should not be seen as a checklist. Entities do not need to include irrelevant disclosures, and disclosure requirements apply only to material items. (ASC 606-10-50-2; IFRS 15.111)

The Standard significantly increases the required disclosures. Some are consistent with those currently required for multiple-element arrangements, but many are completely new. Entities will have to consider

- the level of detail necessary to satisfy the Standard's objectives,
- how much emphasis to place on each requirement, and
- which information to aggregate or disaggregate to make sure decision-useful information is available to their users and not obscured by insignificant detail or aggregated with items that have different characteristics.

(ASC 606-10-50-2; IFRS 15.111)

Entities do not have to duplicate disclosures made elsewhere in the financial statements.

The Standard is principles-based and, therefore, requires more judgment. Documenting how those judgments are made is critical.

Relief for U.S. Nonpublic Entities

In general, the Standard provides relief by requiring qualitative disclosures instead of tabular, quantitative reconciliations for certain disclosures. The Standard also provides some relief for nonpublic entities, specifically for disclosures related to

- quantitative disaggregation disclosures,
- contract balances,
- transaction price allocated to remaining performance obligations,
- certain information related to significant judgments,
- use of practical expedients, and
- certain information related to costs incurred to obtain and fulfill a contract with a customer.

For U.S. GAAP reporters, public entities include public business entities and certain not-for-profit entities and employee benefit plans. IFRS standards do not have public versus nonpublic requirements, and IFRS 15 does not apply to nonpublic entities. Entities with no public accountability can apply IFRS reporting for small and medium-sized entities. Nonpublic entities can elect to provide the disclosures required for public entities. In addition to considering the needs of their lenders, private companies considering going public may want to consider potential filing requirements and present the public entity disclosures.

Exhibit 8.5 Summary of annual disclosure requirements[1]

Disclosure Type	Requirements	Disclosure Relief for Nonpublic Companies—U.S. GAAP Only[2]
Contract with customers	Revenue recognized from contracts with customers, disclosed separately from other sources of revenue. (ASC 606-10-50-4a; IFRS 15.113a)	
	Impairment losses recognized on receivables or contract assets, disclosed separately from other impairment losses. (ASC 606-10-50-4b; IFRS 15.113b)*	
Disaggregated revenue	Disaggregated into categories that show: • How economic factors affect the amount, timing, and uncertainty of revenue and cash flows. (ASC 606-10-50-5; IFRS 15.114)	May elect not to provide the quantitative disaggregation disclosure. If election is chosen, must disclose • revenue disaggregated by timing of transfer of goods or services, and • qualitative information about how economic factors affect the nature, amount, timing, and uncertainty of revenue and cash flows. • (ASC 606-10-50-7)
	• Information that enables users to understand the relationship between the disclosures of disaggregated information and segment information. (ASC 606-10-50-6; IFRS 15.115)	May use the expedient in ASC 606-10-50-7 above.
Contract balances	Opening and closing balances of receivables, contract assets, and contract liabilities. (ASC 606-10-50-8a; IFRS 15.116a)	
	Amount of revenue recognized in the current period that was included in the opening contract liability balance. (ASC 606-10-50-8b; IFRS 15.116b)	May elect not to make this disclosure. (ASC 606-10-50-11)
	Amount of revenue recognized in the current period from performance obligations satisfied or partially satisfied in the previous periods. (ASC 606-10-50-8c; IFRS 15.116c)	May elect not to make this disclosure. (ASC 606-10-50-11)

---

[1] These are disclosures for annual financial statements. Disclosure in interim statements is an area of IFRS and U.S. GAAP difference. See the "Interim Financial Statement Disclosure Requirements" section later in this chapter.

[2] Nonpublic companies for this purpose are entities other than public business entities, not-for-profit entities that have issued, or are conduit bond obligors for, securities that are traded, listed, or quoted on an exchange or an over-the-counter market, or employee benefit plans that file or furnish financial statements with or to the Securities and Exchange Commission (SEC)

Disclosure Type	Requirements	Disclosure Relief for Nonpublic Companies—U.S. GAAP Only[2]
	Explanation (may use qualitative information) of how the timing of performance obligations and the entity's contracts' payment terms will affect its contract asset and contract liability balances. (ASC 606-10-50-9; IFRS 15.117)	May elect not to make this disclosure. (ASC 606-10-50-11)
	Qualitative and quantitative information about the significant changes in contract asset and liability balances. (ASC 606-10-50-10; IFRS 15.118)	May elect not to make this disclosure. (ASC 606-10-50-11)
Performance obligations	Descriptive information about an entity's performance of obligations, including: • When the entity typically satisfies its performance obligations. • Significant payment terms. • Nature of the goods or services promised to transfer (highlighting any performance obligations for another entity to transfer goods or services). • Obligations for returns, refunds, and other similar obligations. • Types of warranties and related obligations. (ASC 606-10-50-12; IFRS 15.119)	
	Aggregate amount of the transaction price allocated to remaining performance obligations unsatisfied or partially satisfied** (ASC 606-10-50-13a; IFRS 15.120a)	May elect not to make this disclosure. (ASC 606-10-50-16)
	Either a quantitative (using time bands) or a qualitative explanation of when the entity expects the aggregated amount of the transaction price allocated to remaining performance obligations to be recognized as revenue. (ASC 606-10-50-13b; IFRS 15.120b)	May elect not to make this disclosure. (ASC 606-10-50-16)
	Practical expedient: Entities may elect not to disclose the information required by ASC 606-10-50-13 if the related contract has an original expected duration of one year or less, or the entity recognizes revenue for the performance obligation in accordance with ASC 606-10-55-18. (ASC 606-10-50-14; IFRS 15.121)	May elect not to make the disclosure in ASC 606-10-50-15. (ASC 606-10-50-16)

Disclosure Type	Requirements	Disclosure Relief for Nonpublic Companies—U.S. GAAP Only[2]
	An entity choosing this election should include qualitative explanation of whether any consideration is not included in the transaction price. (ASC 606-10-50-15; IFRS 15.122)	May elect not to make this disclosure. (ASC 606-10-50-16)
	For IFRS reporters: For all reporting periods presented, before the date of initial application may elect not to disclose the amount of the transaction price allocated, to the remaining performance obligations and an explanation of when the entity expects to recognize that amount as revenue. [Clarifications to IFRS 15 C5(d)][***]	
Significant judgments	Judgments and changes in judgment that affect the determination of the amount and timing of revenue recognition, particularly the timing of satisfaction of performance obligation and the transaction price and the amounts allocated to performance obligations. (ASC 606-10-50-17; IFRS 15.123)	
	Methods used to recognize revenue for performance obligations satisfied over time. (ASC 606-10-50-18a; IFRS 15.124a)	
	Why the method used to recognize revenue over time provides a faithful depiction of the transfer goods or services. (ASC 606-10-50-18b; IFRS 15.124b)	May elect not to make this disclosure. (ASC 606-10-50-21)
	Significant judgments related to transfer of control for performance obligations satisfied at a point in time. (ASC 606-10-50-19; IFRS 15.125)	May elect not to make this disclosure. (ASC 606-10-50-21)
	Information about the methods, inputs, and assumptions used to determine and allocate transaction price. (ASC 606-10-50-20a and c; IFRS 15.126a and c)	May elect not to make this disclosure. (ASC 606-10-50-21)
	Assessing whether an estimate of variable consideration is constrained. (ASC 606-10-50-20b; IFRS 15.126b)	
	Measuring obligations for returns, refunds, and other similar obligations. (ASC 606-10-50-20d; IFRS 15.126d)	May elect not to make this disclosure. (ASC 606-10-50-21)
Cost to obtain and fulfill a contract	Judgments made to determine cost to obtain or fulfill a contract and method of amortization. (ASC 340-40-50-2; IFRS 15.127)	May elect not to make this disclosure. (ASC 340-40-50-4)

Disclosure Type	Requirements	Disclosure Relief for Nonpublic Companies—U.S. GAAP Only[2]
	Closing balances of assets and amount of amortization and impairment. (ASC 340-40-50-3; IFRS 15.128)	May elect not to make this disclosure. (ASC 340-40-50-4)
Practical expedients	Use of the practical expedient regarding the existence of a significant financing component. (ASC 606-10-50-22; IFRS 15.129)	May elect not to make this disclosure. (ASC 606-10-50-23)
	Use of the practical expedient for expensing incremental costs of obtaining a contract (ASC 340-40-50-5; IFRS 15.129)	May elect not to make this disclosure. (ASC 340-40-50-6)

[*]Upon implementation of ASU 2016-13, *Financial Instruments – Credit Losses (Topic 326) Measurement of Credit Losses on Financial Instruments*, this item for U.S. GAAP reporters will be superseded by: "Credit losses recorded on any receivables or contract assets from contracts with customers, disclosed separately from credit loss from other contracts." The IFRS language will remain the same.

[**]See discussion later in this chapter for a practical expedient related to this requirement.

[***]See Technical Alert at the beginning of this chapter for a related change in an FASB proposal.

Disaggregated Revenue

Revenue in the statement of comprehensive income may represent revenue from many contracts with customers. Revenue may result from the transfer of different categories of goods and services, and the transfer to different types of customers or markets. The disaggregated disclosures are intended to show how the nature, amount, timing, and uncertainty about revenue and cash flows are affected by economic factors. These disclosures will provide users with a deeper understanding of the entity. (ASC 606-10-50-5; IFRS 15.114) *Note for IFRS preparers:* this is the only disclosure requirement that is required in both interim and annual financial statements.

Some entities may have to use only one disaggregation category, while others may need to use more than one to meet the requirement. (ASC 606-10-55-89; IFRS 15.B87) The Standard does not dictate specific categories or a minimum number of categories for disaggregation, but instead provides principles and examples. The Standard suggests entities consider how revenue is presented for other purposes, including all of the following:

- disclosures presented outside the financial statements;
- information used by the chief operating decision maker when evaluating the financial performance of operating segments;
- other similar information used by the entity or users of its financial statements to evaluate financial performance and make resource allocation disclosures.

(ASC 606-10-55-90; IFRS 15.B88)

The already existing disaggregated data listed above may be most useful for financial statement users.

When deciding on the specific categories of revenue, entities should consider entity-specific and/or industry-specific factors that would be more meaningful for its business than categories prescribed by standards.

Examples of categories for disaggregation provided by the Standard are listed in Exhibit 8.6. (ASC 606-10-55-91; IFRS 15.B89)

Exhibit 8.6 Examples of items for disaggregation categories

Items to Consider Disaggregating	Examples
Type of good or service	Major product lines
Geographical region	Country or region
Market or type of customer	Government and nongovernment contracts
Type of contract	Fixed-price and time-and-materials contracts
Contract duration	Short-term and long-term contracts
Timing of transfer of goods or services	Revenue from goods or services transferred to a customer at a point in time and revenue from goods or services transferred over time
Sales channels	Goods sold directly to consumers and goods sold through intermediaries

ASC 606-10-55-91; IFRS 15.B89

Entities must also describe the relationship between the disaggregated revenue disclosures required by the Standard and those required by ASC 280, *Segment Reporting* and IFRS 8, *Operating Segments*. (ASC 606-10-50-5 through 50-7; IFRS 15.115) Users must understand not only the composition of the revenue, but also how it relates to segment information, like cost of goods sold, expenses, and assets used. If the information provided on operating segments is presented in accordance with the guidance in the Standard and it meets the objectives of disclosing disaggregated revenue, then additional disclosures are not needed.

Example 8.4: Disaggregation of Revenue

Conglomerate reports the following segments:

- office supplies
- computers
- home products.

For investor presentations, Conglomerate disaggregates its revenue by

- primary geographic markets
- major product lines
- timing of revenue recognition.

After analyzing the data, Conglomerate decides that the categories used in the investor presentation will meet the objectives of the Standard. Conglomerate will also include a schedule reconciling the disaggregated revenue to the operating segments.

Segments	Office Supplies		Computers		Home Products		Total	
Primary geographic markets								
United States	CU	1,200	CU	350	CU	1,000	CU	2,550
Canada		250		100		180		530
Latin America		1,000		300		620		1,920
	CU	2,450	CU	750	CU	1,800	CU	5,000

Major product lines

	Office Supplies		Computers		Home Products		Total	
Filing supplies	CU	1,450					CU	1,450
Paper		1,000						1,000
Computers—laptops			CU	500				500
Computer peripherals				250				250
Appliances					CU	1,000		1,000
Mattresses						500		500
Outdoor furniture						300		300
	CU	**2,450**	CU	**750**	CU	**1,800**	CU	**5,000**

Segments	Office Supplies		Computers		Home Products		Total	
Timing of revenue recognition								
Goods transferred at a point in time	CU	2,450	CU	500	CU	1,800		4,750
Goods transferred over time				250				250
	CU	2,450	CU	750	CU	1,800	CU	5,000

Contract Balances

Users need to understand the relationship between revenue recognized and changes in the balances of total contract assets and contract liabilities during the reporting period. Reconciliation of account balances gives the user information about the amount of revenue recognized in the current period that is not a result of current-period performance. To limit the costs of providing the information, tabular data is not required and formatting of this information is flexible. However, entities must disclose qualitative and quantitative information about an entity's contract balances. The items listed in Exhibit 8.3 are required to be disclosed. (ASC 606-10-50-8; IFRS 15.116)

Part of the explanation should include how the timing compares with the typical timing of payments and the effect on contract asset and contract liability balances. This information can be qualitative. (ASC 606-10-50-09; IFRS 15.118)

The Standard provides examples of significant changes in contract assets and contract liabilities that require disclosure, for instance:

- changes from business combinations;
- cumulative catchup adjustments to revenue that affect the corresponding contract asset or contract liability;
- impairment of a contract asset;
- changes in timeframe for a right to consideration to become unconditional and, therefore, for a contract asset to be reclassified to a receivable;
- changes in the timeframe for a performance obligation to be satisfied, that is, for the recognition of revenue arising from a contract liability.

(ASC 606-10-50-10; IFRS 15.118)

Example 8.5: Disclosure of Contract Balances

Manufacturer discloses its trade receivables as a line item in the statement of financial position. To comply with the Standard, it must also disclose the following information in the financial statement notes.

	20X3	20X2	20X1
Contract asset	7,500	11,250	9,000
Contract liability	(1,000)	(4,250)	(2,500)
Revenue recognized in the period			
Amounts included in the contract liability at the beginning of the period	3,250	1,000	500
Performance obligations satisfied in previous periods	1,000	625	1,000

We receive payments from customers based on a billing schedule in our contracts. The contract asset represents the cost incurred related to contracts in advance of scheduled billing. The contract liability relates to payment received in advance of performance. Performance under contracts is represented in the changes in contract assets and contract liabilities. In 20X3, we recorded an impairment of CU 2000 to contract assets because of a change in the customer's credit risk.

Performance Obligations

Entities are required to disclose the amounts of revenue recognized in the current period that were at least partially satisfied in prior periods. This could occur, for example, because of changes in transaction price or estimates related to the contract and revenue recognized. This disclosure gives users information about the timing of revenue recognition and useful information about current-period operating results, trends, risks, and predicting future results. Bear in mind that this information is not disclosed elsewhere in the financial statements. As with other disclosures, these disclosures are not required for immaterial amounts.

Separate disclosure of remaining performance obligations should help users analyze the nature, amount, timing, and uncertainty of revenue and cash flows from contracts with customers. Disclosures should not be boilerplate and should supplement the entity's policy disclosures. Note that disclosures about remaining performance obligations in particular will require judgment, especially if the timing might be affected by external forces. In the remaining performance obligations disclosure, entities should use the constrained amount. The disclosure can be presented on a quantitative basis or on a mix of qualitative and quantitative information. Quantitative information may be disclosed, for example, in time bands.

Entities should provide a qualitative explanation of any consideration that is not included in the transaction price, like constrained variable consideration or contract renewal options that do not represent a material right, and are not included in the remaining performance obligation disclosure.

Transaction Price Allocated to Remaining Performance Obligations—Practical Expedient

To address concerns about the costs of preparing these disclosures, the Standard offers a practical expedient related to the transaction price allocated to remaining performance obligations. Entities can omit these disclosures if

- the related contract has a duration of one year or less, or
- the entity recognizes revenue equal to what it has the right to invoice when that amount corresponds directly to the value to the customer of the entity's performance to date.

(ASC 606-10-50-14; IFRS 15.121)

Users indicated to the Boards that their primary interest in this information related to long-term contracts. This practical expedient should ease the cost burden without compromising significantly the usefulness of the information for users. (See also the Technical Alert at the beginning of this chapter for a proposed change to this guidance.)

Example 8.6: Disclosure of the Transaction Price Allocated to the Remaining Performance Obligations—Purchase Obligations Satisfied Over Time—Quantitative Disclosure

Eastern Maintenance Services enters into a contract to provide Office Complex with cleaning and lawn maintenance services for CU 600 per month beginning July 1, 20X1. The services are provided as needed and are capped at a maximum of four visits per month over two years. Eastern Maintenance Services analyzes the terms of the contract and decides to measure progress toward satisfaction using a time-based measure.

Eastern is required to disclose the amount of the transaction price that has not yet been recognized as revenue. Eastern Maintenance Services uses a table with quantitative time categories. This table quantifies when they expect to recognize revenue.

	20X3	20X2	Total
Revenue expected to be recognized on the Office Complex contract as of December 31, 20X1	3,600	7,200	10,800

Example 8.7: Disclosure of the Transaction Price Allocated to the Remaining Performance Obligations—Qualitative Disclosure

On January 1, 20X1, Builder enters into a contract with Medical Practice to construct an office building for CU 5,000,000. Builder assesses the contract and decides that the construction of the office building is a single performance obligation satisfied over time.

As of December 31, 20X1, Builder has recognized CU 2,800,000 in revenue. Current estimates call for the project to be completed in 20X2, however, it is possible that the work could spill over into 20X3. Because of the uncertainty about the timing of revenue, Builder decides to disclose the transaction price allocated to the remaining performance obligation qualitatively rather than quantitatively in time bands. Here is Builder's disclosure:

> *As of December 31, 20X1, the aggregate amount of the transaction price allocated to the remaining performance obligation is CU 2,200,000. Builder will recognize revenue as the building is completed, which is expected to occur in the next 12–18 months.*

Example 8.8: Disclosures of the Transaction Price—Quantitative Time Bands

Eastern Maintenance Services enters into a two-year contract to provide maintenance and irrigation services to Office Complex when or as needed, beginning on July 1, 20X1. Office Complex pays CU 200 per month plus a one-time variable consideration payment, varying from CU 0 to 2000. This is to provide a one-time regulatory review of the irrigation system's backflow system. Based on past experience, Eastern Maintenance Services estimates that it will be entitled to CU 1200 of the variable consideration related to the backflow system inspection. Because it is probable that a significant reversal in the amount of cumulative revenue recognized will not occur, Eastern Maintenance Services includes the CU 1200 estimate in the transaction price. Progress toward completion is time-based.

In a table with quantitative time bands, Eastern Maintenance Services discloses the amount of the transaction price that has not yet been recognized. The disclosures are made in a table with quantitative time bands that illustrate when it expects to recognize revenue. Eastern Maintenance

Services also includes a qualitative discussion of any significant variable consideration not included in the quantitative disclosure.

	20X2	20X3	Total
Revenue expected to be recognized as of December 31, 20X1	CU 3000*	CU 1500**	CU 4500

* Transaction price = CU 6000 (CU 200 × 24 months + CU 1200 variable consideration) recognized over 24 months, or CU 3000 per year.

** CU 3000 ÷ 2 = CU 1500 for the six months remaining on the contract.
   CU 1500 was recognized in the 20X1 financial statements.

Example 8.9: Remaining Performance Obligations—Application of the Practical Expedient

On May 1, 20X1, RVC Cleaning Services enters into a contract to provide weekly cleaning services to Brower Pharmacy. The contract is for two years, and RVC has the right to invoice the customer for the work performed to date. RVC recognizes revenue equal to what it has a right to invoice, and the amount corresponds directly to the value to Brower of RVC's work performed to date. The contract fits one of the criteria for using the practical expedient in ASC 606-10-50-14(b) and IFRS 15.121(b). RVC's right to consideration corresponds directly to the entity's perform-ance to date. RVC elects to apply the practical expedient and no disclosure is necessary.

Significant Judgments

Legacy standards contain general guidance about disclosing significant estimates and judg-ments. Because of the importance of revenue information, the Standard includes specific disclosures about estimates used and judgments made. Not only must an entity disclose the significant judgments it made in determining the transaction price, allocating the transaction price, and determining when performance obligations are satisfied, it must also disclose changes in that judgment that significantly affect the amount and timing of revenue from contracts with customers. Entities can be expected to exercise significant judgment when estimating transaction prices for contracts including variable consideration and when determining standalone selling prices.

Costs to Obtain or Fulfill a Contract

It is helpful for users to understand the types of cost recognized as assets and how these assets are subsequently amortized or impaired. Mindful of cost, the Standard requires disclosure of only the most critical information. Entities must disclose information about

- judgments made in determining the amount of costs incurred to obtain or fulfill a contract,
- methods to determine amortization,
- closing balances of assets recognized from costs incurred to obtain or fulfill a contract by main category of asset, and
- amount of amortization and impairment losses.

The assets are separated by main category (acquisition costs, pre-contract costs, setup costs, and other fulfillment costs), and the amount of amortization and impairment loss recognized in the period. (ASC 340-40-50-1 to 50-4; IFRS 15.127 to 128) Nonpublic U.S. entities may choose not to make these disclosures.

Practical Expedients

Applying practical expedients may lead to financial results different from full application of the Standard. If the entity uses the practical expedient related to the existence of a significant financing component or the incremental cost of obtaining a contract, it should disclose that fact and whether any amounts have been excluded from the transaction price. (ASC 606-10-50-22; IFRS 15.122) Likewise, the entity should disclose if it uses the practical expedient regarding disclosure of the information related to the transaction price allocated to the remaining performance obligations. See also the Technical Alert at the beginning of this chapter.

Interim Financial Statement Disclosure Requirements

Interim reporting requirements are an area where the IASB and the FASB came to different conclusions. Both do, however, require entities to disclose information about disaggregation of revenue.

U.S. GAAP Only. The Standard requires public entities to disclose information required under ASC 270 and the same disclosures about revenue information in the year-end statements:

- disaggregation of revenue;
- receivables, contract asset and contract liability opening and closing balances and significant changes in those balances since the previous period end;
- revenue recognized in the current period that was included in the opening contract liability balance;
- transaction price allocated to the remaining performance obligations.

(ASC 270-10-50-1A)

IFRS Only. In addition to information required under IAS 34, IFRS 15 requires disclosure of the disaggregation of revenue and impairment losses generated from contract costs. Disaggregation of revenue is considered crucial to users and is already required by IAS 34, so there should be no significant incremental costs to provide that information. None of the other annual revenue disclosures are required by the IASB to be included in the interim statements.

Requirement to Disclose the Future Impact of the Standard

IFRS Reporters. IAS 8.30 through 8.31 requires IFRS reporters that have not applied a new IFRS that is issued but not yet effective to disclose that fact, and known or reasonably estimable information relevant to the possible impact of the new IFRS on the entity's financial statements in the initial period of application.

The entity should consider including the following.

a. The title of the new standard or interpretation.
b. The nature of the impending change or changes in accounting policy.
c. The date by which application of the IFRS is required.
d. The date at which it plans to apply the IFRS initially.
e. Either

    i. a discussion of the impact that initial application of the IFRS is expected to have on the entity's financial statements, or
    ii. if that impact is not known or reasonably estimable, a statement to that effect.

(IAS 8.30 and 8.31)

Example 8.10: Disclosure of New Guidance—IFRS Reporter

IFRS 15, *Revenue from Contracts with Customers* was issued in May 2014 and amended in April 2016. It is effective for accounting periods beginning on or before January 1, 2018 and the Company will adopt it on April 1, 2018. IFRS 15 is expected to have a material impact on the Company's reporting of revenue and costs, as follows.

- IFRS 15 requires entities to identify promises in contracts with customers that qualify as performance obligations. The transaction price receivable from customers must be allocated between the entities' performance obligations under the contracts on a relative standalone selling price basis. Currently, the Company's revenue allocated to deliverables is restricted to the amount that is receivable without the delivery of additional goods or services; this restriction will no longer be applied under IFRS 15. The primary impact on revenue reporting will be that when the Company sells cell phones together with data service agreements to customers, revenue allocated to equipment and recognized when control of the device passes to the customer will increase and revenue recognized as services are delivered will reduce.
- Under IFRS 15, certain incremental costs of acquiring a contract with a customer are deferred on the balance sheet and amortized as revenue is recognized under the related contract; this will generally lead to later recognition of charges for some commissions payable to third-party dealers and employees.
- Under IFRS 15, certain costs incurred in fulfilling customer contracts will be deferred on the balance sheet and recognized as related revenue is recognized under the contract. Such deferred costs are likely to relate to the provision of deliverables to customers that do not qualify as performance obligations and for which revenue is not recognized; currently such costs are generally expensed as incurred.

U.S. SEC Registrants. The SEC, in SAB 74 (Topic 11M), has a similar provision and requires public entities to provide disclosures regarding new authoritative guidance which has been issued, but not yet adopted, including:

- description of the new requirements;
- date when adoption is required;
- alternative, allowable transition methods;
- transition method the entity plans to use;
- discussion of the anticipated impact of the new requirements on the financial statements or, if unknown or not reasonably estimable, a statement to that effect;
- any other significant consequences of adopting the new requirements, such as debt violations or change in business practices.

SEC registrants have begun to include these disclosures. They may be found in the front portion of the 10-K filings or in financial statement footnote disclosures only. Here are two examples.

Example 8.11: Disclosure of New Guidance—U.S. GAAP Reporter

In May 2014, the FASB issued ASU 2014-09, *Revenue from Contracts with Customers* (Topic 606), an amendment to the FASB Accounting Standards Codification. The core principle of this guidance is that an entity should recognize revenue to depict the transfer of goods or services to customers in an amount that reflects the consideration to which the entity expects to be entitled in exchange for those goods or services. In August 2015, the FASB issued ASU 2015-14, delaying the effective date of adoption. This update is now effective for annual and interim periods beginning after December 15, 2017, which will require us to adopt these provisions in the first quarter of fiscal year 2018. Early adoption is permitted. This update permits the use of either the retrospective or cumulative effect transition method. The Company is currently evaluating the impact the guidance will have on our consolidated financial statements.

Example 8.12: Disclosure of New Guidance—U.S. GAAP Reporter

In May 2014, the FASB issued amended guidance on contracts with customers to transfer goods or services or contracts for the transfer of nonfinancial assets, unless those contracts are within the scope of other standards (e.g., insurance contracts or lease contracts). The guidance requires an entity to recognize revenue on contracts with customers relating to the transfer of promised goods or services to customers in an amount that reflects the consideration to which the entity expects to be entitled in exchange for those goods or services. The guidance requires that an entity depict the consideration by applying the following steps.

Step 1: Identify the contract(s) with a customer.
Step 2: Identify the performance obligations in the contract.
Step 3: Determine the transaction price.
Step 4: Allocate the transaction price to the performance obligations in the contract.
Step 5: Recognize revenue when (or as) the entity satisfies a performance obligation.

The amendments in this ASU were deferred by ASU 2015-14 for all entities by one year, and are effective for annual reporting periods beginning after December 15, 2017, including interim periods within that reporting period. Earlier application is permitted only as of annual reporting periods beginning after December 15, 2016, including interim reporting periods within that reporting period. This amendment is to be either retrospectively adopted to each prior reporting period presented or retrospectively with the cumulative effect of initially applying this ASU recognized at the date of initial application. Adoption of this guidance is not expected to have a material impact on the Company's consolidated financial statements.

The Company is currently assessing the impact of these accounting changes. The changes listed above are expected to have a material impact on the income statement and statement of financial position.

When IFRS 15 is adopted, entities have the option of applying it either on a full retrospective basis, requiring the restatement of the comparative periods presented in the financial statements, or with the cumulative retrospective impact of IFRS 15 applied as an adjustment to equity on the date of adoption. When the latter approach is applied, entities must disclose the impact of IFRS 15 on each line item in the financial statements in the reporting period. The Company currently intends to reflect the cumulative impact of IFRS 15 in equity on the date of adoption.

COMPARISON WITH LEGACY GUIDANCE

Presentation

IFRS. Under legacy guidance, entities using the percentage-of-completion method present the gross amount due from customers for contract work as an asset and the gross amount due to customers as a liability. For other contracts, entities present accrued or deferred income, or payments received in advance, to the extent that payment is received before or after performance.

The Standard streamlines guidance by containing a single, systematic approach to presentation. The Standard does not distinguish between different types of contract.

U.S. GAAP. Legacy U.S. GAAP contains separate guidance for construction- and production-type contracts. There is also guidance for specialized industries. The Standard does not distinguish between different types of contract and uses a single approach to presentation. In addition, an entity does not recognize work in progress or its equivalent for performance obligations satisfied over time, because the entity controls the asset as it is created or enhanced.

Disclosure

IFRS. The Standard requires significantly more disclosures than those required under IAS 18 and IAS 17. The detailed disclosures about performance obligations, among others, are not required under legacy guidance.

U.S. GAAP. Legacy U.S. standards require disclosure under the general revenue topic, ASC 605, and under the specialized industry topics. The Standard requires streamlined revenue accounting in general by eliminating many of the specific industry requirements and putting the requirements in ASC 606. However, the Standard requirements are generally more extensive than those in the legacy standards.

9 IMPLEMENTATION ISSUES

Technical Alert

Subsequent to the issuance of ASU 2014-09 and IFRS 15, questions arose regarding the effective date, implementation of the modified and full retrospective methods, and definition of a completed contract. Related changes instituted by the Boards are incorporated into the guidance in this chapter. The Boards continue to monitor implementation efforts, have proposed and made changes, and may continue to add changes in the early years of the Standard's implementation. The Executive Summary and its appendix contains information on TRG issues, the FASB's ASUs and the project's status, and information about the IASB's Clarifications to IFRS 15. For the latest information on the revenue recognition project, readers should consult each board's project page.

In addition as a purchaser of this book, you have exclusive access to a companion website, with the latest technical developments and other useful information. See the back of the book information on accessing the site.

EFFECTIVE DATES

In deciding on effective dates, the Boards wanted to strike the right balance between improving reporting standards as soon as possible and giving entities enough time to implement the Standard's broad and significant changes. Ultimately, the Boards decided on a longer-than-usual implementation period, because of the number of entities and line items affected. Despite that added time, soon after the release of the Standard, the Boards heard from many entities that they needed more time to implement the new guidance and both boards decided to defer the effective dates.

Changes to Effective Dates

U.S. GAAP. In response to constituent concerns, the FASB issued ASU 2015-14, *Revenue from Contracts with Customers (Topic 606): Deferral of the Effective Dates.* For all entities, the ASU allows

- a one-year deferral from the original effective dates, and
- early adoption using the original adoption dates.

The effective date for U.S. GAAP reporters depends on whether they are public or nonpublic entities. The Standard includes an expanded definition of a public entity. Under the Standard, U.S. GAAP public entities include

- public business entities,
- not-for-profit entities that have issued (or are conduit bond obligors for) securities that are traded, listed, or quoted on an exchange or over-the-counter market, and
- employee benefit plans that file or furnish financial statements to the SEC.
(ASC 606-10-65-1a)

The ASU is effective as follows.

- For public entities, the guidance in the Standard is effective for annual reporting periods beginning after December 15, 2017, including interim reporting periods within that period— that is, beginning in the first interim period within the year of adoption. Early application is permitted, but not earlier than the original effective date of annual reporting periods beginning after December 15, 2016, including interim reporting periods within that reporting period.
- For nonpublic entities, the new guidance is required for annual reporting periods beginning after December 15, 2018, and interim periods within annual periods beginning after December 15, 2019. A nonpublic entity may elect early application, but no earlier than the original effective date for public entities. That is, either

  - annual reporting periods beginning after December 15, 2016, or
  - annual reporting periods beginning after December 15, 2016 and interim reporting periods within annual reporting periods beginning one year after the annual reporting period in which an entity first applies the Standard.
(ASC 606-10-65-1 and 1b)

Notice that for some options, U.S. nonpublic entities are not required to apply the guidance in interim periods in the year of adoption.

For public entities, it may be more cost effective to wait to adopt. With time, entities can learn from the experience of others and many implementation and practice questions will be resolved. Another consideration is that some entities may want to coordinate the Standard's implementation with their implementation of the FASB's new leases standard. There is some interaction between the two standards, particularly for lessors.

IFRS. IFRS 15 was originally effective for annual periods beginning on or after January 1, 2017. Partly because, in the near future, some companies will transition from national to international standards, the IASB allows for early adoption for current and first-time IFRS preparers, provided that fact is disclosed. In September 2015, the IASB issued an amendment to IFRS 15, *Effective Date of IFRS 15*, deferring the effective date for one year until January 1, 2018. (IFRS 15.C1) Entities still have the option of adopting early.

Exhibit 9.1   Summary of deferred effective dates

	IFRS	**U.S. GAAP Public**	**U.S. GAAP Nonpublic**
Effective Date	Annual periods beginning on or after January 1, 2018	Annual periods (and interim periods within) beginning after December 15, 2017	Annual periods beginning after December 15, 2018
Early Adoption	Yes	Yes, but no earlier than the original effective date	Yes, but no earlier than the original effective date for U.S. Public entities

KEY TERMS

To understand the implementation requirements, it is necessary to understand the following terms as described by the Standard.

- **The date of initial application.** The start of the reporting period in which an entity adopts the Standard.
- **Completed contract.**
  - **IASB.** A contract in which an entity has transferred all of the identified goods and services before the date of initial application in accordance with IAS 11 and IAS 18 and related interpretations. As a result, entities do not need to apply the Standard to contracts for which they have completed performance before the date of initial application. This applies even if the entity has not received the consideration, and the consideration is variable.
  - **FASB.** A contract for which all (or substantially all) of the revenue was recognized under legacy guidance before the date of initial application of the Standard.
  (ASC 606-10-65-1c; IFRS 15.C2)

Understanding what constitutes a completed contract is important, because it affects how entities treat uncompleted contracts and the application of practical expedients.

To clear up questions regarding the definition of a completed contract, the FASB issued ASU 2014-12, *Narrow-Scope Improvements and Practical Expedients*. The ASU's clarified definition of a completed contract is reflected above. Additionally, the ASU states that accounting for elements of a contract that do not affect revenue under legacy guidance would be irrelevant to the assessment of whether a contract is completed. (ASU 2016-12, Summary of Amendments) These would be items that would not have existed under legacy guidance, such as historical cost accruals for loyalty points.

The IASB decided not to make a similar amendment to IFRS 15 to clarify the definition of a completed contract. The IASB affirmed that the definition of a completed contract includes a contract in which all the goods or services have been transferred to a customer, but for which revenue may not have been fully recognized because of collectibility issues or uncertainties in measurement. An entity would not apply IFRS 15 in subsequent periods to account for such a completed contract. The contract would be accounted for under legacy IFRS.

IMPLEMENTATION METHOD OPTIONS

Overview

Entities have the option to implement the guidance through

- full retrospective application, or
- modified retrospective application.

(ASC 606-10-65-1d; IFRS 15.C3)

The choice of implementation date and method dictates the years that revenue and the effects of a change in accounting principle will have to be restated.

Full Retrospective Approach

The full retrospective approach requires considerable effort. However, it is transparent and preserves trend information, making it useful for investors and analysts. U.S. nonpublic companies with public company competitors or intending to go public may want to consider using the full retrospective approach to ease comparisons. It may also be useful for entities expecting to recognize revenue earlier than under previous guidance.

Under this method, all prior periods presented must be restated and reflected in equity in accordance with ASC 250, *Accounting Changes and Error Corrections* or IAS 8, *Accounting Policies, Changes in Accounting Policies, and Errors*. That is, entities must report the cumulative effect for the earliest year reported and apply the Standard as if it had been applied since the inception of all contracts with customers presented in the financial statements. For a public U.S. company that does not adopt early, this means that financial statements must be restated for 2016 and 2017. Deferral of the effective date may make the full retrospective method more viable for some entities.

The full retrospective approach can also be adopted using one or more of the optional practical expedients below.

Practical Expedients. *Completed Contracts* For completed contracts, entities can elect not to restate contracts that

- begin and per FASB: "are completed"; or per IASB: "end" within the same reporting period.

[ASC 606-10-65-1f(1); IFRS C5(a)]

In addition, in its Clarifications, the IASB added a practical expedient that permits entities electing the full retrospective approach to elect not to restate completed contracts as of the beginning of the earliest period presented. The FASB has not added a similar practical expedient. [IFRS 15.C5a(ii)]

Entities using the full retrospective method may elect any combination of the following practical expedients.

1. For completed contracts that have variable consideration, an entity may use the transaction price at the date the contract was completed rather than estimating variable consideration in the comparative reporting period. [ASC 606-10-65-1f(2); IFRS C5(b)]
2. For all reporting periods presented before the date of initial application, an entity does not have to disclose the amount of the transaction price allocated to remaining performance obligations and an explanation of when the entity expects to recognize that amount as revenue.
[ASC 606-10-65-1f(3); IFRS 15.C5(c)]

Modified Contracts   For modified contracts, an entity can select a practical expedient and elect not to retrospectively restate the contract. Rather, the entity can reflect the aggregate effect of all the modifications that occur before the beginning of the earliest period presented by the following.

1. Identifying all the satisfied and unsatisfied performance obligations in the contract at the contract modification adjustment date (CMAD) reflecting all modifications from contract inception to the CMAD.
2. Determining the transaction price at the CMAD reflecting all modifications from inception to the CMAD.
3. Allocating the transaction price to the performance obligations identified at the CMAD based on the historic standalone selling price of each good or service.
[ASC 606-10-65-1f(4); IFRS 15.C5(c)]

Entities electing the full retrospective transition method should use the beginning of the earliest period presented as the CMAD.

Application and Disclosure. If an entity uses any of the practical expedients above, the entity must apply the expedient consistently for all contracts within the reporting periods presented and disclose:

- the expedients used, and
- to the extent reasonably possible, a qualitative assessment of the estimated effect of applying each of those expedients.
[ASC 606-10-65-1(g); IFRS 15.C6]

The FASB also made a technical correction in ASU 2014-12, which provides that an entity using the full retrospective method would not be required to disclose what the financial information would have been under the legacy guidance in the period of adoption of the Standard. However, the entity does have to disclose the effect of the changes on any prior periods that have been retrospectively adjusted. (ASC 606-10-65-1e)

Modified Retrospective Approach

The modified retrospective approach is intended to reduce transition time and effort. Under this approach, entities will

- present comparative periods in accordance with legacy guidance,

- apply the Standard to existing and new contracts from the effective date forward, and
- recognize a cumulative catchup adjustment to the opening balance of retained earnings or other appropriate components of equity.

[ASC 606-10-65-1(h); IFRS 15.C7]

If the entity issues comparative statements, then it reports revenue for prior years under the guidance in effect before adoption (legacy guidance). Comparative prior years are not adjusted.

Practical Expedients. The modified retrospective approach can also be adopted using one or more of the optional practical expedients that follow.

Completed Contracts For entities using the modified retrospective method, both boards added a practical expedient that permits an entity to apply the modified retrospective approach either

- to all the contracts at the date of initial application, or
- only to contracts that are not completed contracts at the date of initial application.

[ASC 606-10-65-1(h); IFRS 15.C7]

Use of this election must be disclosed.

Modified Contracts For modified contracts, an entity can select the practical expedient allowed for modified contracts under the full retrospective method and elect not to retrospectively restate the contract. (See above for detailed information.)

For U.S. GAAP reporters, as mentioned previously, entities electing the modified retrospective transition method must use the date of initial application as the CMAD. In a departure from the FASB, the IASB:

- Permits an entity using the modified retrospective transition method and electing to apply the contract modifications practical expedient allowed for modified contracts under the full retrospective method to apply the expedient either

  - at the beginning of the earliest period presented in the financial statements in which IFRS 15 is first applied, or
  - at the date of initial application of IFRS 15.

[IFRS 15.C7(a)]

Disclosures. While the modified retrospective approach is intended to be easier to implement, in weighing their options, entities should factor in the extensive disclosures required in the year of initial application. Entities using the modified retrospective method must provide the following additional disclosures in reporting periods that include the period of initial application.

a. The amount by which each financial statement item is affected in the current period by the application of the revenue recognition standard compared with legacy guidance. This option has the effect of an entity applying both the Standard and legacy guidance in the year of initial application.

b. An explanation of the reason for significant changes in (a) above.

[ASC 606-10-65-1(i); IFRS 15.C8]

Exhibit 9.2   Example of transition options

Using the required implementation date for IFRS reporters and U.S. public entities and not electing early adoption, assuming December 31 year end, these are the transition options.

Full retrospective approach

- January 1, 2018 apply the Standard to all contracts.
- 2016 and 2017 restate all contracts.
- Date of cumulative adjustment January 1, 2016.

Full retrospective method using one or more practical expedients

- January 1, 2018 apply the Standard to all contracts.
- 2016 and 2017 restate all contracts under the Standard except for contracts using the practical expedients elected (see 606-10-65-1).

Modified approach

- Cumulative effect at the date of adoption.
- January 1, 2018 apply the Standard to all contracts at the effective date for uncompleted contracts, that is, those that still require performance by the entity in the year of adoption and disclose the amount by which each financial statement line item was affected by applying the Standard. Financial statement line items affected by the Standard, in addition to revenue, gross margin, operating profit, and net income, include
    - assets for costs to obtain or fulfill a contract,
    - employee compensation, and
    - current deferred tax balances.
- 2016 and 2017 no contracts restated, report using legacy guidance.
- Date of cumulative adjustment January 1, 2018.

Exhibit 9.3   Transition and related disclosures, assuming January 1, 2018 implementation

	2016	2017	2018
Full retrospective method	Cumulative catchup adjustment at 1/1/2016		
	Contracts reported in accordance with new standard	Contracts reported in accordance with new standard	Contracts reported in accordance with new standard
Modified retrospective method	Cumulative catchup adjustment at 1/1/2018–new and existing contracts only		
	Contracts reported in accordance with legacy standards	Contracts reported in accordance with legacy standards	New and existing contracts reported in accordance with new standard

CHANGE MANAGEMENT ASPECTS OF IMPLEMENTING THE STANDARD

Successful implementation of the new standard will be critical to ensuring comparable, high-quality financial reporting for investors.

James Schnurr, Chief Account, Office of the Chief Accountant
(remarks before the 2014 AICPA National Conference on
Current SEC and PCAOB Developments)

Overview

For each entity, the degree of change brought on by the Standard depends on the nature of an entity's revenue stream and its contracts. By the nature of their customer contracts, some industries are affected more than others. For instance, retailers need to align their policies and procedures with the Standard, but the changes may not have a significant effect on the timing and amount of revenue, whereas the revenue recognition policies of the software industry may significantly change the timing and amount of revenue recognized. The changes in specific industry guidance will especially affect these industries:

- entertainment and media
- software
- telecommunications
- real estate.

Some changes in the Standard that may affect entities' revenue include the following.

- The focus on transfer of control for timing of revenue recognition.
- Estimates of variable consideration included in the transaction price and recognized sooner than under legacy guidance.
- Incorporation of the time value of money into the measurement of significant financing components.
- A switch to one approach to account for licenses and multiple-element arrangements instead of general or industry-specific approaches.
- Capitalization of costs previously expensed or with the option to do so.

For instance, a telecommunications company must allocate part of its revenue from a contract that includes a handset and services to the "free" handset. Under IAS 18, revenue may not have been allocated to the handset at contract inception. Therefore, under the Standard, revenue may be recognized earlier than previously.

Management must also gather information for strategic planning and budgeting.

Project Approach

Many entities will require a significant effort to implement the Standard. Entities need to prioritize a change management project that involves management and audit committees. Sufficient resources and appropriately skilled personnel should be assigned to the project. In addition to the in-depth inventorying and analysis of contract terms and decisions related to the technical implementation of the Standard, management must make subjective assessments related to

- the time value of money for significant financial components,
- variable fees, and
- licenses.

Exhibit 9.4 Approach to implementation

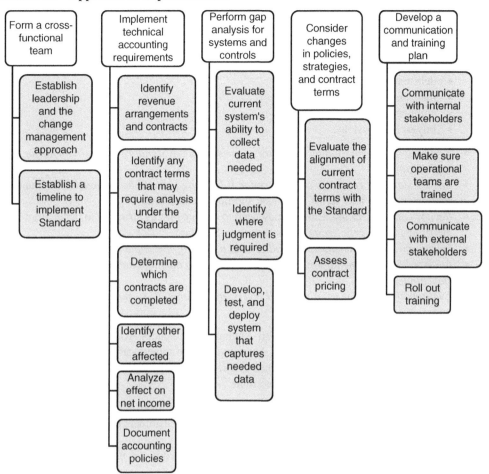

When implementing its project plan, management should take these tasks into consideration.

- *Review existing contracts.* Identify any terms that may require deeper analysis under the Standard. For example, does a contract have variable consideration? Contracts with variable consideration require more analysis. Does an entity have a contract with both a good and a service? This would require the entity to identify performance obligations.
- *Evaluate the ability of current systems to collect and maintain all the data necessary for compliance.* Ensure that IT systems capture data for proper period or date related to disclosures. Currently, an entity may track at the contract level. Under the Standard, the entity may have to drill down deeper and look at contracts from a performance obligation level. Systems must have the ability to capture data to aggregate or disaggregate contracts.
- *Draft disclosures required by the Standard.* This exercise may surface gaps in processes or systems.

- *Identify where more judgment is required.* Implement processes and controls to make sure adequate processes and controls are in place. Also, make sure adequate documentation is in place to respond to auditors or regulators.
- *Determine whether the Standard affects other areas.* For example

  - taxation
  - debt covenant compliance
  - management agreements
  - compensation
  - buy–sell provisions.

- *Review sales commission fee structures considering the Standard's requirements for cost capitalization.*
- *Review standard contracts and determine if language should be changed.* The Standard introduces some new terms and those should be considered.
- *Review contract pricing.* Entities may want to change pricing structure to better align with the timing of revenue recognition under the Standard.
- *Decide on which transition method to use, assessing the impact of each method.*
- *Analyze how implementation affects net income and communicate it internally, but also to stakeholders.*
- *Evaluate the need for training at all levels: audit committees, management, operational units.*

In a March 2016 speech before the 12th Annual Life Sciences Accounting and Reporting Congress,[1] James Schnurr, the SEC's Chief Accountant, gave some examples of implementation project tasks related to the life sciences industry. Mr. Schnurr explained entities in that industry should look closely at their contracts to determine

- if their research and development arrangements are collaborative arrangements, which would be out of scope of the Standard, contracts with customers under the Standard, or a combination of both
- if the contracts' terms involve variable pricing terms common in research and development contracts, and
- if the contracts include rights of returns or concessions such as agreements to cover costs or profit guarantees.

While Mr. Schnurr mentioned these in the context of a specific industry, they may well apply to other industries.

Debt Covenants. Debt covenants are often based on a measure of net income. Entities must be careful not to unintentionally violate an agreement. Debt covenants may have to be modified in preparation for change, while at the same time keeping their original intent.

Compensation Arrangements. Concerns have arisen regarding how the Standard will affect compensation plans. Some entities have plans tied to revenue goals. Depending on the structure of the plan and whether an entity using the Standard recognizes revenue sooner or later than under legacy guidance, compensation will affect entities and individuals. Entities with compensation plans expected to be affected should task human resources and their legal team to determine how agreements should be restructured to meet human resource goals.

---

[1] www.sec.gov/news/speech/Schnurr-remarks-12th-life-sciences-accountning-congress.html.

Tax Implications. U.S. Federal income-tax regulations contain specific rules for recognizing revenue for tax purposes. In some cases, such as when an entity receives advance payments, revenue for tax purposes depends on revenue recognized in the financial statements. In those areas, the Standard could have a significant effect on an entity's cash tax position. The Standard could also affect book-tax differences and deferred taxes. Entities should consider the effects on transfer pricing, state and local taxes, and foreign-controlled subsidiaries. There may also be implications for sales, excise, telecommunications, and other specialty taxes. To understand the implications, entities should involve their tax experts.

ABOUT THE COMPANION WEBSITE

This book includes a companion website, which can be found at http://www.wiley.com/go/revenuerecognition.com. Enter the password: flood123.

This website includes:

- The latest news from the standards' setters – including any new related standards or interpretations and
- Digital ancillaries featuring:
  - Useful implementation tools and
  - Disclosure checklists

As the Revenue Recognition Standard is implemented, it is important for professionals to keep abreast of the latest developments and make use of the valuable tools on the website.

INDEX